ECONOMIC THEORY

Gary S. Becker

University of Chicago

Alfred A. Knopf, New York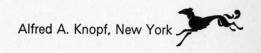

ECONOMIC
THEORY

With the assistance of MICHAEL GROSSMAN and ROBERT T. MICHAEL

Copyright © 1971 by Alfred A. Knopf, Inc.

All rights reserved under International and Pan-American Copyright Conventions. Published in the United States by Alfred A. Knopf, Inc., New York, and simultaneously in Canada by Random House of Canada Limited, Toronto. Distributed by Random House, Inc., New York.

ISBN: 394–31492–1

Library of Congress Catalog Card Number: 71–137992

Manufactured in the United States of America.

First Edition

9 8 7 6 5 4

To my girls JUDY and CATHY

Preface

For more than a decade I gave a course on price theory to first-year graduate students at Columbia. The course tries to present a rigorous and systematic statement of the principles economists have developed to understand the allocation of resources. The emphasis of the course, however, has been on the value of these principles in understanding the world about us.

The lectures during the academic year 1967–1968 were recorded, and Michael Grossman and Robert Michael converted the transcribed oral presentation into a readable written draft. Their task was formidable since an oral presentation is more repetitive and relies more on diagrams, discussion, and even "atmosphere" than a written presentation should. They did an excellent job and their appearance on the title page is only a small expression of my indebtedness to them.

Although I converted their draft into a final draft, I tried to preserve the flavor and content, including the informality, of the lectures rather than to aim at a complete text on theory. In particular, since the lectures reflect my own interests and approach to different subjects, some important subjects, such as activity analysis, are only discussed in passing, and the approach to consumer behavior, for example, is not the typical one. The more difficult lectures are marked with an asterisk (*) and can be omitted on a first reading.

The most efficient way to learn economic theory is to solve many problems that test one's understanding. To this end I encourage discussion during the lectures, including the discussion of queries that I put to the class. Many of these queries are included, usually in the form of a Why? after a sentence, and students should try seriously to answer them before passing on to new materials. More difficult problems have been assigned each week for students to take home, write up, and discuss at a weekly lab session. A number of these are included at the end of each lecture, as well as some easier ones from written examinations. Students should try to solve all the easier problems and at least some of the more difficult ones (marked with an asterisk).

It is difficult to choose the appropriate mathematical level of the presentation, especially since the mathematical sophistication of students has improved rapidly in recent years. I have placed extended mathematical discussions in footnotes and appendixes, and mathematically prepared readers should study these carefully. Practically all statements proved mathematically are also proved geometrically or verbally in the body of the text, and other students can rely on these.

The perhaps presumptuous title of *Economic Theory* is used instead of a title like *Micro Theory* or *Price Theory* because of my belief that there is only one kind of economic theory, not separate theories for micro problems, macro problems, nonmarket decisions, and so on. Indeed, the most promising development in recent years in the literature on unemployment and other macro problems has been the increasing reliance on utility maximization and the other principles used to study micro problems.

Armen Alchian read an earlier draft thoroughly and gave me numerous valuable suggestions and criticisms. I also received helpful comments from Jack Hirshliefer, Jacob Mincer, and George Stigler. Sara Paroush drew the charts. Last, but far from least, let me record my appreciation to the able students who were in charge of the lab sessions and did much of the teaching in the course: Isaac Ehrlich, Reuben Gronau, Gerald Jantscher, William Landes, John Owen, Michael Rahm, and Robert Reischauer.

Gary S. Becker

Contents

PART TWO
Supply of Products

PART THREE
Production and the Demand for Factors

PART FOUR
Supply of Factors of Production

chapter 1

Introduction

LECTURE 1

What Is Economics?

What is economics? One definition by a well-known economist is that economics is what economists do. This is obviously circular and was meant to illustrate the difficulty of rigidly defining a subject matter that has changed so much over time. A more serious definition is that economics is the study of the allocation of scarce means to satisfy competing ends. Air is not usually scarce, and ordinarily there is no economic problem in the use of air since nothing else must be forfeited. In recent years, however, especially in our urban communities, there has been considerable interest in and concern about air pollution. We can make the air cleaner than it is; for example, Con Edison and the City Government of New York (probably the two major pollutors in New York City) can use more costly methods to reduce their discharge of air pollutants. So *clean* air is often scarce, and cleaner air can be achieved only by using resources that could be used to satisfy some other end. The ends must be competing in order that value judgments or choices of different kinds are involved. When there are no alternatives, there is no problem of choice and, therefore, no economic problem.

Most important, observe how wide the definition is. It includes the choice of a car, a marriage mate, and a religion; the allocation of resources within a family; and political discussions about how much to spend on education or on fighting a Vietnam war. These all use scarce resources to satisfy competing ends.

In terms of what most economists generally do, however, this definition is too broad. Particularly in Western countries, economists are primarily concerned with the operation of the market sector in an industrialized economy. Yet I will often argue, and this is perhaps the unique theme of these lectures, that the economic principles developed for this sector are relevant to all problems of choice.

For example, economic analysis has been useful in understanding the labor force participation of children and wives, the allocation of time to various nonmarket activities, and family formation. It has also been used with some insight in understanding competition among political parties for elected office. Even illegal behavior and the forces, both monetary and psychic, that determine entry into criminal activities can be usefully analyzed within an economic framework.

Similarly, in recent years economists in Communist countries, such as Russia, Yugoslavia, Hungary, and Czechoslovakia, have discovered that the principles developed by Western economists—involving profits, prices, and interest rates—are of great relevance to their own economies. They often call them by different names, but the concepts are the same. Within our own economy, economic principles are currently being applied with some effect to rather inefficient nonprofit organizations like hospitals and universities.

It is frequently asserted that traditional economic principles are of little relevance in underdeveloped countries having large subsistence sectors and small market sectors. Dean[1] has studied the allocation of labor in a poor African country between a subsistence, a cash crop (tobacco), and a hired labor sector. He shows that shifts among these sectors resulting from changes in wages and tobacco prices are similar to those observed in the United States and other developed countries.

Although much of our discussion is also related to the market sector in industrialized economies, the principles being developed are frequently applied to other sectors and different kinds of choices. It is my belief that economic analysis is essential in understanding much of the behavior traditionally studied by sociologists, anthropologists, and other social scientists. This is a true example of economic imperialism! In other words, I argue that the broad definition of economics in terms of scarce means and competing ends should be taken seriously and should be a source of pride rather than embarrassment to economists since it provides insights into a wide variety of problems.

At the same time, our coverage is severely limited in a number of ways. The emphasis is on the allocation of resources under full employment conditions, and little attention is given to fluctuations in the price level, unemployment, or aggregate output. We do not, however, abstract from growth, and we plan to say a fair amount about growth in output, capital, labor, and technology. But fluctuations around trends, including serious fluctuations like the Great Depression, are not covered even though the same basic economic principles are also useful in understanding fluctuations.

In different words, we can say that microeconomics, not macroeconomics, is the subject matter of these lectures. The lectures are most emphatically, however, not confined to microeconomics in the literal sense of microunits like firms or households. Our main interest, as is that of most economists, is in the market behavior of aggregations of firms and households. Although important inferences are drawn about individual firms and households, we try mainly to understand aggregate responses to changes in basic economic parameters like tax rates, tariff schedules, technology, or antitrust provisions.

[1] Edwin Dean, *The Supply Response of African Farmers* (The Netherlands: North Holland Publishing Company, 1966).

Another important restriction is that these are primarily lectures on what is called positive economics—the *actual*, not the desired, behavior of markets and economies. We try to determine, for example, what happens to employment or housing when the government imposes a minimum wage or rent control, without asking very extensively whether these policies should be followed. It is significant that the analysis developed by economists to understand actual behavior has been their major contribution to determining desired behavior, so that indirectly these lectures are also of great relevance to what is called welfare economics.

The Role of Prices

Every society, regardless of its methods of organization, must somehow determine what is produced, how it is produced, and how that product is distributed. The basis of economics is choice, and an economy certainly has many choices among different products, including the choice of how much to set aside for future growth. Choice enters again in determining how to produce, for a variety of techniques and combinations of factors (different kinds of labor, capital, and raw materials) can usually be used to produce the same thing. Finally, there is choice in how to distribute what is produced, that is, choice about the personal distribution of income.

In a complete dictatorship, which even the most centralized economies have never experienced, one person or group makes all these choices. In decentralized market economies like our own, families, governments, and other organizations influence what to produce. They do so not primarily through the ballot box but by the way they spend their resources in the market place. There is a kind of proportional representation in which the influence of each person is not fixed nor shared equally, but is strictly proportional to his command over resources. Influence is exerted by offering to exchange these resources for the goods and services that are desired.

In this process prices play a crucial role even in the nonmarket sector where monetary prices do not exist, for economists have ingeniously discovered "shadow prices" that perform the same function. Because prices are so important, lectures on microeconomic theory can be said to be lectures on price theory. For example, an increase in the demand for product A and a decrease in that for B will bid up the price of A and force down that of B. These price movements encourage resources to enter the industry producing A and leave the industry producing B and thus help accommodate the change in influence.

In addition, prices determine how production is organized. If the price of capital decreased relative to the price of labor, firms would use more capital relative to labor, or if the price of skilled labor decreased relative to that of unskilled labor, they would use relatively more skilled labor. It is quite obvious that prices of factors, together with the personal distribution of the supplies of factors, in turn determine the personal distribution of income.

The latter determines the distribution of influence, and the process starts over again.

A central planning bureau could in principle determine what to produce, methods of production, and the distribution of products without relying on prices, but relying instead on input-output tables, resource constraint equations, and the like. Efforts to downgrade prices, however, have led to bottlenecks, unwanted surpluses, and a myriad of problems and complaints. This is why the main thrust of economic reform in Eastern Europe countries has been toward greater reliance on market prices in guiding economic decisions. One of the important goals of these lectures is to demonstrate how market prices influence these decisions.

These lectures cover systematically the various parts of price theory. We begin at one end of the economic system with the demand for final products, and move from there into the rest of the system. A discussion of the supply of final products leads directly into cost conditions. Implicit in the latter is the derived demand for factors of production, which in turn leads into an analysis of production functions. Finally, the supply of factors of production is considered—the supply of labor in general and to particular occupations and the supply of nonhuman capital. This discussion naturally directs our attention to savings, investment, and other forces determining economic growth, that is, to changes over time in the aggregate level of resources.

LECTURE 2

Supply and Demand Analysis

The three basic economic decisions are obviously closely related: what to produce may depend on the distribution of income, just as the latter may depend on what and how it is produced. Thus it has been said that in economics everything depends upon everything else. Critics have even accused economists of circular reasoning when describing the operation of the interdependent pricing mechanism.

The French economist Walras analyzed this problem of interdependence and showed that there is no circular reasoning, just mutual determination or general equilibrium. Anyone who has studied high school algebra knows that each of the unknowns in a system of simultaneous equations can be determined[1] provided a sufficient number of independent relations are

---

[1] Assume that the variable X_1 depends on X_2 according to the relation

$$X_1 = 5X_2 - 4$$

and that X_2 at the same time depends on X_1 according to

$$X_2 = X_1 - 8$$

The reader can easily verify that these equations are mutually consistent if, and only if, $X_2 = 3$ and $X_1 = 11$.

available. Walras similarly demonstrated that all prices and quantities in the economic system can be simultaneously determined because there are a sufficient number of independent supply and demand equations. Walras' demonstration was a major achievement with far-reaching implications, perhaps the greatest achievement of nineteenth-century economics—simple as it appears to a modern student.

The problem facing someone trying to learn about the economic world is: Given its apparent complexity and interdependency, how can it be made amenable to analysis? One approach is to say: "The world is complex, there is no escape from this. Realistically, it must be recognized that the demand for, say, butter, depends not only on the price of butter but also on the prices of margarine, lard, apples, beef, automobiles, machinists, economists; you name it, it is relevant." This approach takes the Walrasian equations and their interdependencies seriously and makes no attempt to reduce them to a simpler form.

A second approach, more pragmatic and in the English tradition, argues that to solve practical problems one must find a way to break into Walras' complex system. The analyst must be able to concentrate on the few variables he considers important for a particular problem and neglect the variables he considers unimportant. In the economist's own language, he must allocate the limited resources available to him for a particular study in the most efficient manner, which means considering just enough variables to obtain sufficiently accurate answers.

To continue with the butter illustration, the more pragmatic economist would want to consider the price of butter and probably the level of income, the price of margarine, and the size of the population as well. But he would neglect thousands and thousands of other variables that in principle might have an influence—the prices of beef, labor, and capital, tariff policies, and so on. The variables considered would not always remain the same. A law that prevents the artificial coloring of margarine could be quite important because it would reduce the demand for margarine and increase the demand for butter. Although the variables considered are not rigidly fixed, they are always a small fraction of the number entering Walras' system.

The major tool that has been invented to simplify the economic world is supply and demand analysis, brought to its highest development by Alfred Marshall. Supply and demand are the "engines of analysis" that enable an investigator to discuss systematically the variables he considers pertinent for a particular problem. They enable him to use his limited resources efficiently to obtain sufficiently accurate answers. Although often called partial-equilibrium analysis, a more accurate name for the supply-demand approach would be "practical general equilibrium analysis."

On one level, supply and demand analysis is simply a language or classification scheme: How does variable X affect the demand function, variable Y the supply function, and variable Z both? The classification of animals has been a useful language in zoology, and many other languages have been extremely useful in other scientific fields. The language of supply and demand has been

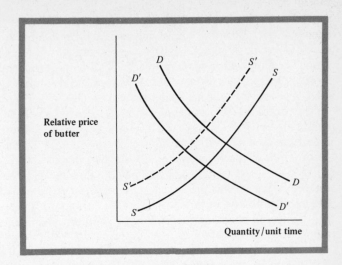

FIGURE 2.1

especially fruitful in solving economic problems because of the assumption that many variables affect either demand functions or supply functions, but not both. This assumption is no longer simply part of a language, but is a strong condition imposed on behavior. Its great empirical significance is that it permits one to reach conclusions about the effects of various changes on prices and outputs with relatively little information.

Suppose, for example, the price of margarine declined because an excise tax was removed. This would shift the supply curve of margarine to the right, lowering its price and thereby inducing the public to substitute margarine for butter, which would shift the demand curve for butter to the left. But it would have a negligible impact on the supply curve since butter and margarine are produced with very different resources, although soybean fields can make good cow feed. The hypothesis that the demand curve and not the supply curve for butter is altered by a change in the price of margarine, along with some other assumptions, permits a simple analysis of the responses in the butter market. In Figure 2.1, DD and SS are the initial supply and demand curves for butter drawn on the assumption that the price of margarine is fixed, and the initial market equilibrium is given by their intersection. Removal of the tax reduces the price of margarine and thus reduces the demand for butter at any given butter price, but does not change supply conditions. The leftward shift of the demand curve to $D'D'$ reduces both the price and quantity of butter.

To reach these important qualitative conclusions, we assumed (1) the direction of shift in the demand curve, (2) no shift in the supply curve, and (3) the signs of the slopes of the demand and supply curves. From such limited information, the direction of price and quantity movements in the butter market could be predicted. These predictions explain why butter producers lobby for higher taxes on margarine regardless of whether the form is anti-coloring provisions or a straight excise tax.

Such predictions could not be made if the supply curve of butter also shifted. If it shifted upward, to $S'S'$ in Figure 2.1, the quantity produced would fall even more than before, but the direction of change in the price of butter would not be known a priori and would depend on the relative shifts in the supply and demand curves. Therefore, the assumption that a removal of the tax on margarine has a negligible effect on the supply curve of butter *compared* to its effect on the demand curve greatly simplifies the analysis.

It would be still better if something could be said about the size, as well as direction, of the movements in prices and quantities. To do this requires information on the shapes of the supply and demand curves, and on the magnitude of their "shifts." Such information is not easily acquired although research in the last two decades has exponentially increased our empirical knowledge. Nevertheless, qualitative conclusions are extremely important and are sufficient, for example, to predict the attitudes of butter producers toward a tax on margarine.

These lectures are organized within the supply-demand framework. The discussions of final products, intermediate products, and factors of production are unified by a common treatment within this same framework. It is not only useful in handling relatively simple problems, such as the butter-margarine example, but also complicated ones, including the effects of unions on wages and the savings-investment equilibrium.

PART ONE

Demand Analysis

chapter 2

The Scarcity Principle

LECTURE 3

Definition of Demand

Perhaps the most fundamental finding in economics is the "law" of the negatively sloped demand curve. Other variables held constant, an increase in the relative price of any good would decrease the amount consumed of that good. Another useful relation is that a change in income necessarily changes total expenditures on goods by the same amount. Expenditures on individual goods may change by percentage amounts that differ from the percentage change in income, and expenditures on a "few" goods might even move inversely to the income change.

In the next three lectures we probe behind the fundamental law and the income relation. First, a demand curve is defined exactly, and its most important parameter, the price elasticity, is discussed. Then a model of irrational behavior by households is developed to show that the basic demand relations are derived fundamentally from scarcity alone rather than from an assumption that behavior is "rational."

The demand curve for a good by any group can be defined as the locus of points giving the amount of the good that the group would purchase per unit of time at different unit prices. It could also be defined in terms of the price that the group would pay for any given quantity. Notice that a demand curve can be defined for final products like butter or haircuts, intermediate products like sheet steel or polyethylene, or factors of production like engineers or machines. As is shown later, however, the demand for all goods and services is ultimately derived from the demand for final products.

Notice too that a demand curve can be defined for any group. Sometimes we speak of the demand by an individual household, other times of the demand by all persons in a city or by all members of a particular income or education class. Similarly, there are demand curves by a single firm, a collection of firms in an industry, or a collection of industries. Even the world demand for, say, wheat or rubber or oil is discussed. Indeed, the world demand for oil was in the headlines in 1967 when the Suez Canal was closed.

11

The amount that a group would purchase if the group could have all it wanted at a given unit price would be different from the amount it would purchase if offered, for example, either a certain amount or nothing at all at that price.

Time is used in two basic senses. The quantity is a flow per unit of time and increases in proportion to the time unit. A firm demands so many manhours per week, approximately 4 times that per month, or 52 times that per year. This use of time increases one's confidence in the continuity of the demand curve. A piano is purchased only in discrete units, say, once every ten years, but the rate of purchase can be considered continuous: 1/120 of a piano per month or 1/10 per year.

A demand curve measures alternatives as of a moment in time or under given conditions. Since these conditions include the history of purchases, a single demand curve would not necessarily predict the sequence of purchases as prices actually change over time. These dynamic patterns are partly captured in the differences between short and long run curves and are discussed later.

Elasticity of Demand

The most important property of the demand curve is the negative relation between price and quantity. At first blush, the magnitude of this relation could be summarized by the absolute value of the slope of the demand curve, $-dq/dp$. But this simple measure has the grave defect that it is not independent of units; measuring quantity and price in pounds instead of tons would significantly raise the slope[1] even though the basic relation between price and quantity has not changed. One measure that is independent of units is the ratio of the proportional change in quantity to the proportional change in price. This measure, called the elasticity of demand, is defined as

$$\epsilon = -\frac{dq}{dp}\frac{p}{q} \qquad (3\text{-}1)$$

It indicates the amount that quantity increases as price falls in a way that is independent of the units in which they are measured.

The elasticity is defined at each point on a demand curve and may be quite different at different points even on the same curve. If only a few points along a curve were known, the elasticity at any point would depend on the shape of the unknown curve connecting the known points. The job of the economic statistician is to fit the "best" curve to the known points, perhaps a straight line or a constant elasticity curve. Obviously, the notion of best becomes less ambiguous as more observations become available, which is our first

---

[1] The dimensions of the slope of a demand curve are a^2, where a is the unit of measure. If a' and a'' represent pounds and tons respectively, and since $a'' = 2,000a'$, a shift from a'' to a' would raise the slope by a factor of $(2,000)^2 = 4,000,000$.

encounter with the voracious appetite that applied economists have for "facts."

The elasticity is an important concept primarily because it is a convenient summary of the effect of a change in price on total expenditure (which equals total revenue of the sellers). If, for example, price falls by 1 percent, an elasticity of 1 implies that quantity increases also by 1 percent, thus leaving total expenditure unchanged; the additional units purchased just offset the reduction in expenditure per unit. An elasticity greater than 1 means that the percentage change in quantity exceeds that in price, and total expenditure increases whereas the converse holds if the elasticity is less than 1. A useful summary of these effects is given by the formula[2]

$$ MR = p\left(1 - \frac{1}{\epsilon}\right) \tag{3-2} $$

where MR refers to marginal revenue or expenditure, the change in the total as quantity changes. If $\epsilon = 1$, $MR = 0$ and total expenditure is unaffected by a change in quantity (or price) whereas if $\epsilon > 1$, $MR > 0$ and total expenditure increases as quantity increases or price falls.

To illustrate the importance of the elasticity concept, consider the following examples. A layman thinks that farmers should prefer good to bad weather, for good weather brings larger crops and presumably more profits. And, indeed, individual farmers looking only at their own situation generally do hope for good weather. Yet it often means less total revenue and profits, for although an outward shift in the supply curve of all farmers—say due to good weather—increases the quantity sold, it reduces their total revenue through a greater than proportionate reduction in price because the elasticity of demand for many agricultural products is less than unity. This explains why farmers throughout the world attempt, in effect, either to raise the elasticity or reduce the quantity offered by instigating agricultural storage programs and acreage restrictions.

A second example is in the field of industrial organization. Economists predict that industries with relatively inelastic demands at their competitive equilibrium positions are more likely to collude and develop other monopolistic policies. (Other factors, such as the elasticity of cost curves, are assumed to be the same. See the discussion in Lecture 21.) The gain from output restrictions would be greater in these industries because total revenue, and thus profits, would tend to increase more.

If, however, the elasticities of demand at the actual equilibrium position of each industry are compared, we may find a positive rather than negative correlation between the degree of monopoly and the elasticity. Although monopolies are more likely to develop in competitive industries that operate in inelastic sections of their demand curves, monopolistic industries have an

---

[2] This formula is easily derived by differentiating total revenue with respect to quantity:

$$ \frac{d(pq)}{dq} = MR = p + q\frac{dp}{dq} = p\left(1 + \frac{q}{p}\frac{dp}{dq}\right) = p\left(1 - \frac{1}{\epsilon}\right) $$

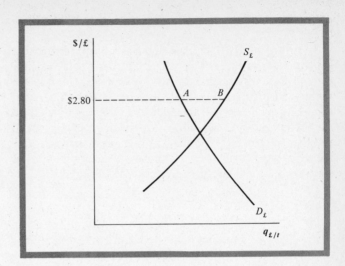

FIGURE 3.1

incentive to reduce output until they are in elastic sections. For industry profits are necessarily increased by a reduction in output in inelastic sections since total revenue would go up and total costs down. Consequently, the magnitude and even sign of the correlation between the degree of monopoly and the elasticity of demand would depend on whether the elasticity was measured before or after the monopoly developed.

A third example is drawn from the foreign-exchange market. The price of the British pound in terms of dollars was fixed at about $2.80 until late 1967. Since the demand for dollars exceeded the voluntary supply of pounds at that price, say by the amount AB in Figure 3.1, the British government supported the pound by selling dollars. Since their holding of dollars is limited, this process could not continue indefinitely. If the supply and demand curves for pounds were like those shown in the figure, the gap could be reduced by devaluing the pound, which is what Britain did. The shapes of these curves partly depend on the elasticities of the underlying demands for British imports and exports. For example, if the elasticity of the British demand for imports exceeded 1, devaluation would tend to reduce the supply of pounds in the foreign-exchange market since the percentage decline in the quantity imported would exceed the percentage increase in the pound price of imports.

LECTURE 4

The Opportunity Set

Our discussion of the demand function starts with the demand by individual households and builds from that to market demand. Since we are not pri-

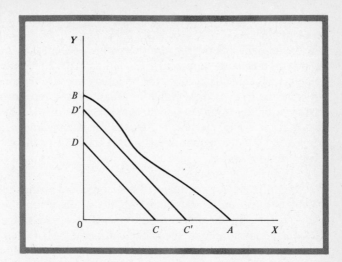

FIGURE 4.1

marily interested in households, the analysis of household demand is just an intermediate step useful in understanding the market. In fact, one of our models pays little direct attention to households and proceeds almost directly to market behavior.

Initially, we avoid utility functions, indifference curves, rational behavior, transitivity, and the other paraphernalia of modern demand analysis. We intend to demonstrate that the main conclusions of demand analysis stem from a much more general principle than rational behavior—the scarcity of resources that defines an economic problem (see Lecture 1). Accordingly, we are able to derive the usual demand functions even when households behave "irrationally."

The geometrical discussion is considerably simplified, without any loss in generality at this stage, by assuming that each household consumes only two goods, X and Y. The amounts of X and Y available or feasible are limited because both goods are assumed to be scarce relative to a household's resources. The set of all feasible combinations of goods is called the opportunity set and is illustrated by the area OAB in Figure 4.1, where the outer boundary AB shows the maximum combinations of X and Y available. A household may choose any point in the opportunity set, be it on the boundary or in the interior, and the point chosen may change from week to week according to a simple pattern or in an erratic fashion.

The shape of the boundary depends on the institutions prevailing in the market. For example, it would have kinks with rationing and other forms of multiple pricing. We usually assume, as a major and empirically valid simplification, a single price for each household that is independent of its purchases. The boundary is then simply a straight line, like CD in Figure 4.1, for since the slope of the boundary at any point measures how much Y can be acquired in exchange for a unit of X, it would equal the price of X divided by the price of Y. (Why?) If prices were independent of the quantities consumed, the slope would be constant, and the boundary would necessarily be a straight line.

A household's income per unit time, which depends on the labor and other factors its members supply to the market, determines the location of the boundary. Income determines the boundary because the amount spent could not continue to exceed the value of a household's resources. The X and Y intercepts of the boundary must equal income divided by the prices of X and Y, respectively. Hence, if I stands for income and p_x and p_y for these prices, the boundary equation of budget constraint can be written as

$$I = Xp_x + Yp_y \tag{4-1}$$

For several reasons we assume that a household spends all its income and thereby ends up on the boundary. If the whole income were not spent on X and Y, then by our definition of "spent" it would be spent on something else, which may simply be the accumulation of cash. Then by defining cash balances or whatever as additional goods, total expenditure on goods so defined would have to equal income.[1] Even if this definition of spent were dropped and households were permitted to be in the interior of opportunity sets, the analysis would not be greatly affected.

Income Effects

If a household's income increased with no change in relative prices, perhaps due to uniform technological progress, the boundary would move out parallel to itself, say from CD to $C'D'$ in Figure 4.1. At the most general level all that could be said is that expenditures must now shift to some point on the new boundary; in other words, the total change in expenditures would equal the change in income. Put differently and in a more interesting way, a weighted average of the income elasticities for each good would necessarily add up to 1. These elasticities are defined as the percentage change in quantity purchased per 1 percent change in income, and the weights are the fraction of income spent on each good. This formula follows simply from the equality between expenditures and income[2] and consequently holds for all kinds of behavior.

---

[1] Utility maximization in the absence of satiation also implies that a household spends all its income, but since we are not restricting the analysis to such behavior, this way out cannot be taken at present (see, however, the discussion in Lecture 6).

[2] Differentiating the budget constraint with respect to income, holding prices constant, gives

$$\frac{dI}{dI} \equiv 1 \equiv p_x \frac{dX}{dI} + p_y \frac{dY}{dI}$$

If the first term on the right-hand side is multiplied by $X/X \cdot I/I$ and the second term by $Y/Y \cdot I/I$, one gets

$$1 \equiv \frac{p_x X}{I} \frac{dX/x}{dI/I} + \frac{p_y Y}{I} \frac{dY/Y}{dI/I}$$

But $k_x = p_x X/I$ is simply the fraction of income spent on X, and $\eta_x = (dX/X)/(dI/I)$ is the income elasticity of demand for X. Consequently,

$$k_x \eta_x + k_y \eta_y \equiv 1$$

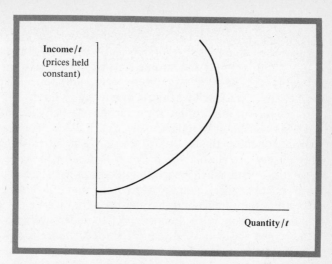

FIGURE 4.2

Market consumption of X or Y is by definition the sum of the consumption of all households in the market, which may be as large as the world or a nation or as small as a single town. If all households in the same market faced the same prices,[3] the market budget constraint relating market income to the market consumption of X and Y would be identical in form to the household constraint:

$$I_m = \sum_{i=1}^{n} I_i = \sum_{i=1}^{n} p_{x_i} X_i + \sum_{i=1}^{n} p_{y_i} Y_i = p_x X_m + p_y Y_m \qquad (4\text{-}2)$$

where the subscript i refers to the ith household in the market, and m refers to the market. Therefore, market choices are also constrained by an opportunity set bounded by a straight line, given by equation (4-2), and the market quantities of X and Y selected must be consistent with this constraint. Just as for an individual household, a weighted average of the market income elasticities for different goods, defined as the percentage change in market consumption per 1 percent change in market income, must sum to one, the weights being the market expenditure shares.

How is this market identity related to the corresponding household identity? In particular, is the market income elasticity "democratically" related to the household elasticities, so that the former is an equally weighted average of the latter? Or, as suggested in the opening lecture, do some households have greater influence? Problem 4.2 indicates that there is proportional representation rather than simple democracy; higher income households have greater influence than others.

One can draw a curve that relates the quantity of a particular good consumed to income, holding prices constant. The curve, usually called an Engel curve in honor of an early student of the relationship, can represent either a single household or an entire market, and typically has the shape

---

[3] Later (see Lecture 14) we discuss the factors determining the degree of price uniformity.

given in Figure 4.2. The quantity becomes positive after income exceeds a certain level, eventually increases at decreasing rates, and may even begin to decline when income becomes sufficiently high. The elasticity of the curve at any point is simply the income elasticity of demand for the good at that income level. The good is said to be "superior" when the curve is positively inclined and "inferior" when it is negatively inclined.

An important implication of the income elasticity identity is that different Engel curves cannot be independent of each other. For example, not all and, indeed, not more than a "few" can have negative slopes (or elasticities) since the average elasticity must equal 1. Or, for the same reason, very high elasticities—those much greater than 1—must be balanced by very low ones— those much smaller than 1. Moreover, goods that take a large share of expenditures are unlikely to have either very high or low elasticities, which explains why economists do not expect an underdeveloped country to have a high income elasticity of demand for food. Since food can take 60 to 70 percent of the budget in these countries, a high income elasticity would imply that the elasticities for other goods, such as manufactures and services, would be negative,[4] an implausible implication.

This entire discussion of income effects does not assume utility maximization, preferences, or any decision rule; it is based solely on the scarcity of opportunities and the identity between income and expenditures. A reader might think that adding utility maximization and transitive preferences would greatly expand the variety of income effects, but he would search in vain among the implications of utility theory for anything else. Consequently, the implications about income usually associated with this theory are in fact consistent with all other behavior, nonrational as well as rational.

PROBLEMS

4.1a.   Write the formula

$$\sum_j K_j N_j = 1$$

where N_j is the market income elasticity of demand for the jth good and K_j is the fraction of total market income spent on j, in terms of the η_{ij} and k_{ij}, where these are the income elasticities and shares of the ith person for the jth good. First derive the N_j in terms of the η_{ij}. Is N_j a simple average of the η_{ij}, or do higher income persons have a greater weight than lower income persons?

b.   If income is redistributed, do those gaining income increase their weight in the N_j?

---

[4] If $k_x = 0.7$ and $\eta_x > 10/7$, then $\eta_y < 0$ since $0.7\eta_x + 0.3\eta_y = 1$.

*4.2.   "There is a presumption that η_i and k_i are inversely related," where η_i is the income elasticity of the ith good and k_i is the fraction of total expenditures going to i.

a. Show that the sign of the correlation coefficient (look up the definition of this term if you don't know it) between η_i and k_i can be determined from knowledge of the various η_i *alone*.

b. Use this result to determine the sign of the correlation in the following bodies of data (supplied by Robert Michael).

Group	η_i (for different classifications of goods that exhaust total expenditures)
U.S. (1960)	0.64, 1.23, 0.76, 1.61, 0.76, 1.11, 0.98, 1.22, 0.94, 0.84, 1.30, 1.59, 1.35
Israel (1956–1957)	0.52, 1.42, 0.47, 2.31, 0.78, 0.78, 1.22, 1.71, 1.28, 1.24, 2.15, 1.70
Canada (1959)	0.53, 0.62, 0.97, 1.38, 1.18, 1.93, 0.77, 0.98, 1.35, 0.94, 0.89, 1.00, 1.28

c. Use the result in 4.2a to show that the sign of the correlation is basically arbitrary since it depends on the classification of goods used.

d. Will there be any correlation between the *direction of change* in k_i over time and the η_i, assuming that incomes rise over time?

LECTURE 5

Substitution Effects

We have indicated that the most important theorem in economics is that a "pure" increase in the relative price (or terms of trade) of good X would reduce the amount of X demanded. This theorem reappears under various guises throughout economic theory. Traditionally, it has been associated with rational behavior since it was derived from, and considered the main implication of, utility and indifference curve analysis. We intend to show, however, that like the income effects just discussed, it is basically implied by scarcity, not rationality, and holds for many other kinds of behavior as well.

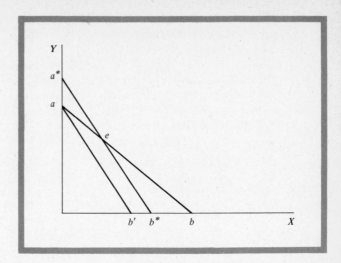

FIGURE 5.1

By a pure change in relative price, we mean a change that does not also change real income. Since the slope of a budget line in Figure 5.1 is p_x/p_y, a shift from ab to ab' would raise the absolute and relative price of X. Since real income or opportunities would clearly decline, opportunities in the set $ab'b$ would no longer be available; thus, the shift from ab to ab' cannot be considered a pure change in relative prices.

One common-sense method of holding real income constant is to change relative prices in a way that permits, yet does not require, the selection of the combination of X and Y chosen before the change. If point e on ab represents this initial combination, then a change to a^*b^* permits the continued selection of e, at the same time that it raises the relative price of X to the level given by the slope of ab'. This change eliminates the region bb^*e from the opportunity set, but compensates by adding the region aa^*e, and, in a sense, opportunities on the average are neither increased nor decreased.

A shift from ab to a^*b^* cannot be accomplished simply by increasing p_x, for the Y intercept, given by I/p_y, increases from a to a^*, which implies that either I increases or p_y decreases. Naturally, if the initial combination is to remain available, an increase in the price of X has to be accompanied either by a decrease in the price of Y or by an increase in money income. This is called a *compensated* price change.

This method of holding "apparent" real income constant by rotating the new budget line through the initial position is the most commonly used method in empirical demand studies that separate relative price from real income changes. The geometry is algebraically equivalent to changing relative prices while holding constant a ratio of money income to a Laspeyres measure of the price level; that is,

$$\frac{I^t}{P^i} = k \qquad\qquad (5\text{-}1)$$

where P^t, the Laspeyres measure of the price level in period t, uses the initial quantities consumed as fixed weights and is defined as

$$P^t = \sum p_i^t Q_i^o = \sum \frac{p_i^t}{p_i^o} (p_i^o Q_i^o) \tag{5-2}$$

where Q_i^o is the initial quantity of the ith good, and p_i^t is the price of the ith good in period t.[1]

Since a compensated increase in the relative price of X shifts opportunities away from X and toward Y, a consumer would be "forced" to consume less X and more Y. The force is not rationality or preferences, but simply the changing relative mix of different opportunities. For example, a shift from ab to $a*b*$ eliminates the region $bb*e$, which contains relatively large quantities of X, and adds the region $aa*e$, which contains relatively large Y. With a variety of decision rules, a shift of the opportunity set toward Y and away from X would result in greater consumption of Y and lesser consumption of X. To illustrate, if a consumer behaved "impulsively" (the model of man beloved by many on Madison Avenue), a shift from ab to $a*b*$ would give him more Y and less X to be impulsive about. One might expect him, therefore, to increase his consumption of Y and reduce his consumption of X.

To derive this conclusion more rigorously, a formal model of impulsive behavior has to be developed. To eliminate every vestige of preference, we define impulsive to mean that each point on the budget line is equally likely to be chosen. Then the expected position—in the mathematical sense of an average position—would be at the midpoint, with $\frac{1}{2}(I/p_x)$ units of X and $\frac{1}{2}(I/p_y)$ units of Y. Moreover, if the market contains a large number of consumers each choosing independently at random, the market demand per consumer, or the average demand, would almost certainly[2] be at the midpoint of the market's budget line with different consumers uniformly distributed around this point. In Figure 5.2, the axes measure the market demand per

[1] If the budget line is rotated through the initial position, then

$$\sum_i p_i^t Q_i^o = I^t$$

and

$$\sum_i p_i^o Q_i^o = I^o$$

Hence the Laspeyres price index would equal

$$L \equiv \frac{P^t}{P^o} \equiv \frac{\sum p_i^t Q_i^o}{\sum p_i^o Q_i^o} = \frac{I^t}{I^o}$$

Therefore, "apparent" real income, given by I/P, would be constant since

$$\frac{I^t}{P^t} = \frac{I^o}{P^o} = 1$$

[2] By "almost certainly" is meant that the variance around this point would be negligible if n, the number of consumers, were large.

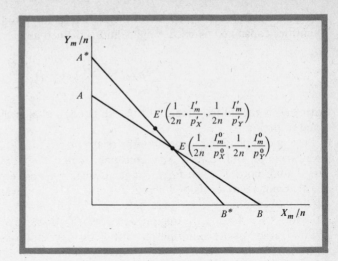

FIGURE 5.2

consumer, and the budget line AB measures the market income per consumer. The equilibrium would be at the midpoint, given by $1/2n(I_m/p_x)$ and $1/2n(I_m/p_y)$, respectively.

Suppose an increase in the relative price of X were fully compensated so that a ratio of market income to a Laspeyres price level with market expenditures as the weights was held constant. This is geometrically equivalent to rotating the budget line AB in Figure 5.2 through the midpoint E to A^*B^*. If each consumer also chose at random from the points on his new budget line, it is possible, and there is even a positive probability, that he would consume more X than initially. There is even a greater probability, however, that he would consume less; his expected behavior is shifted from the midpoint of his old budget line leftward to the midpoint of his new one.[3] What is mathematically expected for a single consumer is virtually certain for the market; it shifts from point E in Figure 5.2 to E'.

To summarize, we would observe a negative relation between the price of X and its market consumption even though every consumer chose at random. The shift in the opportunity set as relative prices change forces the community to respond rationally, at the same time that some consumers respond irrationally with positive relations between quantity and price. This expectation of greater predictability in the aggregate than in a single consumer is almost always confirmed in empirical studies; this is partly the basis for the economist's greater interest in and confidence about aggregate responses.

This model of random behavior not only implies a negatively inclined market demand curve, but a reasonably elastic one as well. The market demand function for X is simply $X_m = \frac{1}{2}(I_m/p_x)$, which can be written as

$$X_m = \frac{1}{2}\left(\frac{I_m}{P}\right)^1\left(\frac{p_x}{P}\right)^{-1} \tag{5-3}$$

---

[3] His new budget line does not necessarily pass through his initial position since his expenditure weights may differ from the average ones found in the market; in other words, his "apparent" real income is not necessarily held constant even though the community's income is.

where P is the Laspeyres measure of the price level. The reader should be able to show from the definition in equation (3-1) that the price elasticity defined with respect to a change in p_x/P, the relative price of X, equals $+1$, the absolute value of the price exponent in equation (5-3). Similarly, the income elasticity equals the exponent of the real income term (I_m/P), or $+1$ as well. Therefore, both the market price and income elasticities would equal $+1$, a response that is far from negligible. Indeed, these elasticities are precisely those implied by rational behavior when all consumers have a Cobb-Douglas utility function (this useful function is discussed in Lecture 11).

Of course, many other kinds of behavior principles could be considered. At the opposite pole from completely random behavior is inert behavior, or as little change as possible. A compensated rise in the relative price of X would literally force inert households consuming large quantities of X (relative to Y) to change, for otherwise they would violate their budget constraint. And since opportunities with relatively little X and much Y have opened up, they are likely to change by reducing their consumption of X.[4]

Of course, some behavior principles imply positively inclined demand curves even at the market level. Our point is not that all imply negatively inclined curves, but rather that strong pressures are exerted in that direction, pressures created by scarcity, the basic raw material of economics. Economists too frequently hear: "People are irrational and, therefore, do not have negatively inclined demand curves." Before the statement can be evaluated, a decision rule describing the irrationality has to be specified, a task seldom attended to by the critics. In any case, we have demonstrated that the "therefore" does not follow because the scarcity of resources usually forces irrational persons to respond in the same direction as rational persons.

PROBLEMS

5.1.   Consider a consumer who purchases 100 units of good X and 75 units of good Y at given money prices and given money income. Suppose that the price of X rose by 3 cents and the price of Y fell by 4 cents.

a. Calculate the change in the cost of the initial bundle.
b. If the individual's money income remained unchanged, will he purchase more, less, or the same amount of good X after the change in prices?
c. Does your answer to 5.1b depend on the income elasticity of demand for X?

---

[4] For an elaboration of this and related arguments, see: Gary S. Becker, "Irrational Behavior and Economic Theory," *Journal of Political Economy* (February 1962), 1–13.

5.2.   Evaluate: A doubling of all prices and money income to each
         consumer would not change the average consumption basket of a
         large group of impulsive consumers.

5.3.   Suppose that a person has an income of $4.00 per month, that there
         are two goods, X and Y, with equal prices $p_x = p_y = 1$. Also
         suppose that only integer values of X and Y can be purchased in
         any month, such as $X = 0$ and $Y = 4$, or $X = 1$ and $Y = 3$, and
         so forth. Suppose, in addition, that he decides what to purchase
         each month by choosing at random, with each integer position on
         the budget line being equally probable.

         a. Plot the quantity of X chosen for each of 12 months (use some
            random mechanism to make your choices).
         b. At the end of 12 months, p_x increases to $1\frac{1}{3}$ and p_y decreases to
            $\frac{2}{3}$. Plot the amount of X for another 12 months. Is there any
            discernible pattern?
         c. Sum the first and second 12 monthly observations into 2 annual
            observations. Plot these points. Is there a clearer pattern now?

         This problem illustrates the effect of changing the time span covered
         by the unit of observation, in particular, why economic patterns
         usually can be seen more clearly with annual than with monthly
         or quarterly observations.

chapter 3

Indifference Curves

LECTURE 6

Rational Behavior

We now begin a discussion of purposive (sometimes called rational) behavior with utility maximization. A reader who has absorbed the lessons of the previous lectures might wonder why we bother. Since we have demonstrated that the market demand curves tend to be negatively inclined even when consumers behave irrationally, and since this is usually considered the main implication of utility maximization, why bother with utility? One weak answer is that this is the common model in the economic literature, and students of economics have to be familiar with it to follow the literature.

There is a more compelling reason as well. Clearly, it cannot simply be the negative slope of demand curves nor even the other implications of utility theory found in major works like J. R. Hicks' *Value and Capital* or Paul Samuelson's *Foundations of Economic Analysis*. Several follow arithmetically from the negative slope of demand curves and would hold, therefore, for irrational behavior as well. An independent one deals with a certain symmetry of effects but has had little practical use.

Instead, the reason has to do with an implication of utility theory that receives insufficient emphasis—namely, that consumers prefer more goods to less. This is an extremely powerful implication that can explain why consumers end up on the boundary of their opportunity sets, why they buy at the lowest price known to them, or even Adam Smith's famous observation about the propensity of people "to truck, barter, and exchange one thing for another." It also provides an incentive to invest in education, on-the-job training, information about the quality and prices of goods, and other human capital. Of course, an assumption that consumers prefer more goods to less could be added to a model of irrational behavior. Although this is not logically inconsistent, a model that implies such behavior, in a sense that will be established shortly, is to be preferred.

One basic query is: What is meant by rational behavior? Consider first what is not meant. Certainly not that people are necessarily selfish, "economic men" solely concerned with their own well-being. This would rule out charity

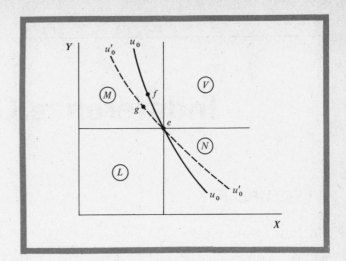

FIGURE 6.1

and love for children, spouses, relatives, or anyone else, and a model of rational behavior could not be so grossly inconsistent with actual behavior and still be useful. A viable definition of rationality must not exclude charity and love; indeed, consistent family behavior probably *requires* love between family members.

Also, rationality should not imply that each household's decisions are necessarily independent of those made by others. Different households are linked ultimately by a common cultural inheritance and background, and they may also be linked in a more proximate way. If household j increases its consumption of X, household i might be led to change its consumption of X. Such interdependencies commonly occur, and should be consistent with our model of rational behavior.

The essence of this model of rational behavior is contained in just two assumptions: each consumer has an ordered set of preferences, and he chooses the most preferred position available to him. Ordering includes transitivity and implies that he could rank any three baskets of goods, α, β, and γ, such that if he prefers α to β and β to γ, then (by transitivity) he necessarily prefers α to γ. When he neither prefers α to β nor β to γ, he is said to be indifferent between them (that is, he would be willing to let the toss of a coin determine his choice), and indifference is also transitive.

The Indifference System

Let the opportunity space be divided into four quadrants intersecting at some initial combination of goods, shown by point e in Figure 6.1. Since more of both goods are preferred to less, point e is preferred to any point in quadrant L and is less preferred than any point in V.

All points in quadrants M or N have more of one good and less of the other than at point e. Presumably, however, the closer the points in these

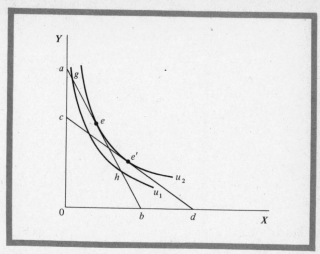

FIGURE 6.2

regions are to V, the more likely they are preferred to e, and the closer they are to L, vice versa. As one moves from points in M or N that are close to L to points close to V, one may pass points that are neither more nor less preferred than e. These points of indifference form a boundary between the less preferred and more preferred regions. This boundary, given by U_o in Figure 6.1, is called an indifference curve; the preference system is simply the complete family of these curves. We assume that each indifference curve is continuous and has no jumps or kinks.

Two indifference curves cannot intersect at a common point, like U_o and U_o' do at point e in Figure 6.1, for by the condition that more goods are preferred to less, a point like f on U_o would be preferred to a point like g on U_o'. By the same condition, each indifference curve has to be negatively inclined. (Why?)

A proof that more of all goods consumed in positive quantities is preferred to less can be developed along the following lines. If less of any good were preferred to more, and if the good had a non-negative price, a consumer would increase his utility by reducing his demand for that good until he either consumed none of it or preferred more to less.[1] If a consumer were "satiated" —indifferent between more and less of all goods—and if work were "irksome," he would reduce his hours worked and thus his income until either his income (or at least his earnings) vanished or he preferred more of some goods to less; he would then consume only these goods in positive quantities. It is in this sense that utility theory implies that more is preferred to less of all goods actually consumed.

Once the indifference curves or preference system of a consumer is known, no other information on his attitudes or personality is required. Information on his preferences, along with information on his income and on market

---

[1] Show that he could prefer less to more of a good with a negative price. If he did, what would be the slope of his indifference curves?

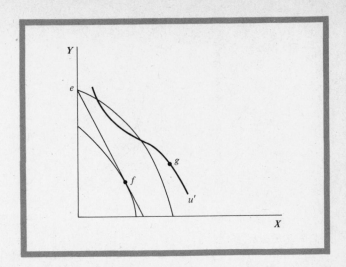

FIGURE 6.3

prices, would be sufficient to determine his choices completely. By assumption, he chooses the point in his opportunity set that touches his highest indifference curve. Clearly the highest indifference curve must be on the boundary; if the boundary were a straight line and if the indifference curves were convex, the equilibrium position would be the point of tangency, where the slope of the budget line equals the slope of an indifference curve (see point *e* or *e′* in Figure 6.2).

If the indifference curves were concave rather than convex to the origin as in Figure 6.3, the point of tangency would not be optimal. A higher indifference curve could be reached by moving away from the tangency point at *f* to specialize in one of the goods, say *Y* at point *e*. Since we consider only goods bought in positive quantities, completely concave indifference curves between these goods must be excluded. Of course, there could be both concave and convex sections, like *U′* in Figure 6.3. But since points like *g* on concave segments would never be optimal, they would never be chosen. For this reason, rather than any introspection about diminishing marginal utilities or rates of substitution, economists assume convex indifference curves for the goods actually consumed. Utility maximizing consumers would never end up in other regions.

The slope of the budget line gives the rate of transferring *X* into *Y* in the market place whereas the slope of an indifference curve gives the rate of transferring *X* into *Y* along the same preference level. Optimality requires equality between these slopes. If the consumer were at point *g* in Figure 6.2, convexity implies that the (absolute value of the) slope of his indifference curve going through *g* would exceed the slope of his budget line. By converting *Y* into *X* along the budget line, he would move to a higher indifference curve since the amount of *X* acquired would be more than sufficient to compensate for the loss in *Y*. Similarly, if he were at a point *h* to the right of *e*, converting *X* into *Y* at the market rate would raise his preference level. The point of tangency *e* is clearly, therefore, the optimal position; he would not leave *e* and would move to *e* from either direction.

PROBLEMS

6.1.   Prove geometrically that (1) a change in relative prices that keeps a household on the same indifference curve is equivalent *for small changes* to (2) a change in relative prices that keeps a ratio of his money income to a Laspeyres measure of the price level constant.

Hint: Prove this by showing the relationship between these two "pure" demand curves.

LECTURE 7

Demand Curves

Indifference curves can be used to analyze reactions to changes in either relative prices or opportunities. With a rational consumer there is an additional interpretation of a "pure" change in relative prices, namely, one that keeps him on a constant indifference curve, which is an interpretation of constant real income that is based on the "principle of substitution." Since our analysis of irrational behavior dispensed with indifference curves, this concept of real income could not be used earlier.

If a decline in the price of *X* were sufficiently compensated either by a rise in the price of *Y* or a decline in money income, the budget line would shift from *ab* to *cd* in Figure 6.2, and the optimality position from *e* to *e'* along a given indifference curve. By the definition of convexity, the slope of an indifference curve, or the rate at which a consumer is willing to substitute *Y* for *X*, would decrease as the amount of *X* increased relative to *Y* along a given indifference curve (this is called diminishing marginal rate of substitution). Consequently, since a decline in the relative price of *X* reduces the slope of the budget line, the tangency position along a given indifference curve would be shifted to the right. The demand curve for *X* (or *Y*) defined in this way would then be negatively inclined.

The elasticity of this demand curve would be greater the smaller the curvature of indifference curves, or the more slowly the marginal rate of substitution fell as, say, *X* was substituted for *Y*. For then the change required in *X* (and *Y*) to bring the marginal rate of substitution into equality with a lower relative price of *X* would be greater.

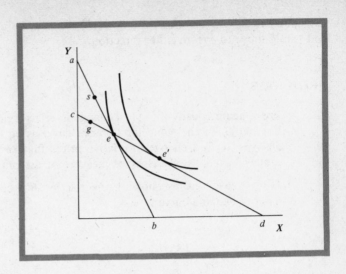

FIGURE 7.1

The trouble with trying to keep a consumer on the same indifference curve is that these curves are not directly observed. It is then virtually impossible in practice (although not in principle) to discover the appropriate changes in other prices or money income that would just compensate a change in the price of X. This is why empirical demand studies use the measurable approximation to constant real income developed earlier, namely, a constant ratio of money income to a Laspeyres measure of the price level. This is equivalent to rotating the budget lines in Figure 7.1 through point e, the initial optimal position.

As Figure 7.1 indicates, a rotation of the budget line from ab to cd through e would give a new optimal position e' that is on a higher indifference curve than e. Consequently, a demand curve derived in this way would not usually be the same as one derived by keeping the consumer on the same indifference curve. Nevertheless, it must also be negatively inclined. For assume the contrary, that the new position is at g in Figure 7.1, to the left of e. The point s on ab must be preferred to g since more goods are preferred to less, and point e is preferred to s since it was chosen over s. By the transitivity of preferences, therefore, e must be preferred to g, and the consumer would never choose g since e is still available. Nor could he stay at e because the indifference curve going through e could not be tangent to both ab and cd at that point.

The conclusion that more of a good would be demanded at lower relative price is of great importance, even though it is primarily a consequence of scarcity, and, therefore, tends to hold even when households behave irrationally. It explains why fewer fresh peaches are purchased in the winter than summer or why salads are more popular in California than in New York. (Why?) Somewhat less obviously, it explains why rural families have more children than urban ones, why women who can earn more in the market sector have fewer children than other women, or why a government allowance for children stimulates the birth rate. (Why? What is the effect, for example, of a government allowance on the cost of children?)

Similarly, a decline in the price of British goods relative to American goods would induce Americans to reduce their regard for "buy American" slogans and to increase their purchases of British goods. Or, the long delays in getting tickets to leading Broadway shows discourages attendance since a significant cost of attending these shows is the amount of advance planning required.

These conclusions are not inconsistent with patriotic behavior, love for children, or interest in cultural activities, as is frequently suggested by critics of the negatively inclined demand curve. Just as a negative relation between price and quantity is consistent with irrational behavior, so too is it consistent with patriotism and love. Nor are attitudes required to change as the price of British goods, children, or the theater change. Patriotism, for example, may cause many Americans to buy their own rather than British goods even when the latter are cheaper. But a decline in the relative price of British goods makes patriotism more expensive, which in turn discourages the purchase of this "good" and encourages the purchase of British goods, even with no change in the degree of patriotism. Attitudes like patriotism primarily explain the distribution of expenditures between domestic and imported goods at *given* prices, not the reaction to a change in prices.

Indifference curve analysis is often said to predict something significant about substitution and complementarity, for example, that other goods as a whole must be substitutes for any good X. But this follows only from the negatively inclined demand curve and a definition of substitution, and, therefore, holds for irrational consumers as well. If the demand for a good decreases when the compensated price of X falls, it is said to be a substitute for X. Since the quantity of X is negatively related to its price, the quantity of other goods as a whole *must* be directly related. (Why?)

Indifference curves do provide a framework for the description of substitution and complementarity, but this framework has been criticized precisely because it has no useful content in the two goods-case. An alternative approach is based on the common-sense notion that goods are substitutes if they are alternative ways of satisfying the same end, and complements if used together to satisfy the same end. Fords and Chevrolets are alternative means of transportation, fish and chicken are alternative sources of protein, and exercise and medical checkups are complements in the "production" of good health. A rigorous development of this approach must await the distinction between goods and ends and the introduction of household production functions (see Lecture 10).

Engel Curves

Just as a movement along an indifference curve is one way to define a shift in terms of trade, so a movement from one indifference curve to another, as

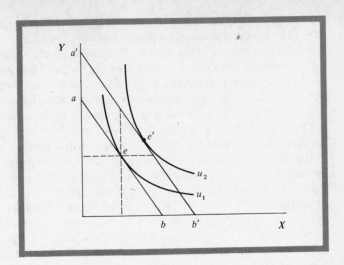

FIGURE 7.2

from U_1 to U_2 in Figure 7.2, is one way to define a shift in opportunities. Since the difficulty again is that indifference curves cannot be directly measured, empirical studies always measure a change in opportunities by the change in (real) money income. Clearly, these methods are equivalent in the sense that there is always a shift in income that corresponds to any given shift in preference level and vice versa.

If money income increased with no change in relative prices—if the budget line shifted out parallel to itself—what can be said about the change in X and Y as the optimal position shifted from say point e on ab in Figure 7.2 to a point e' on the higher indifference curve tangent to $a'b'$? Clearly, a weighted average of the income elasticities of X and Y must add up to 1, the result derived earlier from the identity between expenditures and income. The elasticities depend on the relation between the slopes of the various indifference curves. For example, if the slopes of all indifference curves were the same along any ray from the origin, X and Y would change by the same proportion as income, and both elasticities would equal 1. (Why?) On the other hand, if the slopes of the indifference curves declined (in absolute value) along any line parallel to the Y axis, X would decrease as income increased; that is, X would be an inferior good. (Why?)

These and other possibilities are not ruled out by the assumption that preferences are completely ordered. Economists have not managed to accumulate enough information about preferences to place restrictions on the ordering. For example, the assumption that slopes are constant along a given ray is contradicted by the observation that some goods, like food, have income elasticities much less than 1 whereas other goods, like automobiles, have elasticities much greater than 1. Or an assumption that slopes continue to increase along lines parallel to either axis is contradicted by the observation that many goods are inferior at some income levels and superior at others.

A number of useful empirical observations have accumulated, even though they are not sufficient to place any general restrictions on preferences. As incomes rise, consumers usually add many goods that were not purchased before—in developing nations, cars and television sets are being added rapidly—and decrease their consumption of many other goods—in the United States, potatoes, sugar, beer, bread, and subways are inferior over a wide income range. The more narrowly goods are defined, the more both patterns tend to be observed whereas aggregation hides the introduction of new goods and the elimination of old ones. The introduction of goods dominates on balance so that the *variety* of goods consumed is positively related to income.

The relation between consumption and income—that is, an Engel curve—is particularly useful in understanding the consequences of economic development. The agricultural sector has always declined relative to other sectors as countries have experienced significant development. In the United States, for example, agriculture now accounts for less than 8 percent of the labor force and 5 percent of national income whereas in the early nineteenth century it accounted for more than 50 percent of both. In a poorer country like the Soviet Union, agriculture still accounts for almost 50 percent of the labor force and 25 to 33 percent of national income. Part of the explanation is that agricultural products have a low income elasticity; therefore, as a country's income grows, resources are shifted (relatively and at times absolutely) from agriculture into services and manufacturing.[1]

The growth of income also can explain the large secular increase in "leisure" or decline in hours worked in the United States during this century. Some of the increased income has been converted into additional leisure time. To take another and a rather bizarre example, cannibalism may have been eliminated because human meat is a tough, "inferior" variety of meat. As incomes have grown, man has voluntarily shifted to more tender, "superior" varieties. One piece of evidence on the inferiority of human meat is that animals generally eat it only when near starvation—when their opportunities, so to speak, are depressed.

Income elasticities alone, however, cannot explain all the effects of development on consumption, as can be seen in the growth of the service sector (also see footnote 1). Labor employed in this sector (defined broadly to include retailing, wholesaling, professional services, and the like) has grown significantly in the United States during the last 50 years and now comprises more than one-half of the total labor force. The United States has even been called the first "service economy." Since the income elasticity of services is not much higher than that of "material" goods, the secular growth in income can explain only a small part of the redistribution of labor to the service sector.[2]

---

[1] This is not the whole story, however, since agricultural products also have a low price elasticity. The secular decline in the relative price of agriculture, especially during the last 30 years in the United States, has also contributed to its decreasing importance.

[2] Similar conclusions for Latin America can be found in a Ph.D. dissertation at Columbia by Joseph Ramos published under the title *Labor and Development in Latin America* (New York: Columbia University Press, 1970).

Another example of the use of Engel curves can be found in the analysis of fertility. It used to be commonly observed that higher income families had fewer children; children were an "inferior" good in the economist's perhaps unfortunate language. Recently, however, richer families in developed countries appear to have slightly more children than poorer ones. There is also evidence of a positive relation between income and family size across countries, if a number of variables—urbanization, child mortality, and so forth—are held constant. Therefore, children now appear to be a "superior" good. The income elasticity is only slightly positive because most of the increased expenditure on children at higher income levels goes not to increased numbers, but to increased expenditures per child—more toys, schooling, space, and so forth. In the same way, most of the increased expenditure on cars, houses, or television sets at higher income levels takes the form of more expensive rather than a greater number of units. This economic interpretation of fertility has become increasingly popular since the 1950s and has made a useful contribution to understanding fertility trends and differentials.

One final and more conventional example is the Engel curve known as the consumption function. The effect of a change in income on either total consumption or total savings (their sum equals income) has been made famous by Keynes. The first "psychological" law proposed by Keynes states that more is consumed as income rises, that total consumption is a superior good. This is plausible if the share of total consumption in income is large. About 90 percent of income is spent on consumption in the United States, leaving only 10 percent for savings. Since a weighted average of income elasticities must equal unity, consumption could be an inferior good only if the income elasticity of savings exceeded $+10$, a rather unlikely situation.

Keynes' second law states that the income elasticity of consumption is less than unity, a not so obvious "law" that is still vigorously debated. There was general acceptance of the second as well as the first law during the first two decades after the publication of Keynes' *General Theory* and both appeared to be supported by empirical evidence. But examination of consumption-income ratios in different countries and in the same country at different stages of development has led to a growing consensus that the income elasticity of consumption is close to unity, perhaps slightly less but not greatly so.[3]

PROBLEMS

7.1. Evaluate: Suppose the change in average prices from period A to period B was estimated by a fixed weight price index, the weights being the consumption basket in A (Laspeyres). Such an index would overestimate the change in money income required to maintain an average consumer on the indifference level he attained in A.

[3] Much of the empirical evidence and theory can be found in the important book by Milton Friedman, *A Theory of the Consumption Function* (Princeton, N.J.: Princeton University Press for the National Bureau of Economic Research, 1957).

7.2. Evaluate: A strike of subway workers would raise the price of a taxi ride.

7.3. Evaluate: If the demand curve for good X has unit elasticity, X would not have any close substitutes since the amount spent on X and on other goods as a whole remains the same as the price of X changes.

7.4. Will a decline in the relative price of black market or stolen merchandise increase the quantity demanded of such merchandise? Is this because people become less "honest" when the price of "crime" is lower? How would you measure, at the margin, a person's preference for legal over illegal merchandise?

7.5. If an indifference curve system is drawn for the two goods, total consumption and total savings,

a. What do Keynes' two laws assume about their shape?
b. What does Friedman assume?
c. Do the implications of 7.5a or 7.5b seem more plausible to you? Why?

7.6. Evaluate:

a. A weighted average of all price elasticities for different goods must add up to unity.
b. If all goods have income elasticities equal to unity, all price elasticities must also equal unity.

*7.7. Treat charitable contributions as a good entering the utility functions or indifference curves systems of the contributor. Assume that contributions can be deducted from income in arriving at taxable income. Assume a proportional income tax rate equal to t.

What would be the effect of an increase in the tax rate for any one person alone on his contributions? Is he more likely to increase or decrease his contributions? How does your analysis compare with the traditional analysis for goods?

LECTURE 8

Combined Demand Curves

We have discussed two variables in the demand function, relative price and real income. A demand curve shows the relation between relative price and quantity demanded, real income held constant, whereas an Engel curve shows the relation between real income and quantity demanded, relative price held constant. Sometimes both relative prices and real income are affected together. A subsidy given to a particular industry and financed by a tax else-where would reduce the relative price of that industry's product, would increase the real incomes of those persons substantially benefited by the subsidy, and would decrease the incomes of those heavily taxed to pay the subsidy. Therefore, a particular sector (an income class or education level) may experience a change in real income as well as in relative prices. As another example, if technological progress were greater in good X than in other goods, its relative price would fall as incomes rose (see the discussion in Lecture 25). Or, devaluation of currencies would reduce the relative price of domestic goods and sometimes also real incomes because the command over foreign goods would sometimes be reduced.

These examples illustrate how relative prices and opportunities often change together, and a method must be developed for dealing with their joint effects. The most direct way is to introduce explicitly a multivariate function, that is, a function with several variables where the quantity of X demanded D_x depends on the relative price of X, p_x/p, real income I/p, and the relative prices of any close substitutes or complements p_z/p. Symbolically,

$$D_x = f\left(\frac{p_x}{p}, \frac{p_z}{p}, \frac{I}{p}\right) \tag{8-1}$$

If income and price elasticities were constant, f has a simple form often used in empirical studies

$$D_x = \alpha\left(\frac{p_x}{p}\right)^{-a}\left(\frac{p_z}{p}\right)^{\pm b}\left(\frac{I}{p}\right)^{+c} \tag{8-2}$$

where a is the price and c is the income elasticity (show this!), b is positive if x and z are substitutes, and b is negative if x and z are complements.[1] This approach treats relative prices and income as separate variables in a more general function of several variables, a simple and natural procedure that is followed in most modern quantitative studies of demand.

Yet many economists use a special case that is applicable only in a small number of situations. A decline in the price of X is assumed to occur inde-pendently of any change in other prices and money income; the budget line is shifted from ab to ab' in Figure 8.1, and the optimal position is shifted from e to e'. The relative price of X has fallen and, at the same time, real income has increased; the increase would be greater if the amount of X consumed relative to Y were greater. The multivariate function [equation (8-1)] con-siders the shift from e to e' to be the sum of a relative price and an income effect. The former is isolated by the change from e to e'', where e'' is on a

[1] A direct implication of equations (8-1) and (8-2) is that a proportionate change in $p_x, p_z, p,$ and I would not change D_x: The demand function is said to be homogeneous of zero degree in these variables. Diagrammatically, since a proportionate change in these variables would not change the budget line (or surface), the optimal position would also be unchanged.

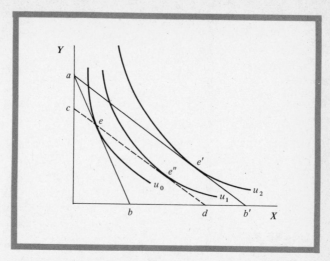

FIGURE 8.1

budget line through point e that is parallel to ab'. The latter is isolated by the change from e'' to e', the change resulting from a parallel shift outward in the budget line cd.

So the demand "curve" that relates changes in the quantity of X to changes in the price of X, holding money income and other prices constant, gives the combined effect of a change in relative prices and in real income—a combined movement along a "pure" demand curve and a "pure" Engel curve. This combined effect is summarized in the famous Slutsky equation, which states that the elasticity of the (combined) demand curve ϵ_x is the sum of the "pure" price elasticity E_x (the substitution effect) and the product of the "pure" income elasticity η_x (the income effect) and the fraction of income spent on X:

$$\epsilon_x = E_x + k_x\eta_x{}^2 \tag{8-3}$$

The combined demand curve is only *usually* negatively inclined, as distinguished from the pure demand curve, which is *necessarily* so. For any given substitution effect, the combined demand curve is more likely to be positively inclined, the more inferior the good and the larger the fraction of income spent on that good. But even a "very" inferior good that took a large fraction of income need not have a positively inclined combined demand curve if the substitution effect were sufficiently powerful. Of course, since inferior goods are the exception, the substitution and income effects usually reinforce each other to produce a negatively inclined combined demand curve that is more elastic than the pure demand curve. (Why?)

There is considerable doubt among economists whether a positively sloped combined demand curve (the so-called Giffen paradox) has ever existed. The

[2] For a simple geometrical derivation of the Slutsky equation, see M. Friedman, *Price Theory* (Chicago: Aldine, 1962), pp. 53–55. For a rigorous derivation, see, among others, Slutsky's classic "On the Theory of the Budget of the Consumer," reprinted in K. Boulding and G. J. Stigler, *Readings in Price Theory* (Chicago: Richard D. Irwin, 1952).

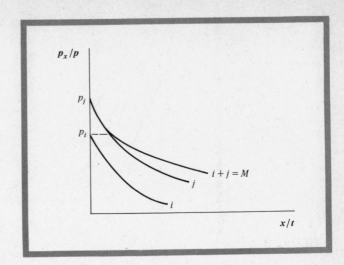

FIGURE 8.2

absence of a clear-cut empirical example may partly result from the economist's confidence in the ubiquity of the negatively sloped demand curve.
When preliminary results suggest a positive slope, the data are usually ingeniously "reworked" until a negative one emerges.[3] A second reason is that
most demand curves estimated nowadays are "pure" demand curves that
hold real income constant, and these curves are not expected to be positively
inclined (as we saw in Lectures 5–7).

The combined demand curve is an anachronism of the historical development of economics and should be used with extreme care. It is directly applicable only in a small number of relevant situations and is misleading or
downright wrong in others. The multivariate approach given by equation
(8-1) can systematically handle all situations, including those where relative
price and real income move in opposite directions, or where the increase in
income per unit decrease in relative price is very different from that assumed
in the combined curve. It is no accident that the latter is almost never used
any longer in statistical studies and that the simultaneous treatment of separate relative price and income effects via a multivariate approach dominates
these studies.

Market Demand and Engel Curves

Having derived demand and Engel curves for a single consumer, we now
consider market curves for groups of consumers. Two assumptions are made:
(1) all consumers face the same market prices (see Lecture 14), and (2) the
demand by any consumer is independent of the demand by others (see
Problem 8.4).

[3] Henry Moore, a pioneer in the use of econometrics, was confident and bold enough to publish
a finding of a positively sloped demand curve. But subsequent analysis indicated that he had
really "identified" a supply curve, which is expected to be positive.

The market's demand curve is then simply the horizontal sum of each consumer's demand curve. If in Figure 8.2, i is the demand for X by consumer i and j the demand by j, then M, the horizontal sum of their separate curves, is the market demand curve of i and j together. The demand curves of any number of consumers could be summed horizontally to get a market demand curve. The market can refer to a few people, a city, a nation, or the world, depending on the problem: it could be the effect of the Watts riot on the prices paid by Negroes in Los Angeles or the effect of the closing of the Suez Canal on the world demand for large tankers.

Since each consumer's pure demand curve is negatively inclined, the horizontal sum must also be; in this sense, the market curve is simply a blown-up version of the individual curves. In the relations between individual and market elasticities, however, some new considerations enter. Different consumers may have different points of entry into a market, different prices at which they begin to consume positive quantities of the good. In Figure 8.2, i consumes X only when p_x/p is below p_i, the entry point for i.[4] The market curve M is identical with js demand curve until p_i is reached; M develops a kink and becomes more elastic when i enters the market. Market consumption expands as price falls not only because each person in the market consumes more, but also because additional consumers enter the market. Since the distribution of entry points affects the shape of the market curve, the latter cannot depend solely on the "typical" individual's elasticity of demand.[5]

The distribution of entry points is partly related to the distribution of income. Consumption is usually dominated by the rich at very "high" prices, but poorer consumers enter and eventually dominate as prices become lower. This basically is what is meant by the statement that a firm has captured a mass market by lowering the price of its product. Since many consumers are concentrated in a narrow income range, a sufficient fall in price to encourage their entry would rapidly expand consumption, and market demand curves would be quite elastic in that price interval. For example, color television was "expensive" when first introduced and the market quite limited; the market has expanded rapidly, however, as the price has fallen significantly. This expansion has primarily been the result of entry by additional (somewhat lower income) consumers, not of an increase in the number of color sets per consumer.

If all persons were assumed to have the same income, the individual Engel curves could be aggregated in the same way to derive a market Engel curve.

---

[4] At prices above p_i, the optimality condition for i would not be equality between p_x/p_y and the slope of an indifference curve between X and other goods Y, but a "corner" solution at which p_x/p_y exceeded the slope. (Why?)

[5] Suppose that an increase in, say, the price of X was compensated by a decline in the price of other goods (Y) so that the ratio of money income to a Laspeyres price index using *market* expenditures as weights was held constant. Then the apparent real income of each consumer would not be held constant; the real income of consumers who spend a relatively large fraction of their income on Y would increase, and that of consumers who spend a relatively large fraction on X would decrease. (Why?) Therefore, market elasticities estimated by holding real income constant in this manner would be larger than those of typical consumers. (Why?)

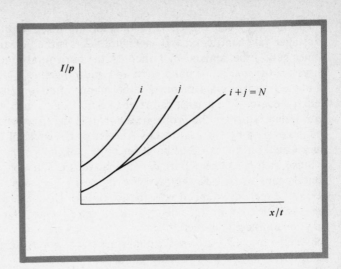

FIGURE 8.3

In Figure 8.3 the Engel curves of the ith and jth consumers are added horizontally to get a market Engel curve N, which shows the relation between the market demand for good X and income, relative prices held constant. The different entry points would be related to differences in preferences for good X.

Market Engel curves are not usually derived in this way because the assumption that all consumers have the same income is grossly contradicted by the sizable inequality in the distribution of income. Market Engel curves are usually derived from the aggregate income (or average income) of all those in the market and show the change in market consumption as aggregate income changes. If the income received by each consumer were uniquely related to the level of aggregate income, the market Engel curve would also be unique. It would, however, generally depend on the distribution of income because the income elasticities of persons with relatively large incomes would have a relatively great influence on the market elasticity. (See Problem 4.2. What if all persons had the same income elasticity?)

PROBLEMS

8.1.   Evaluate: In the United States real income per capita has risen over time whereas the number of domestic servants per capita has fallen. This means that domestic service is an inferior good.

8.2.   Evaluate:

     a. Goods that take a small part of a household's budget (like salt) are apt to have inelastic demand curves.

b. At any given price, the demand curve of a rich person is apt to be less elastic than that of a poor person for the same good.

*8.3.   Evaluate: Suppose that potatoes are a strongly inferior good and their relative price is reduced because price supports are removed. This would reduce the market consumption of potatoes.

*8.4.   Assume that each household's demand function for good X depends not only on the relative price of X, its real income, and so on, but also on the *market's* consumption of X.

a. What is the relation between each household's demand or Engel curve and the market curves? Show how to derive the market curves if one knew the individual curves.

b. Are the market curves more or less elastic than the household ones? Could a market demand curve be positively inclined? If so, how?

c. To help in answering 8.4a and 8.4b, derive the market functions, knowing that each household has the demand function for the jth good

$$X_j = K\left(\frac{p_x}{p}\right)^{-a_j}\left(\frac{I}{p}\right)^{b_j}X^{c_j}$$

where a_j is the elasticity of a household's demand function, b_j is its income elasticity, c_j is the "elasticity of interdependence," and prices and income are assumed to be the same for all households. If you knew that the a_j, b_j, and c_j were uncorrelated from good to good, what could you say about the correlation between the market elasticities, if c_j varied from good to good?

d. Can you use your analysis of the effects of interdependence to explain why a new process, like hybrid corn in the 1930s, or a new product, like television in the late 1940s and 1950s, typically spreads throughout the population initially at an increasing rate as shown in the figure?

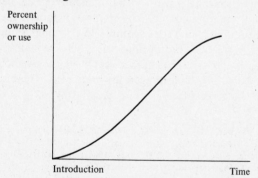

Percent ownership or use

Introduction   Time

What explains the eventual slowdown in the rate of spread?

LECTURE 9

Differences in Tastes

Differences in relative prices and real income, the two variables discussed in previous lectures, explain a large part of the differences in consumer behavior between geographic areas and time periods. For example, they explain most of the variation over time in the United States in the aggregate consumption of automobiles, refrigerators, and other durables; across states in the consumption of liquor; and even across countries in general consumption patterns.[1] Or to take a less statistical example, families in the Los Angeles area spend more time outdoors and have smaller dwellings than those in New York suburbs because the price of good climate relative to that of land and construction is lower in the former. Similarly, per capita consumption of beef is considerably lower in England than in Argentina, even though incomes are higher in England, because beef is much cheaper in Argentina.

Income and price usually appear even more important when care is exercised in matching the empirical measures and the theoretical constructs. By this is partly meant care in the statistical treatment of data so that differences in quality are not mistaken for differences in prices, or inflation-induced increases in money incomes are not mistaken for increases in real opportunities. Care is also necessary in developing the concepts of prices and income. For example, the lectures on the allocation of consumption over time show that the amount spent on consumption out of a given level of current income would tend to be greater, the more rapidly income is expected to increase in the future. This explains why unemployed persons consume a relatively large fraction of what income they do receive or why Negroes tend to consume less than whites with the same current incomes. (Why?)[2] The relevant concept of income should, therefore, take account of future as well as current income.

Time is required in the consumption of all goods: dining takes shopping, preparation, and eating time; certainly travel, education, and the theater take much time. Since time is scarce it has a shadow price, perhaps the earnings foregone, and the total price of consuming any good is the sum of its market price and the value of the time required to consume a unit of the good. Incorporation of the value of time into prices helps explain why married women who can earn more in the market sector have fewer children than other married women and why teen-agers are more willing than adults to wait in line many hours for tickets to the World Series. (Why?)

[1] See A. C. Harberger, ed., *The Demand for Durable Goods* (University of Chicago Press, 1960); J. L. Simon, "The Price Elasticity of Liquor in the United States and a Simple Method of Determination," *Econometrica*, 32 (January, 1966); and H. Houthakker, "An International Comparison of Household Expenditure Patterns," *Econometrica*, 23 (October, 1957).

[2] For answers see Friedman, *A Theory of the Consumption Function* (Princeton, N.J.: Princeton University Press for the National Bureau of Economic Research, 1957).

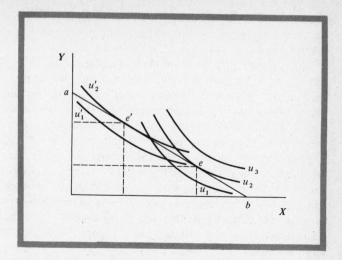

FIGURE 9.1

Even when considerable care is taken in the theoretical formulation and empirical analysis, differences in price and income do not explain all of the differences in consumer behavior, especially when the unit of analysis is the individual family. The demand function [equation (8-1)] has, therefore, frequently been expanded to include additional variables:

$$D_x = d\left(\frac{p_x}{p}, \frac{p_z}{p}, I/p, q_1, \ldots, q_n\right) \tag{9-1}$$

where the q_i may refer to trend in a time series analysis or to the age, education, sex, race, climate, and so forth of a particular consumer or group. These additional variables not only raise the "explanatory" power of the demand function, but also permit the effect of differences in prices and income to be disentangled from other effects.

The behavior of a utility-maximizing consumer is entirely determined by prices, income, and his "tastes." If different consumers behaved differently after adjustment for prices and income, the conclusion would have to be that their tastes differed. For example, consumers faced with the budget line ab in Figure 9.1 would consume more X and less Y if their preference system were given by $U_1, U_2, \ldots$ rather than by $U_1', U_2', \ldots$. If tastes were entered as a variable into equation (9-1) instead of the q_i, the resulting function would necessarily explain 100 percent of the variation in consumption among maximizing consumers.

The variables q_i in equation (9-1) must, therefore, be considered proxies for tastes: persons differing in, say, age, education, or the climate where they live also differ on the average in tastes. For example, evidence that more educated persons, after adjustment for price and income, have fewer children and spend more on services than less educated ones is taken to indicate that education increases the taste for services and decreases the taste for children. Or evidence that persons in warmer climates spend less on heating fuel is taken to indicate that they have less taste for fuel.

Although demand functions such as equation (9-1) can be used to *describe* the effects on tastes of various personal and environmental characteristics, they cannot be used to *predict* these effects in the way that they predict the effects of changes in prices, since economic theory does not explain the formation of tastes. Nor can one usually look to sociology or psychology since the theory in these fields has not been developed sufficiently to be of much help. The outcomes frequently are ad hoc theories about, say, the effect of education on the taste for children or the effect of race on savings that are not only usually bad theories but are also unrelated to any broader framework. The heavy reliance on presumed differences in tastes when explaining differences in consumer behavior is, therefore, a weakness of the traditional theory of choice; we would have a more useful theory if less were attributed to tastes and more were attributed to income and prices.

The main difficulty in the traditional theory is the assumption that goods purchased in the market place, food, clothing, theater tickets, heating fuel, medical care, and so forth are the objects of choice that directly enter the preference system. Obviously, this assumption is not literally true; for example, food does not directly give utility, but only contributes to the "production" of meals that do give utility. Preparation time, shopping time, stoves, refrigerators, knowledge of cooking, and many other inputs are also used in producing a meal, and food no more directly produces utility than do these other inputs. What is convincing for food becomes overwhelmingly obvious for medical services. Surely most consumers do not visit doctors or take medicines because these directly provide utility; on the contrary, many persons are frightened by doctors and medicines. The end presumably is good health, and medical care is one input into the production of health along with proper diet, exercise, recreation, knowledge of symptoms, inherited traits, and many others. Christian Scientists even eliminate most medical care with no apparent major loss of health. To take a still different example, individuals do not generally desire cash balances for their own sake, although many economic models do place them in preference functions. Cash balances are held to protect consumption plans against illness, unemployment, and other hazards.

If purchased goods were considered inputs into the production of "commodities" that entered directly into preferences, differences in tastes would become less important in explaining differences in behavior. Persons in warmer climates would use less heating fuel not because their taste for fuel was less, but because "comfortable indoor temperatures" could be achieved with less fuel input. Similarly, an advance in medical technology would change expenditures on medical care not because tastes were changed, but because the best combination of inputs to achieve "good health" was changed. Again, older persons could spend more for snow removal without suggesting that age affects the taste for clean sidewalks and roads.

PROBLEMS

9.1.   Evaluate: Budget studies show an income elasticity of demand for food of 0.5 for urban families and of 0.35 for farm families. This implies that farm families have different tastes from urban families.

*9.2.   The income elasticities of demand for market services, like haircuts, estimated from different households at a moment in time generally exceeds those estimated from the same households over time. Can you explain this by integrating the cost of time into the analysis?

*LECTURE 10

Revised Approach to Consumer Choices

We now formally introduce a revised theory of choice in which purchased goods are one of the inputs into the production of "commodities" that directly enter preferences. This approach reduces the need to rely on differences in tastes and increases the importance of differences in prices and incomes, the two parameters that can be treated by our framework. In addition, it incorporates the value of time systematically into the price structure and "full" income into the budget constraint.

Preferences are assumed to be an ordered function of a set of commodities $Z_1, \ldots, Z_m$, and for the reasons discussed earlier, the indifference curves between different Z_i can be considered strictly convex. Households themselves "produce" these commodities by combining different market goods, own time, and other inputs in the production functions:

$$Z_i = f_i(X_1, X_2, \ldots, X_i, t_1, t_2, \ldots, t_p; R) \qquad (10\text{-}1)$$

where

$$f_i = \text{production function for } Z_i$$
$$X_1, \ldots, X_i = \text{inputs of different goods purchased into } Z_i$$
$$t_1, \ldots, t_p = \text{inputs of different kinds of time}$$
$$R = \text{other variables}$$

The production of a meal, for example, may require the input of bread, wine, steak, shopping time, preparation time, chairs, cookbooks, and so forth. This approach abandons the traditional separation between production and consumption and makes households producers as well as consumers.

Choices are restricted to the opportunity space determined by various constraints, one being the set of production functions. The total expenditure on market goods is limited by the money income available, as in

$$\sum_{i=1}^{m} p_i X_i = I \qquad (10\text{-}2)$$

where X_i represents all the goods used to produce Z_i. During any period, the sum of the time used to produce different commodities plus the time spent at work must equal the total time available:

$$\sum_{i=1}^{m} t_i + t_w = t \qquad (10\text{-}3)$$

where t is 168 hours per week, 720 hours per month, and so forth. An implication of equation (10-3) is that any time not spent at work, including time spent sleeping, would be an input into the production of some commodity. In rich countries especially, the time "budget" constraint is important as time is probably the major limitational factor.

Income not only equals the total expenditure on goods but also the sum of all factor payments, and can be written as

$$wt_w + V = I = \sum p_i X_i \qquad (10\text{-}4)$$

where w = the average wage rate
$\quad\;\; V$ = other income

Hence, the separate goods and time constraints can be converted into a single total resource constraint by substituting for t_w from equation (10-3):

$$\sum_{i=1}^{m} p_i X_i + \sum_{i=1}^{m} wt_i = wt + V = S \qquad (10\text{-}5)$$

If w were constant, the term S on the right would be a measure of income, not the actual income I, but the "full" income that would be realized if all time were devoted to market work. Unlike I, S is not affected by variations in time worked caused by unemployment, overtime, illness, or retirement. Thus, by using S to measure the constraint on resources, the major causes of the difference between actual and "permanent" earnings are automatically eliminated.

The terms on the left show that full income is "spent" partly on goods and partly by forgoing earnings to use time in household production. The first term gives the goods component of the price of commodities and the second the time component. This interpretation becomes more transparent if a fixed amount of X_i and a fixed amount of t_i are always required to produce a unit of Z_i. Then the general production functions f_i could be written in the simple form

$$X_i = a_i Z_i;\ t_i = b_i Z_i \qquad (10\text{-}6)$$

where a_i and b_i are fixed input-output coefficients.

If equation (10-6) is substituted into (10-5), one gets

$$\sum_{i=1}^{m} a_i p_i Z_i + \sum_{i=1}^{m} b_i w Z_i = \sum_{i=1}^{m} \pi_i Z_i = S \qquad (10\text{-}7)$$

The term

$$\pi_i = a_i p_i + b_i w \qquad (10\text{-}8)$$

is the sum of the cost of goods per unit of Z_i, given by $a_i p_i$, and the "shadow" or opportunity cost of time, given by $b_i w$, and is, therefore, the "shadow" price of a unit of Z_i. The cost of time is fully integrated into the analysis and treated symmetrically to the cost of goods; indeed, in the United States, the opportunity cost of time may be more important than the direct cost of goods.

Each household can be said to choose the Z_i subject to the single resource constraint given by equation (10-7). Put in this form, the analysis is formally the same as in the conventional approach, and the theorems derived earlier still hold. A weighted average of the full-income elasticities of the Z_i would add up to unity, and a "pure"[1] decline in the relative price of Z_i would increase its quantity consumed. A major novelty of the new approach is in the effect of wage rates on consumption. An increase in the wage rate would increase the cost of all the Z_i, but especially of those Z_i with a relatively important time component. (Why?) The *relative* prices of these commodities would increase, and their consumption would be discouraged.

Environmental Variables

In the new approach, the effects of age, education, climate, ability, and other "environmental" variables on behavior can be introduced through the household production functions instead of through tastes. These variables would be represented by R in equation (10-1); a change in R would change the amounts of the X_i and t_i required to produce a given amount of Z_i—the a_i and b_i coefficients in equation (10-6). For example, households in warm climates could produce a "comfortable indoor temperature" with smaller inputs of heating fuel, insulation, and clothing than could those in cold climates. Similarly, educated persons may be able to produce a given level of "health" with relatively small inputs of food and medical care because of

---

[1] One way to define "pure" is to hold constant a ratio of S to a Laspeyres measure of the price level of the π_i.

greater awareness of the vitamin content of different foods, the deleterious effects of cigarette smoking, or the benefits of exercise. Again, "abler" house-wives could produce better "meals" from a given expenditure on food and time.

If an increase in one environmental variable, say, education, improved efficiency by reducing the a_i and b_i input coefficients, it would reduce the cost of producing commodities, and thus would expand opportunities, *even if full income were not affected*. If all input coefficients fell by the same percentage, all commodity prices would also fall by the same percentage (Why?), and no substitution effects would result.[2] An income effect would result from the expansion in opportunities, and the Z_i would be increased in proportion to their income elasticities.

What would be the effect on the demand for different goods and time, which are more directly observable than the Z_i? If an increase in education reduced all input coefficients by the same percentage, the percentage increase in output from given inputs would be the same for all commodities. This would, however, be too small an increase for commodities with income elasticities greater than unity, too large for those with elasticities less than unity, and just right for those with elasticities equal to unity. Consequently, more of the goods and time entering the first set of commodities (the "luxur-ies") would be used, less of those entering the second set (the "necessities"), and the same amount of those entering the third.[3]

In this model, education and other environmental variables enter the de-mand functions for goods not because they change tastes, as in the traditional approach, but because they change the efficiency of household production. Moreover, their effects on demand can not only be *described* statistically, but can also be *predicted*. For example, even if (full) money income were held constant, an increase in education would tend to increase the demand for goods (and time) with high income elasticities and reduce the demand for those with low elasticities. By reducing the reliance on ad hoc shifts in tastes, this method of handling environmental variables is a powerful tool for greatly expanding the predictive content of economic theory.

APPENDIX

1. Since the price of Z_i is $\pi_i = a_i p_i + b_i w$, the effect on π_i of a change in, say, education that did not change wage rates or market prices would be

$$\frac{d\pi_i}{dE} = p_i \frac{da_i}{dE} + w \frac{db_i}{dE} \tag{A-1}$$

or

$$\tilde{\pi}_i \equiv \frac{d\pi_i}{dE}\frac{1}{\pi_i} = s_i\tilde{a}_i + (1 - s_i)\tilde{b}_i \tag{A-2}$$

[2] See section 1 of the Appendix.
[3] Section 2 of the Appendix. A more general analysis is found in section 3.

where

$$s_i = \frac{a_i p_i}{\pi_i}, \qquad \tilde{a}_i = \frac{da_i}{dE} \frac{1}{a_i}, \text{etc.}$$

If $\tilde{a}_i = \tilde{b}_i$, clearly

$$\tilde{\pi}_i = \tilde{a}_i = \tilde{b}_i \tag{A-3}$$

and if $\tilde{a}_i = \tilde{b}_i = \tilde{a}_j$, all i and j, then

$$\tilde{\pi}_i = \tilde{\pi}_j \tag{A-4}$$

If real full income is defined as

$$S^* = \frac{S}{\pi} = \frac{S}{\sum v_i \pi_i} \tag{A-5}$$

where the v_i are fixed weights, then abstracting from the effect of E on S,

$$\tilde{S}^* = -\tilde{\pi} = -\sum \left(\frac{v_i \pi_i}{\pi}\right) \tilde{\pi}_i \tag{A-6}$$

If equation (A-4) held, (A-6) reduces to

$$\tilde{S}^* = -\tilde{\pi}_i \tag{A-7}$$

2. If the income elasticity of demand for Z_i were η_i, the increased demand for Z_i would be [if equation (A-7) held],

$$\tilde{Z}_i^D = \tilde{S}^* \eta_i = -\tilde{\pi} \eta_i = -\tilde{\pi}_i \eta_i \tag{A-8}$$

The increased supply of Z_i from given inputs of X_i and t_i would be

$$\tilde{Z}_i^S = -\tilde{\pi}_i \tag{A-9}$$

and, therefore, the induced change in demand for X_i (or t_i) would be

$$\begin{aligned}
\tilde{X}_i^D &= \tilde{Z}_i^D - \tilde{Z}_i^S \\
&= -\tilde{\pi}_i(\eta_i - 1) \\
&= -\tilde{\pi}(\eta_i - 1)
\end{aligned} \tag{A-10}$$

3. If equation (A-4) did not hold, the demand for Z_i would also be affected by a substitution effect; the total change would be

$$\tilde{Z}_i^D = -\tilde{\pi} \eta_i - \epsilon_i(\tilde{\pi}_i - \tilde{\pi}) \tag{A-11}$$

where

$$\epsilon_i = -\frac{\partial Z_i}{\partial(\pi_i/\pi)} \cdot \frac{\pi_i/\pi}{Z_i} \tag{A-12}$$

is the "pure" price elasticity of demand. Since $\tilde{Z}_i^s$ is still given by (A-9),

$$\tilde{X}_i^P = -\tilde{\pi}\eta_i - \epsilon_i(\tilde{\pi}_i - \tilde{\pi}) + \tilde{\pi}_i \tag{A-13}$$

or, by adding and subtracting $\tilde{\pi}$,

$$\tilde{X}_i^P = -\tilde{\pi}(\eta_i - 1) - (\tilde{\pi}_i - \tilde{\pi})(\epsilon_i - 1) \tag{A-14}$$

The derived demand for X_i and t_i would move in the same direction as the relative price of Z_i if the price and income elasticities of demand for Z_i both exceeded unity, and in the opposite direction if they both were less than unity.

PROBLEMS

*10.1.   When income, age, and a few other variables are held constant, more educated persons are healthier than less educated ones; yet probably the former spend less on medical care than do the latter. Can you explain this?

*10.2.   When permanent income is held constant, an increase in education appears to reduce the number of children and television sets a family has, and the pounds of food it consumes, at the same time that the amount spent per child, per television set, and per pound of food increases. Can you explain these effects by using the model of household production of commodities?

LECTURE 11

Utility Analysis

I have made only a few casual remarks about utility functions, although in Alfred Marshall's *Principles of Economics* and other great neoclassical works, the theory of demand was based on diminishing marginal utility. In this lecture, the utility approach is presented and related to the indifference curve approach.

Each consumer is assumed to try to get as much "utility" as is consistent with his budget constraint. The function measuring the "utility" received from different combinations of commodities can be written as

$$U = U(Z_1, Z_2, \ldots, Z_m) \qquad (11\text{-}1)$$

The optimality condition is that all the ratios of marginal utility to price be the same:

$$\frac{MU_1}{\pi_1} = \frac{MU_2}{\pi_2} = \cdots = \frac{MU_m}{\pi_m} = \lambda \qquad (11\text{-}2)$$

where $MU_i = \partial U/\partial Z_i$ is the marginal utility provided by the ith commodity. A proof is straightforward. Each ratio gives the utility from spending an additional dollar on a particular commodity. If the ratio were higher for Z_i than Z_j, the utility from a given total expenditure could be increased by shifting some expenditures from Z_j to Z_i. This shifting would continue until the ratios were exactly the same.[1] The term λ measures the utility from spending an additional dollar on any commodity and can be called the marginal utility of income.

The optimality condition in equation (11-2) implies that the ratio of the marginal utilities of any two commodities equals the ratio of their prices. We derived earlier the condition that the slope of an indifference curve equals the ratio of prices; if these two conditions are consistent, they imply that the slope of an indifference curve would equal the ratio of marginal utilities. Indeed, a unique set of indifference curves with these properties can always be found from any utility function, and a utility function can be found from any set of indifference curves.

A consumer with the utility function (11-1) would be indifferent between all combinations of the Z_i that yielded the same utility. The slope of the indifference curve between any two commodities—the others held constant— is easily shown to be

$$\text{slope } (Z_1, Z_2) = \frac{-MU_1}{MU_2} \qquad [2] \qquad (11\text{-}3)$$

---

[1] Mathematically, the problem is to maximize U subject to the budget constraint. By maximizing the Lagrangian expression

$$G = U(Z_1, \ldots, Z_m) + \lambda(S - \Sigma_i \pi_i Z_i)$$

with respect to the Z_i, one gets

$$MU_i = \lambda \pi_i$$

or

$$\frac{MU_i}{\pi_i} = \lambda$$

[2] The total differential of the utility function between two commodities is

$$dU = MU_1\, dZ_1 + MU_2\, dZ_2$$

If all combinations of Z_1 and Z_2 were to be on the same indifference curve, then $dU = 0$, and

$$\left.\frac{dZ_2}{dZ_1}\right|_{dU=0} = \text{slope } (Z_1, Z_2) = -\frac{MU_1}{MU_2}$$

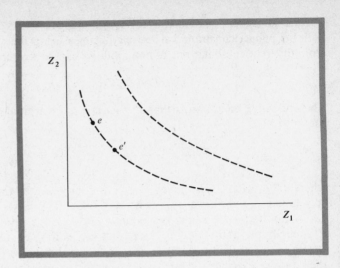

FIGURE 11.1

Likewise, if an indifference curve system were given, a numerical value could be attached to each level and called utility. Then every combination of commodities would give one and only one utility value, and these values are the utility function.

A consumer's indifference curves are in principle derivable from behavior, in the sense that they could be constructed with enough information on his choices. If he selected point e in Figure 11.1 at known prices, the slope of the indifference curve through e must equal the ratio of these prices, and is given by the line-segment through e. Similarly, if he selected e' at different prices, the slope through e' would also be known, and is given by the line-segment through e'. With enough observations, the opportunity space would be covered with a large number of slopes, as illustrated by Figure 11.1, and the shape of his indifference curves would emerge. Although in principle his indifference curves could be derived, in practice usually only a small part of the information required is available.

Can the same principle be established for utility; namely, would sufficient information permit the derivation of a unique utility function? Since we have shown that some utility function could always be constructed from any set of indifference curves, the only question is its uniqueness. Let the constructed function be U and consider a family of different functions $U' = U + a$, where a is a constant greater than zero. Since every combination of commodities that gave the same value of U, say U_o, would also give the same value of U', equal to $U_o + a = U'_o$, the indifference curves of U' and U would be identical; therefore, U' as well as U could be constructed from these curves. The same is obviously true for the utility functions $U'' = kU$, where k is a constant greater than zero, and, indeed, for any function U^* that is a monotonic transformation of U, a transformation that preserves the ordering of commodity combinations.[3]

[3] Let

$$U^* = g(U)$$

Consequently, a unique set of indifference curves and an infinite number of utility functions could be constructed from sufficient knowledge of choices. When this conclusion was first established it had a revolutionary impact, for economists had heavily relied on utility functions to understand behavior.

Take, for example, the apparently plausible principle that an additional dollar is "worth less" to a rich man than to a poor one because the marginal utility of income is decreasing. Alfred Marshall partly inferred this principle from behavior: a rich man is more likely than a poor man to take a cab in a rainstorm. The principle was used normatively to provide theoretical support for the progressive income tax. Yet diminishing utility cannot be derived from consumer behavior; indeed, if one utility function had diminishing marginal utility of income, another one equally consistent with behavior would have increasing marginal utility of income.[4] Even with increasing marginal utility, a rich man might take a cab where a poor man did not if the *ratio* of the utility foregone by taking a cab to the utility foregone by walking were smaller to the rich man.

The important point is that *ratios* of marginal utilities, not marginal utilities themselves, determine indifference curves and behavior. The convexity of indifference curves implies only that the marginal utility of Z_1 declines *relative* to that of Z_2 as Z_1 increases relative to Z_2 along any indifference curve; the marginal utility of Z_1 itself might increase. This is why diminishing utility of income or of commodities cannot be inferred from any evidence on consumer choices.

Unable to justify diminishing marginal utility from consumer choices, economists have frequently turned to other evidence and arguments. Perhaps

---

where

$$g' = \frac{dg}{dU} > 0$$

Then

$$\frac{MU_1^*}{MU_2^*} = \frac{g'MU_1}{g'MU_2} = \frac{MU_1}{MU_2} = \text{slope of the indifference curve}$$

Hence, U^* has the same indifference curves as U.

[4] Define the marginal utility of income for the function U by

$$MU_s = \frac{dU}{dS}$$

(In equilibrium, this equals $\lambda = MU_i/p_i$.) If the marginal utility of income were decreasing,

$$MU_{ss} = \frac{d(dU/dS)}{dS} < 0$$

Introduce a new utility function $U^* = U^n$, $n > 0$, that has the same indifference curves and ordering. Then

$$MU_s^* = nU^{n-1}MU_s$$

and

$$MU_{ss}^* = nU^{n-1}MU_{ss} + n(n-1)U^{n-2}(MU_s)^2$$

The first term on the right side is negative by assumption, but the second term is positive if $n > 1$. The second term would dominate if n were sufficiently large because it increases in proportion to n^2 whereas the first term increases only in proportion to n. Therefore, MU_{ss}^* is necessarily greater than zero for large values of n.

the most common argument is based on the fixed stomach capacity, surface space, physical size, and time of human beings. Diminishing marginal utility of income is alleged to result from the barriers to enjoyment created by these constraints. These barriers are important in explaining behavior. For example, the fixed stomach capacity and surface space can explain why increases in income have small effects on the physical amount of food consumed and clothes worn, and large effects on the quality of food and clothing (including attention to fashion). Or the limited time available for consumption explains why an increase in husbands' incomes reduces the time worked by wives. Again, however, only changes in *relative* marginal utilities can be inferred. An increase in money income decreases the marginal utility of money income *relative* to that of stomach capacity and time; but the absolute marginal utility of money income (as well as of stomach capacity and time) is as unobservable as ever.[5]

Although economists now recognize that diminishing marginal utility cannot be inferred from behavior, many still advocate progressive taxation and other redistributive measures. The currently popular way to evaluate these measures is to introduce a "social welfare function" that, in essence, compares the "social worthiness" of the marginal consumption of different persons. An alternative approach that has developed recently is based on interdependencies between the preferences of different consumers.[6]

Instead of the search for a unique utility function, there is now a search

---

[5] The most natural way to incorporate variables like stomach capacity is to place them in the household production functions along with other environmental variables. Each consumer tries to maximize

$$U = U(Z_1, Z_2, \ldots, Z_m) \tag{1}'$$

subject to, among other constraints,

$$Z_i = f_i(X_i, t_i; E, C) \tag{2}'$$

and

$$\sum_i p_i X_i = I; \ C = C_0 \tag{3}'$$

where C_0 measures the given value of stomach capacity. The first-order conditions for the X_i and C are

$$MU_i MP_i^x = \lambda p_i \tag{4}'$$

$$MU_i MP_i^c = \mu$$

where

$$MP_i^x = \frac{\partial Z_i}{\partial X_i} \qquad MP_i^c = \frac{\partial Z_i}{\partial C} \tag{5}'$$

are the marginal products of goods and stomach capacity, and λ and μ are the marginal utilities of money income and stomach capacity. Then

$$\frac{MP_i^x}{MP_i^c} = \frac{\lambda}{\mu} p_i \tag{6}'$$

An increase in I, C_0, and p_i held constant, would reduce the ratio of marginal products on the left side of equation (6)' because of the law of variable proportions (see the discussion in Lecture 24), and consequently, would reduce λ/μ, the ratio of the marginal utility of income to that of stomach capacity. What happens to either λ or μ separately cannot be determined.

[6] See, for example, H. M. Hochman and J. D. Rodgers, "Pareto Optimal Redistribution," *American Economic Review*, 59 (September 1969).

for the most convenient function among the infinite number consistent with behavior. In other words, there is a search for the utility equivalent of the centigrade scale used in measuring temperature: Fahrenheit and other scales are equally "correct," but centigrade is more "convenient." Commonly suggested for their convenience are the Cobb-Douglas function

$$U = cZ_1^{a_1}Z_2^{a_2}, \ldots, Z_m^{a_m} \tag{11-4}$$

the constant elasticity function

$$U = \left(\sum_i a_i Z_i^{-\beta} \right)^{-1/\beta} \tag{11-5}$$

and the additive function

$$U = \sum_i h_i(Z_i) \tag{11-6}$$

None of the functions suggested are fully consistent with behavior. For example, the functions in equations (11-4) and (11-5) imply unitary income elasticities for all commodities (Why?),[7] which clearly contradicts observed behavior.

PROBLEMS

11.1.   Evaluate: Two goods, X and Y, are substitutes if an increase in the consumption of one good reduces the marginal utility of the other.

11.2.   Evaluate: Income should be redistributed from the rich to the poor because the marginal utility of income is lower to the former.

11.3.   A utility function $U = U(X_i, \ldots, X_n)$ can be said to be *strongly separable* if $U_i = g_i(X_i)$, where U_i is the marginal utility of the ith good, and g_i is a function of X_i alone.

   a. Is strong separability so defined a property of the indifference curve system?
   *b. What restrictions on the income elasticities are implied by such a utility function? Can any goods be inferior? If so, how many?

*11.4.   A utility function can be said to be *weakly separable* if

$$\frac{U_i}{U_j} = h_{ij}(X_i, X_j)$$

---

[7] Hint: Show that the ratio of marginal utilities of different commodities is unaffected by a uniform increase in all commodities.

a. Is weak separability a property of the indifference curve system?

b. If $h^i_{ij} = \partial h_{ij}/\partial X_i < 0$, and $h^j_{ij} > 0$, could good X_k be a substitute for X_i and a complement for X_j, or vice versa? For this purpose, define substitution, complementarity, and independence by the sign of the effect of an uncompensated increase in the price of any good X_k on the demand for any good X_i.

c. Can you show from your answer to 11-4b that all goods must be either substitutes, complements, or independent?

d. Is the "Cobb-Douglas" utility function given by $U = a_o X_1^{a_1} X_2^{a_2}, \ldots, X_n^{a_n}$ weakly separable? Prove that with this function, all goods must be independent.

chapter 4

Uncertainty

LECTURE 12

Uncertainty

The previous lectures on demand theory have generally assumed that preferences, prices, income, and the quality of goods are all known with certainty, yet there is uncertainty about every product—from an orange to a surgeon to a political candidate. There is, for example, uncertainty about the condition of a new car's transmission system and carburetor; new-car warranties shift some of the uncertainty from automobile consumers.

Uncertainty can be neglected without serious consequences in many consumer decisions, but with some, uncertainty is the heart of the matter. Consumers buy life, fire, theft, and other insurance only because they do now know when they will die, have a fire, or be robbed; if they did, the need for "insurance" would vanish. Speculation in the stock market and gambling at a race track would not exist if everyone knew the outcome: "It is differences of opinion that make a horse race." Consumers buy insurance, gamble, and speculate precisely to change the economic consequences of their uncertainty. Similarly, they are willing to pay more for new cars that have warranties in order to shift some of the uncertainty about a car's performance back to the manufacturers, or they buy drugs (and other products) by brand rather than generic name because of the confidence they have in the quality control exercised by certain companies.

To introduce uncertainty into the formal analysis, let p_i be the probability of purchasing a good specimen of commodity Z_i and $(1 - p_i)$ the probability of purchasing a bad one. Consumers do not know in advance which specimen they will receive; only the set of probabilities is known. For example, the quality of a pineapple or a car is not fully known until purchased and put to use. Each combination of different commodities with the probabilities of good and bad varieties attached is called a "prospect," and we assume that a consumer can order every prospect. A change in the probabilities would generally change the ordering, but since the influence of the probabilities on the ordering has not been specified, the direction of the change is not clear as yet.

If (full) income and the prices of commodities were known with certainty, equality between the slope of an indifference curve and relative prices would still be the optimality condition, and the basic demand theorems would be unchanged; namely, a "pure" decline in the relative price of Z_i would still increase the quantity of Z_i consumed, and a weighted average of all income elasticities would still be unity. Consequently, convenience of exposition, not necessity, explains why uncertainty is ignored in the usual presentations of demand theory.

Insurance and gambling would be covered simply by calling them separate commodities that are ranked in prospects along with other commodities. The unit premium would be the price of insurance, the brokerage fee would be the price of speculation on the stock market, the bookie's "take" would be the price of betting on horse races, and so forth. A pure decline in, say, the insurance premium would increase the amount of insurance purchased because all demand curves are negatively sloped, and a pure increase in income would increase insurance in proportion to its income elasticity. A consumer might both insure and gamble in the same way that he might buy both salt and sugar.

Although valuable, this treatment of uncertainty is not fully satisfactory. A satisfactory theory should be able to predict the effects of changes in probabilities, for example, the effect on the demand for life insurance of the large secular increase in life expectancy or the effect on the amount wagered of a change in the odds on a prize fight.

Moreover, insurance and gambling, like medical care, are not basic commodities, but inputs in the production of some commodity, call it "stability of consumption." These inputs alter the fluctuations in future consumption.

Expected Utility Theory

If a consumer were asked to choose between two prospects, P_0 containing only a unit of the good variety of commodity Z_1, and P_1 containing the probability p of a unit of the good variety and $(1 - p)$ of a unit of the bad variety, the "sure thing" principle says that he would always choose P_0 if $p < 1$. It is called a "sure thing" because he can never do worse by choosing P_0, and has a probability $(1 - p)$ of doing better. In this form the "sure thing" principle is persuasive. An objection that the prospect P_1 might be preferred by consumers who value uncertainty per se really amounts to saying that a second commodity Z_2 is also included in the prospect P_1, where Z_2 is the source of the utility from uncertainty. By assumption, however, only one commodity is included in P_1. Difficulties with the principle arise only when it is applied directly to goods rather than to the basic objects of choice.

If consumers can order all prospects, and if the ordering satisfies the "sure-thing" principle, then it has been proved with some additional assumptions that a single class of utility functions would always be consistent with any set of indifference curves between prospects. This is the class of expected utility functions. "Expected" simply refers to the mathematical operation of taking the average or mean and has nothing to do with "anticipations" or "expectations" about the future. Thus the expected utility from prospect P_1 would be

$$U(P_1) = pU(Z_1^q) + (1 - p)U(Z_1^b) \tag{12-1}$$

where $U(Z_1^q)$ is the utility from one unit of the good variety of Z_1,[1] and similarly for $U(Z_1^b)$. In general, if a prospect P_2 contained different baskets of commodities where each had a known probability p_i, the expected utility from P_2 would be

$$U(P_2) = \sum p_i U(B_i) \tag{12-2}$$

where $U(B_i)$ is the utility from having the basket B_i with certainty. This formulation is perfectly general since each B_i can contain any combination of commodities, including different varieties.

Expected utility functions are an infinitely large class, whose members differ only by an origin and unit of measure. That is, a linear transformation of a given expected utility function U:

$$U^* = aU + b \qquad a > 0 \tag{12-3}$$

would also be an expected utility function,[2] and if two functions are members of this class, they can differ only by an origin and a unit of measure.

Not only would a class of expected utility functions always be consistent with any given ordering of prospects, but a monotonic transformation of any member would give the same indifference curves and thus would be equally consistent. The frequent use of expected utility functions does not rest on their being more correct than these other functions but on their being more convenient. Their convenience lies in the calculation of the effects of changes in probabilities, which is precisely what we have been unable to do. Notice that this convenience is applicable only to comparisons under uncertainty and that convenience was also used to justify the search for simple utility functions in comparisons under certainty.

---

[1] Therefore, the expected utility from the prospect P_0 is

$$U(P_0) = 1U(Z_1^q) = U(Z_1^q)$$

[2] Since by assumption

$$U(P_2) = \sum p_i U(B_i)$$

then

$$U^*(P_2) = a \sum p_i U(B_i) + b$$
$$= \sum p_i [aU(B_i) + b]$$
$$= \sum p_i U^*(B_i)$$

Consider prospect P_3, which contains the same set of baskets as P_2, but with a different set of probabilities, p_i'. Then P_3 would be on a higher indifference curve than P_2 if, and only if,

$$\sum_i p_i'U(B_i) - \sum_i p_iU(B_i) = \sum_i (p_i' - p_i)U(B_i) > 0 \qquad (12\text{-}4)$$

If the utility of each B_i were known, the calculation is easily made by summing the product of these utilities and the differences in probabilities.[3]

All the $U(B_i)$ could be easily determined from sufficient evidence on a consumer's choices. Since the expected utility function is unique only up to an origin and unit of measure, these are arbitrary and can be assigned; therefore, let $U(Z_1^b) = 0$ and $U(Z_1^q) = 1$. To determine the utility from say $2Z_1^q$, he could be offered the choice between a prospect P_0 containing one Z_1^q with certainty, and a prospect P_4 containing $2Z_1^q$ with probability p, and $1Z_1^b$ with probability $(1 - p)$. If p were close to unity, presumably P_4 would be preferred to P_0, and if it were close to zero, P_0 would be preferred. By experimentation, some probability could be found (call it $\bar{p}$) that would make the consumer indifferent between P_0 and P_4:

$$U(P_4) = \bar{p}U(2Z_1^q) + (1 - \bar{p})U(Z_1^b) = U(P_0) = U(Z_1^q) \qquad (12\text{-}5)$$

or since

$$U(Z_1^b) = 0 \text{ and } U(Z_1^q) = 1$$

then

$$U(2Z_1^q) = 1/\bar{p} \qquad (12\text{-}6)$$

By similar experimentation, the utility of any basket could be determined relative to the basket chosen as one unit of utility.

The utility of any full income level, $U(S)$, can be defined as the utility of the optimal basket that can be purchased with S under given prices.[4] Since the utility of each basket could be determined, the utility of each level of income could also be determined. By the assumption that more is preferred to less, the marginal utility of income, $U'(S) = dU/dS$, must be positive. Moreover, the sign of the change in the marginal utility of income is invariant within the class of expected utility functions; they must all either have increasing, decreasing, or constant marginal utility of income. (Why?)[5] Consequently, the sign of the marginal utility of income is unambiguous as long as we restrict ourselves to this class of functions.

[3] Of course,

$$\sum (p_i' - p_i) = \sum p_i' - \sum p_i = 1 - 1 = 0$$

[4] The function

$$U(S; \pi_1, \pi_2, \ldots, \pi_m)$$

is called the "indirect utility function."

[5] Consider U and $U^*(S) = aU(S) + b$, where $a > 0$ to preserve the ordering. Then

$$U''^*(S) = aU''(S)$$

and the sign of both U''^* and U'' must be the same.

PROBLEMS

12.1.   Evaluate: Gambling is irrational because it is inconsistent with diminishing marginal utility of income.

12.2.   Evaluate: With constant marginal utility of income, prospects are ranked solely by their expected income.

12.3.   Suppose a student has no more than t minutes to write an examination consisting of two questions. He receives A points if he gets one of the questions correct and B points if he gets the other one correct. There is no partial credit and the probability that he gets a question correct depends on his initial knowledge and on how much time he puts into answering it.

    a. If he receives constant marginal utility from additional points,

       Derive the equilibrium conditions for his optimal allocation of time between the two questions.
       How is his allocation affected by a change in A and B?
       Does he put more or less time into the question he knows more about to start with?
       What determines whether or not he uses up all t minutes available?

    b. How would his allocation of time be changed if instead of constant marginal utility he received diminishing marginal utility from additional points?

*LECTURE 13

Insurance and States of the World

The expected utility approach is valuable in analyzing the demand for insurance and gambling. Assume that a consumer would receive an income of S_a^0 if he experienced a hazard such as fire, illness, robbery, death, or automobile accident and an income of S_b^0, where $S_b^0 > S_a^0$, if he did not. These outcomes are associated with two mutually exclusive "states of the world": state a occurs when "nature" produces the hazard and state b when it does not. Each state is assumed to have the known probabilities of occurrence, p_a and p_b, and by the assumption that the states are all inclusive and mutually exclusive,

$$p_a + p_b = 1 \qquad\qquad (13\text{-}1)$$

These probabilities are assumed to be fixed (although see Problem 14-1 and Lecture 14).

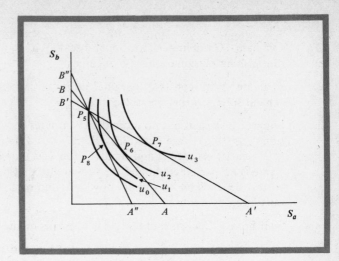

FIGURE 13.1

The utility of the prospect P_5 offering S_a^0 and S_b^0 would be

$$U(P_5) = p_a U(S_a^0) + p_b U(S_b^0) \tag{13-2}$$

Various other combinations of S_a and S_b would give the same utility and be on the same indifference curve. If S_a and S_b were considered different "commodities," the slope of an indifference curve at any point in that "commodity" space, the marginal rate of substitution between S_a and S_b, can easily be shown to be

$$s = \frac{dS_b}{dS_a} = -\frac{p_a}{p_b}\frac{U'(S_a)}{U'(S_b)}\,^1 \tag{13-3}$$

where $U'(S)$ is the marginal utility of an increase in S. The marginal rate of substitution is necessarily negative because p_a, p_b, $U'(S_a)$, and $U'(S_b)$ are all positive, and would be decreasing, constant, or increasing as the marginal utility of income was decreasing, constant, or increasing.[2]

If a consumer with diminishing marginal utility of income were required to accept the prospect given by point P_5 in Figure 13.1, his utility would be

---

[1] Since points are on the same indifference curve if, and only if

$$dU = 0 = p_a U'(S_a)\,dS_a + p_b U'(S_b)\,dS_b$$

equation (13-3) follows immediately.

[2] If p_a/p_b is written as the constant k, then from equation (13-3),

$$\frac{ds}{dS_a} = \left[\frac{-k}{U'(S_b)}\right]U''(S_a) + \left[\frac{kU'(S_a)s}{[U'(S_b)]^2}\right]U''(S_b)$$

or the sign of ds/dS_a would be

$$\text{sgn}\,(ds/dS_a) = [-]\,\text{sgn}\,[U''(S_a)] + [-]\,\text{sgn}\,[U''(S_b)]$$

Hence

$$\text{sgn}\left[\frac{ds}{dS_a}\right] = \overset{+}{\underset{-}{0}} \quad \text{as} \quad \text{sgn}\,(U'') = \overset{-}{\underset{+}{0}}$$

If $U''(S_b)$ and $U''(S_a)$ had different signs, ds/dS_a could either be positive, negative, or zero.

measured by U_0. He might be able, however, to trade away from P_5. If, for example, the budget line AB measured the price of income in state a relative to income in state b, he would give up some income in state b for additional income in state a, and move from P_5 to P_6 at the higher utility level U_2.

In other words, he would, in effect, at least partially "insure" his losses by increasing his income in the hazardous state. The rate of exchange between incomes in states a and b, the slope of a budget line in Figure 13.1, can be said to measure the unit cost of "insurance," π. If π were less than the absolute value of the slope of the indifference curve at the initial prospect P_5, the consumer would buy insurance and move along his budget line toward S_a; if π exceeded the slope he would increase his risk by moving along his budget line toward S_b.

By "fair" insurance is meant that the amount mathematically expected to be paid out in claims to a consumer would equal the amount collected in premiums from him. Then the unit cost π would simply be

$$\bar{\pi} = \frac{p_a}{p_b}^{\,3} \tag{13-4}$$

Since the slope of an indifference curve at any point is given by equation (13-3), it would necessarily exceed $\bar{\pi}$ if $S_b > S_a$ and the marginal utility of income were decreasing. A consumer would then trade away from b by purchasing insurance, and he would continue purchasing until the slope became equal to $\bar{\pi}$. At that point

$$\bar{\pi} = \frac{p_a}{p_b} = \frac{p_a}{p_b} \frac{U'(S_a)}{U'(S_b)} \tag{13-5}$$

or

$$U'(S_a) = U'(S_b) \tag{13-6}$$

which implies that $S_a = S_b$ if everywhere $U'' < 0$. (Why?)

In other words, if insurance were fair, he would trade S_b for S_a until he equalized both incomes, say at point P_6 in Figure 13.1. He would then be completely insured and indifferent to whether the hazard occurred. Fair insurance encourages him to eliminate all the relevant uncertainty.

If insurance were not "fair," if, for example, π were less than p_a/p_b, he would move along a flatter budget line $A'B'$ to the point P_7, which is to the right of P_6. He would "overinsure" in the sense that his income would be greater in state a, the hazardous state, than in state b; indeed, he might even end up with greater risk, measured by the variance of his expected income, than he had at P_5. If π exceeded p_a/p_b, the budget line $A''B''$ would be steeper than AB, and he could go to P_8 to the left of P_6, and "underinsure." A

---

3 The total premium paid by a person out of income in state b is πq, where q is the quantity of insurance purchased in state a; his expected claim in a would be $(p_a/p_b)q$. (Why?) If these two terms are equated, equation (13-4) results.

sufficiently large price would even induce him to go to the left of P_5 and increase his risk. The degree of "fairness" of the insurance, along with the shape of the marginal utility of income function, are the only variables determining how much insurance is purchased.[4]

PROBLEMS

13.1. Let the income endowment of a household in two states of the world be S_a^0 and S_b^0 where $S_b^0 > S_a^0$, with p being the probability of S_a, and let its utility function be U.

  a. Assume that the marginal utility of S is diminishing, i.e., $U'' < 0$. If π is the insurance price of a dollar of income in state a in terms of a dollar of income in state b, show what happens to the amount of insurance bought as π became larger and larger than $p/1 - p$; that is, as insurance became less and less "fair." Would there be a price at which no "insurance" would be bought? If so, which one? Suppose π exceeded such a price (if any). What then would happen?

  b. If $U'' > 0$, what is the equilibrium amount of insurance purchased if $\pi = p/1 - p$?

  c. Assume that U'' is > 0 at S_a^0 and S_b^0, but that as S_b is substituted for S_a, eventually U'' becomes < 0. If $\pi = p/1 - p$, how much insurance is purchased?

*13.2. Assume that each person can reduce (i.e., self-insure) by spending some resources on fire prevention, better diet, and so forth.

  a. If he cannot insure in the market, i.e., trade S_b for S_a in the market, how much would he spend to reduce p?

  b. If he can insure in the market at a fair rate, i.e., $\pi = p/1 - p$, how much would he spend to reduce p, and how much market insurance would he buy?

  c. If $\pi = kp/1 - p$, where k is a constant larger than 1, how much would he spend to reduce p and how much market insurance would he buy?

---

[4] The optimality condition is that

$$\pi = \frac{p_a}{p_b}(1 + \ell) = \frac{p_a}{p_b}\frac{U'(S_a)}{U'(S_b)}$$

where ℓ is the "loading" factor, or

$$(1 + \ell) = \frac{U'(S_a)}{U'(S_b)}$$

Only ℓ and the shape of U', not p_a, p_b, or anything else, are relevant in determining the optimal position. The equilibrium in values of S_a and S_b would differ by enough to have the ratio of their marginal utilities equal one plus the loading factor.

LECTURE 14

Uncertainty and Search

A person can respond to the uncertainty of hazardous events not only by trading income in other states for income in the hazardous states, as when purchasing market insurance or "self-insurance" but also by trading income in all states for a reduction in the probability of the hazardous states. He can install a safe to reduce the probability of a burglary; "fireproof" his house to reduce the probability of a fire; concentrate while driving to reduce the probability of an accident; have a mechanic examine a car he may purchase to reduce the probability of defects; or buy brand-name rather than cheaper generic-name drugs to reduce the probability of contamination.

We focus in this lecture (although see Problem 14.1) on the investment of time and other resources in "search" to reduce the probability of there being cheaper prices elsewhere for the goods and services one buys or higher prices for the goods and services one sells. Both empirical observations and simplified theory are responsible for the common assertion that all persons face approximately the same market prices. Differences in prices appear to be small compared, for example, to the well-known and documented extremes in income. In the United States the range in the prices paid by different persons for the "same" good during any year seldom exceeds 100 percent and is usually much lower whereas extremes in income of more than 500 percent are common.

The theoretical argument for price similarity can be traced back to the conclusion that more goods are preferred to less (see Lecture 6). If different prices were known to be charged for the same good, consumers would buy at the lowest price since that would increase their command over goods. If everyone succeeded in buying at the lowest, all price variation would be eliminated.

And yet prices are not the same even in a given market; different supermarkets in the same neighborhood often sell exactly the same item at different prices on the same day, and "shopping around" when buying a car often leads to significant savings. Price differences may be small compared to differences in income, but they do exist. How can they if consumers prefer to buy at the cheapest price?

One explanation would be that consumers are not rational and do not always prefer more to less; a more appealing approach is to drop the implicit assumption that information is costless. Indeed, information is one of the most valuable and scarce "goods" in modern societies. Although lower prices can generally be found by shopping around, by "searching," searching itself is time consuming and thus costly: a housewife may expect to find lower prices if she canvasses 100 grocery stores than if she canvasses a few, but at some point the gain from additional canvassing would be too small to be worth the cost in time and other resources. Some search—canvassing, reading advertisements and consumer magazines, placing classified ads—frequently pays off handsomely, but there is an optimal amount because search itself is costly.

To formalize somewhat, it pays to spend an additional hour canvassing when the gain exceeds the value of the hour. The cost is related to the foregone wage rate of the canvasser, and the gain is related to the reduction in price. The gain indirectly is related to the dispersion in the prices charged by different sellers: if the dispersion were small, search is unlikely to be profitable. The gain is also related to the fraction of income spent on the good and to its income elasticity (see Problem 14.1).[1]

The value of relating prices to information can be illustrated by the higher prices paid by tourists than by residents: New York City is an expensive place, but it is not as expensive for residents as it is for tourists. Since a tourist stays only for a short period of time, it does not pay for him to invest much time in learning about prices; the cheaper restaurant, bookstore, or department store often eludes him as he frequents the appropriately named "tourist spots." Or consider that the dispersion in wage rates among younger persons generally exceeds the dispersion among older persons partly because the former have had less time to accumulate information about the labor market.

Market demand curves are usually estimated by relating market consumption to the average price paid by different consumers. These curves are not generally independent of the degree of price dispersion (under what conditions would they be?), but if the dispersion were not large (it is not in most markets), and did not change much as the average price changed (it usually does not), the elasticities estimated would not be greatly affected by the dispersion in prices.

PROBLEMS

14.1.   Assume that the cost of a unit of search is the same for all goods and that all have the same price variability in the absence of search.

   a. Show that there will be less search and thus greater equilibrium price variability for goods taking a small part of the budget.
   b. Show that if the cost of search is proportional to income, the rich will search more and thus pay less for goods with income elasticities greater than unity, and search less and pay more for goods with income elasticities less than unity.
   c. On the basis of these results, do you expect the "poor to pay more" for goods?

[1] George Stigler's important article, "The Economics of Information," *Journal of Political Economy*, 69 (June 1961), spells out this model in greater detail.

PART TWO

Supply of Products

chapter 5

Fundamentals of Supply

LECTURE 15

The Firm and Profit Maximization

Demand is just one blade of the scissors determining price and quantity; the other blade, supply, is systematically considered in the next few lectures. Although market behavior is our main interest, much of the time is taken up with the basic micro unit, the firm, because an understanding of the responses of firms contributes to an understanding of market responses.

Following the definition of a demand curve, a supply curve can be said to show the amount of a product that would be supplied per unit of time by any group of firms at different prices under given conditions, or the prices acceptable to the group at different quantities. Therefore, supply curves also show alternative flows that would be forthcoming under given conditions (such as given technology, level of real resources, and factor supply curves) rather than sequences of quantities supplied over time as prices changed from period to period.

A firm is an intermediary between factor and product markets: it purchases a set of factor inputs and transforms them into useful output that is sold.[1] The well-known definition of a firm as an institution that makes internal decisions without the use of exchange[2] does not distinguish firms from households, which also do not generally use exchange internally.

Traditionally, a firm is assumed to maximize its income, often called "profits," defined as the difference between receipts in product markets and outlays in factor markets. The maximization is constrained by a production function that shows the relation between inputs and outputs, and by demand functions in product markets and supply functions in factor markets. Profits are assumed to be spent on consumption goods according to the theory of demand set out in the previous lectures. The assumption of profit maximiza-

---

[1] Households also purchase inputs and transform them into useful output, but households directly consume their output instead of selling it. See Lecture 10 for the analysis of households.

[2] See R. H. Coase, "The Nature of the Firm," reprinted in K. Boulding and G. J. Stigler, *Readings in Price Theory* (Chicago: Richard D. Irwin, 1952).

tion amounts, therefore, to a separation of production from consumption: the former is done in firms and the latter in households.

Several developments in recent decades have stimulated a significant modification of the theory of the firm away from profit maximization. Perhaps the most important is the spread of government-owned and regulated enterprises even in capitalist countries and, of course, more so in other countries. In addition, "nonprofit" private firms have multiplied as education, health, and other service industries have increased their share of output. Economists have also developed a greater awareness of nonprofit motives in "commercial" firms; these motives include an interest in nepotism, discrimination, and size per se. Moreover, the new approach to household decision-making brings production into the household, and sets an example for the theory of the firm.

A natural way to incorporate these developments is to replace profit maximization by utility maximization. A firm may act as if it maximized a utility function that depends not only on profits, but also on the color, sex, and family background of employees; level of outputs; market shares; and so on:

$$U = U(I, y_1, \ldots, y_n, q_1, \ldots, q_m, V) \tag{15-1}$$

where I is profits, y_i and q_i are characteristics of inputs and outputs, and V stands for other variables. We could replace I by the commodities produced by households receiving I, and even the y_i and q_i could be replaced by the commodities they help to produce. Since only indifference curves are relevant for behavior, any order-preserving monotonic transformation of U has the same indifference curves and thus would be equally correct.

The assumption of profit maximization amounts to the strong restriction on U that the marginal utility of I is positive, and the marginal utilities of all other variables are identically equal to zero; in other words

$$\overline{U} = \overline{U}(I)$$

$$MU_I > 0 \tag{15-2}$$

$$MU_k \equiv 0$$

where k is any other variable, is the traditional utility function. Since any function with the same indifference curves as $\overline{U}$ is equally good, the simplest function is the profit function[3]

$$U^* \equiv I \tag{15-3}$$

Since U^* is *identical* to I, utility functions are not even mentioned in the traditional formulations of the firm's behavior. Economists conclude that a

---

[3] From equation (15-2),

$$I = g(\overline{U})$$

with

$$\frac{dg}{dU} = \frac{dI}{dU} > 0$$

Therefore, the transformation

$$U^* = g(\overline{U})$$

is order-preserving.

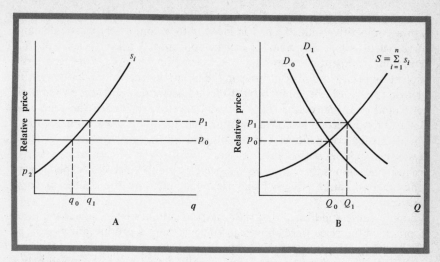

FIGURE 15.1

tax on profit-maximizing firms that is monotonically related to their incomes would not affect their input or output decisions because any monotonic transformation of U^* has the same indifference curves.

The profit-maximizing assumption has performed well in enabling economists to predict, among other things, the effects of an excise tax, collusion, or increase in wage rates on outputs and employment. Therefore, the more recent developments mentioned above are probably best taken account of not by moving directly to the general utility function given by equation (15-1), but by modifying U^*. For example, a firm that discriminates against Negro employees would have a utility function that depends both on its income and its Negro employees[4]; firms whose profits are limited by the government would place unusual emphasis on the attractiveness of their secretaries[5]; or universities would care about the quality of its students as well as its net income. When handled in this manner, the useful theorems derived from the profit-maximizing assumption can also be derived from the analysis that incorporates various nonpecuniary motives.

Firm and Market Supply Curves

Panel A of Figure 15.1 gives the demand and supply conditions for a firm with its output per unit time, q, plotted on the horizontal axis, and the

---

[4] I assume in *The Economics of Discrimination* (Chicago: University of Chicago Press, 2nd ed., 1971), that

$$U = I - dw_i q_i$$

where w_i is the wage rate, q_i the number of Negro employees, and d the firm's "discrimination coefficient."

[5] See A. A. Alchian and R. A. Kessel, "Competition, Monopoly, and the Pursuit of Pecuniary Gain," in *Aspects of Labor Economics* (Princeton, N.J.: Princeton University Press for the National Bureau of Economic Research, 1962).

relative price of the product plotted on the vertical axis. We say that a firm is in a competitive industry if it is faced with a completely elastic demand curve (such as p_0): any amount can be sold at a constant price. By this definition, competition does not necessarily imply, nor is it necessarily implied by, a large number of firms in the industry. Indeed, an industry with a single firm would be competitive if the industry's demand curve were itself horizontal or if many other firms entered the industry when the price was raised above a certain level. On the other hand, an industry with many firms would not be competitive if they colluded with each other. In general, however, industries with many firms are more likely to be competitive (partly because collusion is then more costly; see Lecture 21), and this explains why concentration ratios are used empirically to measure the degree of competitiveness.

Supply curve s indicates that the firm produces more the higher the price is, provided the price were above p_2. Since nothing is produced if $p < p_2$, p_2 is called the entry price for this firm. If the demand curve were p_0, the firm could not sell anything above p_0, and usually would not want to sell below p_0, even if it were not simply profit maximizing. By definition of the supply curve, the quantity q_0 would be supplied at the price p_0.

If the supply curves of all firms in the industry were independent of each other, an assumption modified in Lecture 17, the industry or market supply curve, S in panel B of Figure 15.1, would simply be the horizontal sum of all the s_i. Since each s_i is positively inclined, so is S. Market equilibrium occurs at the intersection of the market supply and demand curves, given by the price p_0 and the quantity Q_0, if D_0 were the market demand curve. The sum of the amounts supplied by each firm would equal Q_0, which would also equal the total quantity demanded.

If the demand curve shifted upward to D_1, say the demand for accountants increased because the income tax laws became more complicated, the equilibrium position would shift along S from p_0 to p_1 and from Q_0 to Q_1. Both price and quantity would increase. The demand curve for each firm would shift from p_0 to p_1, and the amount supplied by the firm in panel A would increase from q_0 to q_1. This example illustrates how supply curves are used to discover the effects of shifts in demand curves.

Supply curves of different firms can differ in both location and elasticity. In Figure 15.2, s_2 and s_3 are always below s_1 whereas s_2 is sometimes below s_3 and sometimes above. The lower the curve, the lower the entry price, or the lower the price at which a firm would be just willing to supply a positive amount of output. The elasticity of a supply curve is defined as the percentage change in quantity per 1 percent change in price. The curve s_2 is clearly more elastic at the quantity q_1 than is s_3. (Why?) The elasticity of all three curves shown in Figure 15.2 falls as quantity increases. (Why?)

If all firms had the same supply curve, the market supply curve would simply be a blown-up version of this curve. If supply curves differed, the elasticity of the market curve would depend both on elasticities of the individual curves and on their entry prices. In price intervals with no entry,

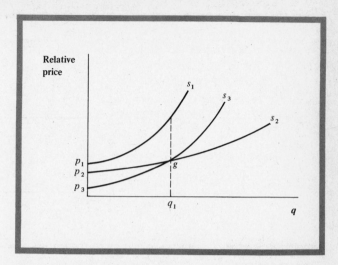

FIGURE 15.2

the market elasticity would be an average of the elasticities of the firms already entered (Why?) whereas entry of new firms would give a concave kink to the market curve, and thereby increase its elasticity. The number of firms in an industry would generally increase with price in a manner determined by the frequency distribution of entry prices. A dense frequency distribution as well as highly elastic firm curves can produce a highly elastic market curve.

An increase in the equilibrium price in response to an increase in the demand curve would usually increase both the number of firms and the outputs of those already producing. The latter would contribute a greater share of the increased output the more elastic were their supply curves and the higher the entry prices of potential additional firms. (Why?) Therefore, industries consistently characterized by few firms, e.g., the automobile and steel industries in the United States since 1900, either have very elastic firm supply curves or large gaps between the entry price of existing and potential firms (or decreasing costs—see Lecture 20).

All the supply curves in Figure 15.2 intersect the vertical axis whereas the firm in panel A of Figure 15.3 has a gap at the entry price between the vertical axis and the quantity q_1: it is indifferent between producing nothing at p and q_1. If a large number of firms N all had the same supply curve s_j, the industry supply curve would essentially be infinitely elastic at the price p until all N firms were supplying q_1. In panel B this is reached at $Q_2 = Nq_1$. The gap between zero and q_1 becomes of negligible importance when measured in industry output units. The rise in industry output at prices above p is determined by N and the rise in s_j. A shift of the demand curve from D_0 to D_1 would not change the price, but would encourage more of the N firms to enter, supply q_1 units, and thereby increase industry output from Q_0 to Q_1. This again illustrates that excessive concentration on the micro unit can be seriously misleading because market and micro responses often differ considerably.

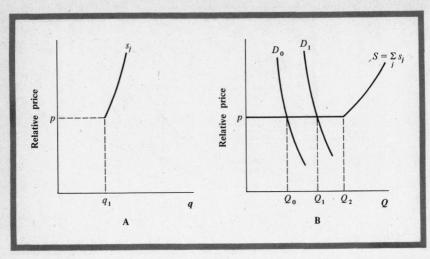

FIGURE 15.3

PROBLEMS

15.1. Suppose that the utility function of a competitive firm is $U = I + dq$ where q is output, d is a constant, and I is the firm's income.

   a. How does the output of this firm compare with what it would be if the firm simply maximized income?

   b. What is the effect of a change in d on output?

   c. How could d be estimated from actual data on prices, output, marginal costs, and so forth?

   d. If all firms in the industry had values of $d > 0$, how would industry output and prices compare to the case where all $d = 0$?

15.2. Evaluate: If a competitive firm maximizes not income but its sales subject to the constraint that it does not make any losses, a reduction in the demand for its product might cause an increase in its output.

LECTURE 16

Marginal and Average Cost

Marginal cost is defined as the change in total cost as the quantity supplied per unit time changes by one unit, or

$$MC = \frac{dTC}{dq} \qquad (16\text{-}1)$$

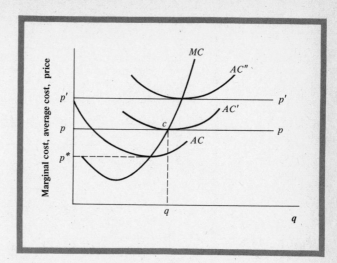

FIGURE 16.1

Average cost is the ratio of total cost to quantity:

$$AC = \frac{TC}{q} \tag{16-2}$$

Marginal and average cost are connected by the same mathematical formula that connects marginal and average revenue (see Lecture 3):

$$MC = AC\left(1 + \frac{1}{\epsilon_{AC}}\right) \tag{16-3}$$

where ϵ_{AC} is the elasticity of the average cost curve. Although this formula is a mathematical relation between different mathematical functions and is not derived from any economic principles, it is useful in understanding the relation between average and marginal cost. Equation (16-3) implies $MC < AC$ where AC is falling ($\epsilon_{AC} < 0$); $MC = AC$ where AC is horizontal ($\epsilon_{AC} = \infty$); and $MC > AC$ where AC is increasing ($\epsilon_{AC} > 0$). These properties are illustrated by the MC and AC curves in Figure 16.1.

The exact relation between supply and cost curves depends on a firm's utility function. The qualitative relation is, however, similar for a variety of functions (as shown in Problem 15-1) and can, therefore, be illustrated by income maximization. Income is maximized where marginal revenue equals marginal cost. If $MR > MC$, an additional unit of output increases income by the amount $MR - MC$; similarly, if $MR < MC$, a reduction in output by one unit increases income by the amount $MC - MR$. Thus, so long as the optimal quantity supplied is positive, it must be where $MR = MC$. The competitive firm which faces the demand curve p^o in Figure 16.1 determines its supply by the intersection of p^o with its marginal cost curve since $p^o \equiv MR$.

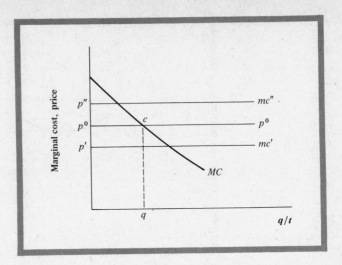

FIGURE 16.2

(Why?) The MC curve is its supply curve as long as its output is positive—
that is, as long as $p \geq p^*$ if AC is its average cost curve; its supply curve
would be on the vertical axis for $p > p^*$ (for p less than the maximum point
on AC), because its income would then be maximized by zero production.

Since the industry supply curve is the horizontal sum of the firms' supply
curves, it would also be the horizontal sum of the relevant sections of the
firms' marginal cost curves. The marginal costs of all firms must be equal
to each other at every point on the industry supply curve, for each is equal to
the same market price. Equality of marginal costs in all firms is necessary to
minimize industry costs; otherwise, they could be reduced by expanding
firms with lower marginal costs and contracting those with higher marginal
costs. Therefore, the industry supply curve can be called the "industry's"
marginal cost curve.

If the marginal cost curve were positively inclined as in Figure 16.1, the
firm's supply curve would also be positively inclined. Could a competitive
firm have a negatively inclined or horizontal marginal cost curve and thus a
supply curve that was not positively inclined? If the marginal cost curve
were negatively inclined, as is MC in Figure 16.2, the intersection of price and
marginal cost at point c would not maximize income; it is clearly greater at
larger quantities.[1] The firm would continue to expand until either MC turned
upward (and again the upward section would determine supply) or the usual
competitive equilibrium, with price equal to marginal cost, broke down (see
Lecture 20).

---

[1] Therefore, equality between MR and MC is not sufficient to maximize income; it is also
necessary that

$$\frac{d\,MC}{dq} > \frac{d\,MR}{dq}$$

or that marginal costs rise more rapidly or fall less rapidly than marginal revenue.

Constant marginal costs cannot be disposed of so readily. If all firms had MC' in Figure 16.2, they would all supply an infinite amount at a higher price than p' and nothing at a lower price. At p' price and marginal cost are equal at all quantities, and the amount supplied by each firm is indeterminate: each has an infinitely elastic supply curve at that price. The industry supply curve would also be infinitely elastic, and the number of firms in the industry would be indeterminate since the distribution of the total supply among different firms is arbitrary.

Economic Rent

The frequent assertion that in full equilibrium firms would produce at the minimum point on their average cost curves is not correct if firms have different marginal costs. If the equilibrium price were p^o in Figure 16.1, the firm shown there would be producing well above p^*, the minimum point on its AC curve. An argument might be made that many firms would enter, supply output, and drive the price back to p^*. But why assume that many firms necessarily have entry prices between p^* and p^o; perhaps all firms in the industry enter at or below p^*? If the number of such firms were finite, p^o could be the equilibrium price. All firms would necessarily be at their minimum AC positions only if an indefinitely large number of firms have identical minima; i.e., identical entry prices.

Some firms have lower entry prices than others because they are more efficient and thus have lower marginal (and average) costs. Greater efficiency can stem from superior managerial and other entrepreneurial abilities or from superior resources. By definition, superior efficiency is limited: there are only a small number of Wilt Chamberlains and Lou Alcindors in basketball, Henry Fords in the automobile industry, Beatles in the entertainment world, and South Africas in the gold mining industry.

Relatively efficient firms in an industry are necessarily above the minimum levels on their average cost curves because the price is high enough to attract less efficient ones. The difference between the revenue and cost of an efficient firm is called "economic rent," and is a reward for the scarcity of superior efficiency that would vanish as it became common. For example, if 500 Wilt Chamberlains were available, each would probably receive no more than $10,000 a year for playing basketball, instead of the quarter of a million dollars he is reported to receive.

If the superior resources and abilities responsible for economic rent can be sold to other firms, as can be with a mine or a patent right, economic rent might justifiably be called a "cost." If it were added to other costs, rent-inclusive total cost would equal total revenue at the equilibrium position and exceed revenue at all other positions. (Why?) Average cost derived from rent-inclusive total cost, therefore, would be tangent to the firm's demand curve at the equilibrium position, as is AC' in Figure 16.1, which is derived from AC by adding the rent at c to costs. Consequently, all firms would be at the minimum point of their *rent-inclusive* average cost curve.

This treatment of rent satisfies the accountant's desire to make both sides of the ledger balance, but has several shortcomings. The most important is that rents are price-determined, not price-determining, as are labor, capital, and other conventional costs. Rent is not price-determining because the marginal cost curve, the basic determinant of supply and indirectly of price, is not affected by the inclusion of rent in costs: the same marginal cost curve MC applies to both AC and AC' in Figure 16.1. (Why?) Rent is price-determined because an upward shift in the demand curve would increase the equilibrium price if the industry supply curve were positively inclined and thus increase the rent of all firms already in the industry. The average cost curve inclusive of rent would shift upward from AC' to AC'' in Figure 16.1, and would be tangent to the new demand curve p'. Since the purpose of cost curves is to help determine equilibrium quantity and price, only price-determining costs should be included in these curves. Hence, rent should be excluded, as should be the conclusion that a firm is necessarily at the minimum point on its average cost curve.

PROBLEMS

16.1.   Evaluate: No firm can be in equilibrium if its marginal costs are negative.

16.2.   Evaluate: A person who enters an industry with no risk instead of a risky industry is a "risk avoider."

16.3.   Suppose there exists a fixed number of physically independent oil fields of varying qualities, i.e., it is cheaper to produce oil with some than with others. The oil industry is assumed to be competitive and all firms are identical except for the quality of field used.

   a. What determines the rental prices of different fields?
   b. How do the cost curves of firms using good fields compare with those using poor ones?
   c. Could any fields have zero rental prices? Why?
   d. If the demand curve for oil increased, what would happen to the number of fields used? To the rental prices of fields? To cost curves?

16.4.   Suppose now that the number of oil fields is increased by the discovery of new ones (say in Alaska).

   a. If they all are of lower quality than the fields already in use, what happens to outputs, prices, and rentals?
   b. What happens to them if the new fields are of higher quality than some of those in use?
   c. If no further discoveries of fields are made and over time those in use begin to wear out (i.e., their marginal cost curves rise), what

happens to the price of oil? Outputs? Rental prices of fields continually in use? Number of fields in use?

16.5.   Evaluate: Racial discrimination would not occur in perfectly competitive industries. Therefore, the market discrimination against Negroes in the United States is evidence of monopoly power in the United States.

16.6.   Let the total output of a competitive industry initially be Q, and let rationing be introduced, e.g., Texas output of oil is rationed. Each firm is given a certain number of coupons, the total number to all firms equaling Q. What happens to the total output if the coupons are not transferable between firms? What if they are transferable and a market price for coupons develops? What is the equilibrium price of coupons?

LECTURE 17

Short and Long Run

We have been relating marginal and average cost per unit time only to the output per unit time, yet these costs depend on several other variables as well. The total accumulated volume of output is relevant, especially for newer firms since firms often become more efficient with greater experience (see Problem 17.4). Fluctuations in the rate of output are also relevant since a steady rate is generally cheaper than a fluctuating rate.[1] In this lecture we discuss a variable that is partly related to the volume of output and partly to the steadiness in the rate; namely, the expected duration of any rate.

The demand for a product can shift permanently, in response perhaps to a growth in education; continuously in a given direction, in response to a trend in income; back and forth in a regular fashion, as the demand for electricity is larger in summer and winter and smaller in spring and fall; cyclically and irregularly, as over the business cycle; or erratically, as the demand for medical care has an erratic component. If the cost per unit time of using all inputs were independent of the duration of use, the same supply curve would be relevant for all demand shifts. The marginal cost per day of producing for a week at a certain rate would be the same as the cost of producing for a decade at that rate.

The cost of using many inputs, however, depends closely and usually negatively on the duration of use. Even unskilled labor has hiring costs that would be cheaper per day if "amortized" over many days of use. Hiring

[1] See G. J. Stigler, "Production and Distribution in the Short Run," *Journal of Political Economy*, 47 (1939), 305–327. Reprinted in *Readings in Income Distribution*, American Economic Association.

costs for skilled labor are even greater, and the often sizable investment in on-the-job training is also cheaper per day when amortized over many days. The cost per day of physical capital is generally lower the longer the duration of use because of sizable transaction costs in the market for capital. Suppose for example, that a \$40,000 machine is uniformly productive for four years and then "dies," and that it is worth \$20,000 in the "used machine" market after one year of use, \$10,000 after two, \$5,000 after three, and nothing after four. Aside from operating costs and interest, it would cost \$20,000 per year if used one year, \$15,000 per year if used two, \$12,000 per year if used three, and only \$10,000 per year if used all four.

The distinction between "fixed" and "variable" factors should not depend on technological considerations, but rather on the relation between cost and duration of use. The cost per unit time of a "pure" variable factor is independent of duration whereas that of a "pure" fixed factor is inversely proportional to duration. Actual inputs fall somewhere between these two extremes: unskilled labor and raw materials are close to the "pure" variable factor and highly specialized labor and physical capital to the pure fixed factor.

The relation between duration and cost is crucial in understanding the difference between short- and long-duration supply curves, which is our almost literal interpretation of the Marshallian distinction between short- and long-"run" supply curves. A competitive firm would react to an increase in market price by increasing output. If the increase in price were expected to be very short-lived, output would be increased primarily by increasing variable factors such as the number of hours worked by men and machines even if overtime, weekend, or night rates had to be paid. If, on the other hand, the increase in price were expected to be permanent, fixed factors would be increased more, and variable factors less—instead of working men and machines overtime and at odd hours, the firm would hire and train additional men and purchase additional machines.

Since fixed factors change more relative to variable ones the more permanent the change in demand, output per unit of a fixed factor would be more affected when the change in output were temporary, as over a business cycle or between seasons, than when it were more permanent, as in response to a secular growth in incomes. This explains why during the brief business downswings that characterized the postwar period in the United States, reductions in output have been several times larger than the reductions in employment.[2] Output has been reduced primarily through reductions in the hours worked by men and machines, not in the number of men and machines. Most of the reduction in employment has been concentrated among the unskilled—Negroes, youths, and so on—presumably also because skilled workers are more of a fixed factor than unskilled ones.

An important implication of the relation between cost and duration is that marginal cost curves and thus supply curves would be more elastic in the

[2] Output has declined about three times more than employment (see Problem 17.3).

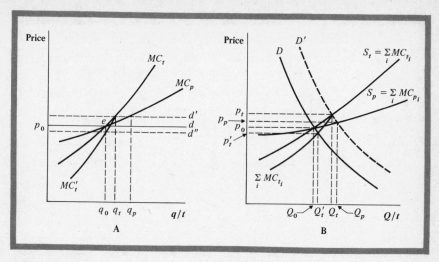

FIGURE 17.1

longer run. Assume that the initial position is point e in panel A of Figure 17.1, where the quantity q_o has been produced for an indefinitely long period, and say demand increases to d'. If the increase in demand were temporary, mostly variable factors would be increased, and let marginal cost be given by the curve MC_t. It would be less costly per unit time to increase output if the increase to d' were permanent because the cost per unit time of fixed factors is a decreasing function of duration of use, the cost of variable factors is independent of duration, and factors with costs that are significantly positively related to duration are not of great empirical importance. Therefore, although the firm could respond to a permanent change in demand by moving along MC_t, it would not choose to do so; it would instead increase its fixed factors more, its variable factors less, and thereby move along MC_p. That is, long-run marginal cost curves are more *elastic* than short-run curves: MC_p is below MC_t at outputs above q_o and above MC_t at outputs below q_o. (Why is the latter part of this statement true? Why is the long-run marginal cost curve *not* the envelope of short-run curves? Show that the reduction in total cost from reducing output in response to a temporary decline in demand to d'' is *less* than the reduction in total cost from reducing output permanently.)[3]

---

[3] For a formal proof, let the marginal cost function be written as

$$MC = f(q, \ell)$$

where ℓ refers to the planned duration of the rate of output. Our analysis implies that

$$\frac{\partial MC}{\partial q} = f_q > 0 \quad \text{and} \quad \frac{\partial MC}{\partial \ell} = f_\ell < 0$$

Therefore,

$$\frac{dMC}{dq} = f_q + f_\ell \frac{d\ell}{dq} > f_q \quad \text{if } \ell \text{ is reduced as } q \text{ increases}$$
$$< f_q \quad \text{if } \ell \text{ is reduced as } q \text{ decreases}$$

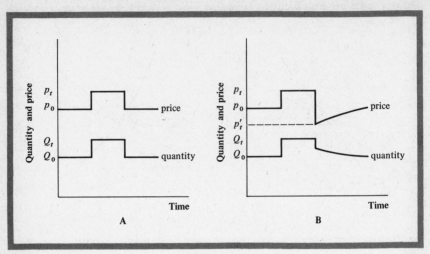

FIGURE 17.2

Since the marginal cost curve is a firm's supply curve, the more permanent the change in price the greater would be the change in output. An increase in price to d' would increase output to q_t if the firm responded along MC_t and to the greater level q_p if it responded along MC_p. Consequently, industry output would increase more and price would increase less, the more permanent the increase in demand. In panel B of Figure 17.1, price and output increase to p_t and Q_t with a temporary increase in demand to D' and to Q_p and p_p with a permanent increase.

If demand increased temporarily to D' and then returned to D, would price and market output return directly to p_o and Q_o from p_t and Q_t? The answer is no, for price would often initially fall below p_o, and output would initially remain above Q_o. Although firms respond to a temporary, say a three-year, increase in demand primarily by increasing their variable factors, they might also increase their fixed factors, even those lasting longer than three years. When demand returned to D, they would often continue to use these additional fixed factors until they wore out, instead of selling them or leaving them idle. Until they did wear out, the reduction in costs from reducing output below Q_t would be less than MC_t, say MC_t'; therefore, market price would fall all the way to p_t', and quantity only to Q_t'. The marginal cost curve would rise as time went by, eventually all the way back to MC_t; market price and output would then be back to p_o and Q_o, respectively.

Instead of following the patterns in panel A of Figure 17.2, price and quantity follow the more cyclical patterns in panel B because of the time it takes to depreciate fully the additional fixed factors. These cyclical patterns in quantities and prices do not require lagged adjustments or uncertainty and are related solely to the time it takes to depreciate certain factors.

The distinction we have drawn between the short and long run has not required either uncertainty about the duration of demand changes or supply responses that lag behind changes in demand. Uncertainty and lags are important, but they are not necessary to explain the different responses of outputs and inputs to erratic, cyclical, seasonal, and secular changes in demand. Moreover, the effects of uncertainty and lags can be analyzed with the same concepts we have been using.

Since erratic, irregular, seasonal, and cyclical changes are important, firms often do not know immediately that a permanent shift in demand has occurred. Initially, they may assume that most of the shift is temporary, and respond primarily with variable factors. As the shift persists, they become increasingly confident of its permanence and respond more with fixed factors.[4] Initially, therefore, output would respond less and price (and inventories) more whereas eventually output would respond more and price (and inventories) less.[5]

Even after a shift in demand was known to be permanent, firms may not immediately expand along their long-run marginal cost curve. Generally, the cost of fixed factors is related not only to their level but also to their rate of increase. It is cheaper, for example, to hire 100 additional skilled workers over a two-year period than over a two-week period if only because the cost of additional inputs into personnel departments could be amortized over a longer period. Similarly, it is usually cheaper to build a plant over a longer period because inputs used in the construction could be amortized over a longer period. Consequently, firms would approach their long-run position through a sequence of short-run adjustments.

PROBLEMS

17.1.   Evaluate: Short-run marginal costs are never below long-run marginal costs.

17.2.   Evaluate: Not only are long-run marginal costs more elastic than short-run marginal costs, but long-run Engel curves are also more elastic than short-run Engel curves.

17.3.   "Okun's Law," that a 1 percent change in employment is associated with about a 3 percent change in output, is consistent with recent cyclical changes in the United States, but not with changes over the last five decades. What explains this difference?

[4] Sometimes, firms have clear information about the duration of demand shifts. For example, the Carvel Co. knows that the demand for ice cream increases only temporarily during warm weather, and, therefore, invests less in their buildings than if the increase were permanent. Many pavilions at the New York World's Fair were built without the use of pilings, even though the fair was on swampy land, because it takes a few years for buildings to sink perceptibly and by that time the fair was rightly expected to be concluded.

[5] In recent years, economists have concluded that expectations of future prices are often partly formed by taking a weighted average of current and past prices. This implies that only part of any change in price would initially be assumed to persist into the future.

17.4. If a firm suddenly discovered that it could "learn by doing," i.e., an increase in its current rate of output would reduce future marginal costs, how would this affect the size of current output?

*17.5. It has been alleged that the shift of shaving from barber shops to homes over time has been partly responsible for the slow growth of productivity in these shops, even though increased specialization on a single product would presumably increase productivity. Can you develop any arguments that would support this allegation? What do your arguments imply about the optimal price of a shave combined with a haircut compared with their prices when taken separately?

LECTURE 18

External Effects

Negative externalities are said to occur when the actions of one behavior unit harm others whereas positive externalities occur when these actions benefit others. For example, an additional car on a crowded highway harms the persons in other cars—it makes their cars go slower and increases the chances of accidents. Similarly, Con Edison harms the residents of New York City when it pollutes the air. Or, many boats fishing in the same waters can interfere with each other's catch. On the other side, Thomas Edison's many inventions benefited the whole world's population. Again, education would confer external benefits if more educated persons made wiser political decisions. As a final example, the antiques industry of New York City is mainly located in a particular section because each dealer benefits from locating near other dealers, for customers can then canvass several dealers more conveniently, which indicates why external effects are also called "neighborhood effects."

Externalities result from imperfect ownership of property, not from defects in the motivations induced by private ownership. Since oceans are not owned by any person or even by any nation, fishing, drilling, and navigation rights are disputed. The air has been easy to pollute because no one owns it, and Edison had only partial ownership of his many inventions. Ownership of all resources would eliminate many externalities. If each person owned the air he breathed, he could charge firms for the right to pollute it, which would discourage pollution. If Edison had full control of the use of his inventions, he could have more fully charged for their use. An owner of a forest (or an ocean) has an incentive to prevent "excessive" cutting (or fishing) because that would decrease the future value of the timber (or fish), and thus the market value of the forest (or ocean).

Imperfect ownership is also related to the cost of "policing" the use of property. It may be difficult—i.e., costly, the only rigorous meaning of "difficult" in economics—to discover who is polluting the air, even if one could charge for the right to pollute; or it may be difficult to discover who is using particular ideas or fishing in an ocean, even if ideas and oceans were owned. Government regulation of the transfer of ownership rights, as in criminal proceedings, is at heart based on a presumption about the cost of policing ownership.

In the past, much of the discussion, especially that in the Marshall-Pigou tradition, focused on externalities among firms in the same industry. It showed that externalities could make market supply curves negatively inclined and government assistance necessary to reach an optimal output. We now derive these implications.

Firm j is said to impose externalities on firm i if an increase in js output changes is costs:

$$\frac{\partial TC_i}{\partial q_j} \neq 0 \qquad (18\text{-}1)$$

Negative externalities are imposed if is costs increase; positive externalities, if they decrease. If all firms in the industry affected each other in the same way, q_j could be replaced by the industry supply Q, and equation (18-1) could be written as

$$TC_i = TC_i(q_i, Q) \qquad (18\text{-}2)$$

The sign of $\partial TC_i/\partial Q$ determines the nature of the externality.

Marginal cost can be defined as the change in total cost per unit change in q_i, with all the other q_j held constant:

$$MC_i(q_i, Q) = \frac{dTC_i}{dq_i} = \frac{\partial TC_i}{\partial q_i} + \frac{\partial TC_i}{\partial Q}\frac{dQ}{dq_i} = \frac{\partial TC_i}{\partial q_i} + \frac{\partial TC_i}{\partial Q} \qquad (18\text{-}3)$$

Competitive equilibrium requires that marginal cost equal price:

$$p = MC_i(q_i, Q) \qquad (18\text{-}4)$$

By inverting equation (18-4), the supply function of the ith firm can be derived:

$$q_i = s_i(p, Q) \qquad (18\text{-}5)$$

Equation (18-5) gives a family of curves, one for each level of Q, which are plotted in panel A of Figure 18.1. With positive externalities, an increase in Q would shift s_i to the right, as in the figure. Obviously, the converse would hold with negative externalities.

Equilibrium requires that price equal marginal cost for all firms and that the sum of all outputs equal industry output. Panel B plots the horizontal

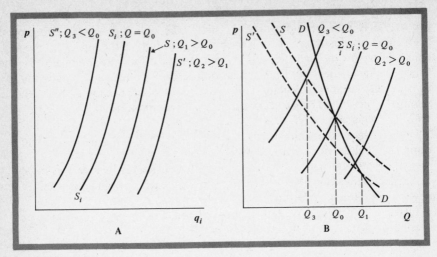

FIGURE 18.1

sum of the s_i in panel A, one summation for each level of Q. Since, in equilibrium, Q must equal the sum of all the q_i, only one point on each curve in B is relevant. The locus of all these relevant points gives the industry supply curve, shown by S.

Positive externalities make the industry supply curve more elastic than the sum of the individual s_i'; negative externalities do the opposite. Sufficiently powerful positive externalities can even make the industry supply curve negatively inclined,[1] as is S in the figure. A negatively inclined industry

---

[1] Consistency requires that

$$\sum_i q_i = \sum_i s_i(p, Q) = Q$$

Then

$$\frac{dQ}{dp} = \sum_i \left(\frac{\partial s_i}{\partial p} + \frac{\partial s_i}{\partial Q} \frac{dQ}{dp} \right)$$

or

$$\frac{dQ}{dp} = \sum_i \left(\frac{\partial s_i}{\partial p} \right) \Big/ \left(1 - \sum_i \frac{\partial s_i}{\partial Q} \right)$$

Therefore,

$$\epsilon_s = \frac{p}{Q} \frac{dQ}{dp} = \left[\sum_i \frac{s_i}{Q} \left(\frac{\partial s_i}{\partial p} \frac{p}{s_i} \right) \right] \Big/ \left[1 - \sum_i \frac{s_i}{Q} \left(\frac{\partial s_i}{\partial Q} \frac{Q}{s_i} \right) \right]$$

$$= \sum_i w_i \epsilon_i / (1 - \sum_i w_i \epsilon_{iQ})$$

where $w_i = s_i/Q$, etc.
Then setting $\sum_i w_i \epsilon_i = E_i$, and $\sum_i w_i \epsilon_{iQ} = E_Q$, one gets

$$\epsilon_s = \frac{E_i}{1 - E_Q}$$

Hence

$$\epsilon_s \gtrless E_i \quad \text{as} \quad E_Q \gtrless 0$$

and

$$\epsilon_s \lessgtr 0 \quad \text{as} \quad E_Q \gtrless 1$$

If $E_Q = 1$, then $\epsilon_s = \infty$; i.e., S is horizontal. The derivation in this footnote provides the answer to part of Problem 8.3.

supply function is not inconsistent with competition; indeed, it was intro-duced by Marshall to reconcile increasing returns and competition (for an application, see Lecture 27). The equilibrium position is stable, however, only if the negatively inclined supply curve is more elastic than the negatively inclined demand curve (as in Figure 17.1).[2]

At every point on the industry supply curve the marginal cost of each firm, as given by equation (18-3), would equal price. The definition of marginal cost in equation (18-3) assumes that the repercussions on other firms of a change in output by any single firm are small enough to be ignored by that firm. Consequently, the industry supply curve would measure "private" marginal costs alone since it would exclude the external effects. Full, or "social," marginal costs would be greater or smaller than private costs as the externalities were negative or positive.

Effects that are "external" to an individual firm would be "internal" to a "holding company," call it H, composed of all firms in the industry. The difference between private and social marginal costs could be seen, therefore, by contrasting the marginal costs of H and a typical firm. These marginal costs differ by the effect of a change in industry output on a firm's marginal costs.[3]

Welfare economics demonstrates that the optimal output is where price and social marginal cost are equal. Therefore, a unit tax or subsidy equal to $(N - 1)(\partial TC_i/\partial Q)$ (by footnote 3 on this page) on firms that were behaving independently would make their tax-inclusive marginal cost equal to social marginal cost. (Why?) The industry supply curve would be raised or lowered depending on whether the externalities were negative or positive. In Figure 18.1, the supply curve would be lowered from S to S' because positive externalities are assumed; output would be raised from Q_0 to Q_1.

---

[2] For a proof, see M. Friedman, *Price Theory* (Chicago: Aldine, 1962), p. 93.

[3] The total cost of H would be the sum of the total costs of the N firms in H:

$$TC_H = \sum_{i=1}^{N} TC_i(q_i, Q)$$

If, for simplicity, all firms are assumed to be identical,

$$TC_H = NTC_i(q_i, Q)$$

Then

$$MC_H = \frac{dTC_H}{dQ} = N\frac{\partial TC_i}{\partial q_i}\frac{dq_i}{dQ} + N\frac{\partial TC_i}{\partial Q}$$

By the assumption that firms are identical, $dq_i/dQ = 1/N$, and hence

$$MC_H = \frac{\partial TC_i}{\partial q_i} + N\frac{\partial TC_i}{\partial Q} = MC_i + (N - 1)\frac{\partial TC_i}{\partial Q} \qquad \text{[by equation (18-3)]}$$

The difference between the marginal cost of H and of each firm would be

$$MC_H - MC_i = (N - 1)\frac{\partial TC_i}{\partial Q} \gtreqless 0 \quad \text{as} \quad \frac{\partial TC_i}{\partial Q} \gtreqless 0 \quad \text{if} \quad N > 1$$

PROBLEMS

*18.1.   A factory located next to a private house makes noise that disturbs
the residents of the house; i.e., it imposes an external cost on the
residents. The amount of noise can be reduced either by reducing
the factory's output or by installing more soundproof walls and
ceilings in the factory. A court could award "property rights in the
air" to the house owner, so that the factory owner would have to get
the house owner to agree to any noise, or to the factory owner, so
that he could make as much noise as he likes. Contrast the effect of
these different "property rights" on the factory's output, sound-
proofing, and profits.

chapter 6

Competition and Monopoly

LECTURE 19

The Comparative Statics of Competitive Equilibrium

Having derived the supply and demand curves for consumer goods, we are in a position to consider their interaction in greater detail. Figure 19.1 plots the quantity of good X along the horizontal axis and its relative price along the vertical axis. The cross-hatched area shows the prices and quantities consistent with both the supply and demand curves, given by S and D, when real income and the prices of close substitutes and complements in production and consumption are held constant. The maximal quantity in this area at point e is the competitive equilibrium position, which is a crude proof that competition maximizes output.

The competitive equilibrium can also be found algebraically from the equation

$$D_x\left(\frac{p_x}{p}; \frac{p_y}{p}, \frac{S}{p}, U\right) = S_x\left(\frac{p_x}{p}; \frac{p_w}{p}, \frac{S}{p}, V\right) \tag{19-1}$$

when real full income, S/p, the prices of close substitutes and complements in production and consumption, p_y/p and p_w/p, and other variables that affect S and D, U and V, are given. A change in variables that raised the demand curve alone would raise the equilibrium price and quantity—compare e and e' in the figure. On the other hand, a change that raised the supply curve alone would raise price and lower quantity—compare e and e_1 in the figure.[1]

---

[1] The effect of a shift in the demand curve on price and quantity can be found algebraically by differentiating equation (19-1):

$$\frac{\partial D_x}{\partial U} + \frac{\partial D_x}{\partial p'_x}\frac{dp'_x}{dU} = \frac{\partial S_x}{\partial p'_x}\frac{dp'_x}{dU}$$

where $p'_x = p_x/p$. Hence

$$\frac{dp'_x}{dU} = \frac{\partial D_x}{\partial U}\bigg/\left(\frac{\partial S_x}{\partial p'_x} - \frac{\partial D_x}{\partial p'_x}\right) > 0$$

89

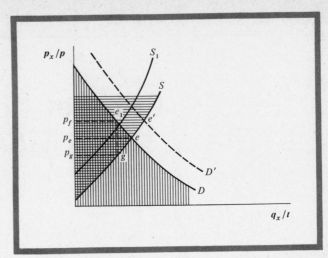

FIGURE 19.1

A change in the price and quantity of X might have significant reper-cussions on the prices and quantities of the close substitutes and complements for X, which in turn would react back on the X market. These repercussions can be formally introduced into the analysis by adding the equilibrium conditions for these goods:

$$D_y\left(\frac{p_y}{p}; \frac{p_x}{p}, \frac{S}{p}, U'\right) = S_y\left(\frac{p_y}{p}; \frac{S}{p}, V'\right)$$

$$D_w\left(\frac{p_w}{p}; \frac{S}{p}, U''\right) = S_w\left(\frac{p_w}{p}; \frac{p_x}{p}, \frac{S}{p}, V''\right)$$

(19-2)

Given S/p and the Us and Vs, equations (19-1) and (19-2) would be sufficient to determine simultaneously the equilibrium prices and quantities in the X, Y, and W markets. An upward shift in the demand curve for X would raise not only the price and quantity of X but also the prices and quantities of substitutes and would lower those of complements.[2]

The number and variety of substitutes, complements, and other variables considered in actual empirical studies depend not only on the goods being

---

since the numerator and denominator on the right side are both positive. (Why?) Similarly,

$$\frac{\partial D_x}{\partial p'_x}\frac{dp'_x}{dV} = \frac{\partial S_x}{\partial V} + \frac{\partial S_x}{\partial p'_x}\frac{dp'_x}{dV}$$

or

$$\frac{dp'_x}{dV} = \frac{\partial S_x}{\partial V}\bigg/\left(\frac{\partial D_x}{\partial p'_x} - \frac{\partial S_x}{\partial p'_x}\right) > 0$$

[2] A geometrical solution can be found in Friedman, *Price Theory*, pp. 23–25. An algebraic solution can be obtained by differentiating equations (19-1) and (19-2). If, to simplify the algebra, the good W is ignored, then

$$\left(\frac{\partial D_x}{\partial p'_x} - \frac{\partial S_x}{\partial p'_x}\right)\frac{dp'_x}{dU} + \frac{\partial D_x}{\partial p'_y}\frac{dp'_y}{dU} = -\frac{\partial D_x}{\partial U}$$

$$\frac{\partial D_y}{\partial p'_x}\frac{dp'_x}{dU} + \left(\frac{\partial D_y}{\partial p'_y} - \frac{\partial S_y}{\partial p'_y}\right)\frac{dp'_y}{\partial U} = 0$$

studied, but also on the availability of data, the resources of the investigator, and the accuracy required. If the resources were fixed, additional variables could be incorporated into a study only by spending fewer resources on improving the accuracy of the data, on experimenting with different functional forms, etc. Reliable results have frequently been obtained simply by including the own price and quantity, and real income, as in studies of the demand for automobiles, computers, and liquor. Sometimes, the price of a single close substitute is also included, as the price of margarine in the demand function for butter, or the price of wheat in the supply function of corn. During the past 20 years, the increasing availability of data and the development of electronic computers have made it feasible to consider the interactions between supply and demand functions in several markets. Although research is properly moving in this direction, many of the best studies still consider only a small number of variables in a single market.

The Stability of Equilibrium

Suppose initially a market with supply and demand curves given by S and D in Figure 19.1 was not at the equilibrium position e, but at some other point g in the feasible region. Would price and quantity be forced to move away from g in the direction of e? If so, e is said to be a stable equilibrium; equilibrium positions receive much attention in economics precisely because they are usually stable.

Since the quantity demanded exceeds the quantity supplied at point g, even competitive firms would not have to take the price p_g as given. Instead, they could charge higher prices, perhaps p_f, and still sell as much as they wanted. Because all firms have this opportunity, the market price of X would rise. Similarly, if the initial position were above e, producers would have an incentive to lower price and to increase quantity. Thus, deviations from e do appear to set in motion pressures returning the market to e.

By Cramer's Rule for the solution of a system of linear equations,

$$\frac{dp'_x}{dU} = -\frac{\partial D_x}{\partial U}\left(\frac{\partial D_y}{\partial p'_y} - \frac{\partial S_y}{\partial p'_y}\right)\Big/\Delta > 0$$

$$\frac{dp'_y}{dU} = \frac{\partial D_x}{\partial U}\frac{\partial D_y}{\partial p'_x}\Big/\Delta \gtreqless 0$$

where

$$\Delta = \left(\frac{\partial D_x}{\partial p'_x} - \frac{\partial S_x}{\partial p'_x}\right)\left(\frac{\partial D_y}{\partial p'_y} - \frac{\partial S_y}{\partial p'_y}\right) - \frac{\partial D_x}{\partial p'_y}\frac{\partial D_y}{\partial p'_x}$$

Clearly, $\Delta > 0$. (Why?) If X and Y were substitutes, then $\partial D/\partial p'_x > 0$, the numerator of dp'_y/dU would be positive, and $dp'_y/dU > 0$. If they were complements, then $\partial D_y/\partial p'_x < 0$, the numerator of dp'_y/dU would be negative, and $dp'_y/dU < 0$. The same approach could be used if there were other substitutes and complements, like W, but the algebra would become more complicated.

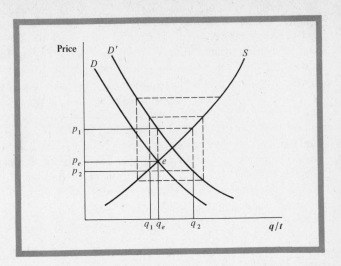

FIGURE 19.2

The stabilizing force is the negative slope of the demand curve and the positive slope of the supply curve because they imply that demand exceeds supply below the equilibrium price, and supply exceeds demand above it.[3] A market can overcome this force and become unstable only if lags are introduced that require demanders or suppliers continually to make erroneous decisions. A good example is the well-known cobweb model. The current supply of many agricultural products depends on decisions made earlier because of the time lag between planting and harvesting. The simple assumptions of the cobweb model are that current supply is based on last season's price—it is expected to persist—whereas current demand is based on current price.

These assumptions generate oscillations in price and quantity that may increase over time. Suppose, for example, that the initial equilibrium position given by point e in Figure 19.2 is disturbed by a shift in demand to D'.

---

[3] A common mathematical formulation of the dynamic process is

$$\frac{dp}{dt} = f[D(p) - S(p)]$$

where p is the (average) market price. If

$$f' = \frac{df}{d(D - S)} > 0 \qquad f(0) = 0$$

and

$$\frac{dD}{dp} - \frac{dS}{dp} < 0$$

then

$$\frac{dp}{dt} \gtrless 0 \qquad \text{as} \qquad p \lessgtr p_e$$

since

$$D - S \gtrless 0 \qquad \text{as} \qquad p \lessgtr p_e$$

Since suppliers expect the price p_e to continue, they produce q_e, which results in the higher price p_1 next season. Since this in turn is assumed to persist, the quantity supplied in the following season increases to q_2, which results in the lower price p_2. As the process continues, the oscillations shown by the cobweb pattern in the figure are generated. The oscillations would increase if the elasticity of supply exceeded that of demand,[4] as assumed in the figure.

Although supply is more elastic than demand for many agricultural and industrial products, we know of no markets that are characterized by increasing oscillations in price; instead, most show fluctuations around a particular price path. This suggests that the cobweb model is not a realistic representation of actual behavior. Increasing oscillations imply that producers' forecasts of prices have increasing errors, and the losses resulting from these errors would encourage, if not compel, them to forecast differently. Perhaps price movements further into the past would begin to affect their forecasts of future prices—the distributed lag forecasts mentioned in Lecture 17—or perhaps the oscillations in price would be discovered and anticipated. Either adjustment would dampen the oscillations and help stabilize the market. Moreover, if producers didn't learn, speculators would, for profits could be made by buying and storing the goods when prices were low and selling in the next period when they were high. These transactions would

---

[4] Let the supply function be given by

$$q_t^s = a_s p_{t-1}^{b_s}$$

and the demand function by

$$q_t^d = a_d p_t^{-b_d}$$

where b_s and b_d are the elasticities of supply and demand respectively. Equilibrium requires that $q_t^s = q_t^d$, or

$$p_t = \left(\frac{a_d}{a_s}\right)^{1/b_d} p_{t-1}^{-b_s/b_d} = k p_{t-1}^a$$

where

$$a = \frac{b_s}{b_d} \quad \text{and} \quad k = \left(\frac{a_d}{a_s}\right)^{1/b_d}$$

Consequently,

$$p_1 = k p_0^a$$
$$p_2 = k p_1^a = k^{1+a} p_0^{a^2}$$
$$p_3 = k p_2^a = k^{(1+a+a^2)} p_0^{a^3}$$
$$\vdots$$
$$p_t = k p_{t-1}^a = k^{(1+a+a^2+\cdots+a^{t-1})} p_0^{a^t}$$

where the exponent of k is a simple geometric series. Therefore, if $b_s < b_d$, then $|a| < 1$, and

$$\lim_{t\to\infty} p_t = k^{1/1-a} = \left(\frac{a_d}{a_s}\right)^{1/(b_s+b_d)} = \text{constant}$$

(Why is this constant equal to p_e?) The limit is evaluated by noting that a^t approaches zero as t approaches infinity, and that $1/(1-a)$ is the sum of the geometric series $1 + a + a^2 + \cdots$. If $b_s > b_d$, then $|a| > 1$, and p_t explodes in ever-increasing oscillations as $t \to \infty$ because $\lim_{t\to\infty} a^t = \pm\infty$. For those who are delighted by discovering that they speak prose, please note that we have solved a first-order nonlinear difference equation.

raise the low prices and lower the high ones (Why?), and thus help stabilize the market. An important lesson illustrated by this example is that knowledge is stabilizing: the cobweb mechanism can generate instability only by permitting an outrageous amount of ignorance. The usual incentives to invest in knowledge would work to stabilize each market. Knowledge is stabilizing because of the negative slope of demand curves and the positive slope of supply curves, for then low prices (relative to equilibrium values) result from "excessive" output and high prices from "insufficient" output.

If there were close substitutes or complements, the change in price in any market would depend not only on the excess demand in that market, but also on the excess demands in closely related markets.[5] If, however, certain extreme complementarities are ruled out, a system of markets would also be stable, again primarily because the excess demand in each market would be inversely related to its own price.

PROBLEMS

19.1.   Either a specific (fixed amount per unit output) or an *ad valorem* tax (fixed proportion of price) is to be imposed on a competitive industry. If both tax rates would be set to yield the same revenue at the initial equilibrium, which would have the greater effect on output?

LECTURE 20

Monopoly

Since a firm is in a competitive position when its demand curve is infinitely elastic, a firm can be said to be in a monopolistic position when its demand curve is negatively inclined. Monopolistic firms cannot simply take prices as given, but determine them as they determine their output. Each increase in output increases (or decreases) income by the difference between marginal revenue and marginal cost. Consequently, a monopolist would maximize his income at that output where marginal revenue (MR) equals marginal cost (if

---

[5] Mathematically,

$$\frac{dp_x}{dt} = f_x(D_x - S_x, D_y - S_y)$$

where

$$\frac{\partial f_x}{\partial (D_y - S_y)} \gtrless 0$$

as x and y are substitutes or complements.

MR is smaller than marginal cost at larger outputs and greater at smaller ones).[1] Geometrically, the maximum occurs at the intersection of the marginal revenue and marginal cost curves (if the former is falling more rapidly or rising less rapidly than the latter).

The equilibrium price can be found by using the relation derived in Lecture 3.

$$MR \equiv p\left(1 - \frac{1}{\epsilon}\right) \tag{20-1}$$

where ϵ is the elasticity of demand. At the equilibrium output, therefore,

$$MR = p\left(1 - \frac{1}{\epsilon}\right) = MC \tag{20-2}$$

or

$$p = MC\frac{\epsilon}{(\epsilon - 1)} \tag{20-3}$$

A firm would be competitive if $\epsilon = \infty$ and, by equation (20-3), then $p = MC$, as shown in the lectures on competition. The smaller ϵ was, the greater would be the monopoly power possessed by a firm, and by equation (20-3) the equilibrium ratio of p to MC would also be greater. This explains why the ratio of price to marginal cost has been suggested as a measure of monopoly power.

For at least the last 200 years, economists have been trying to understand why some industries are competitive and others monopolistic. And for almost an equally long period, two competing explanations have been offered: one stresses the technological conditions that make monopoly inevitable, the other stresses the incentives to collude and suppress competition. These will be discussed and evaluated in turn.

"Natural" Monopoly

The technological or "natural" monopoly argument is based on the assumption that marginal cost curves are declining in the vicinity of the industry demand curve. Examples are supposed to include the postal system, television broadcasting, the telephone and electric power industries. We pointed out

[1] Mathematically, the first-order condition to maximize income is

$$\frac{d}{dq}I = \frac{d[TR(q)]}{dq} - \frac{d[TC(q)]}{dq} = MR - MC = 0$$

and the second-order condition is

$$\frac{d^2I}{dq^2} = \frac{d(MR)}{dq} - \frac{d(MC)}{dq} < 0$$

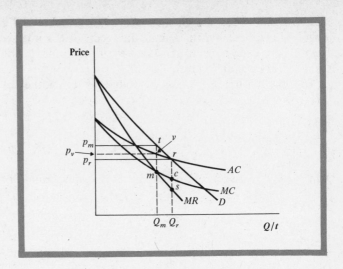

FIGURE 20.1

earlier that competitive firms would not operate in a region of decreasing costs because they could increase their incomes by becoming larger. Eventually they would become large enough to influence price and would no longer be competitive. Consequently, the usual conclusion has been that in the absence of government intervention, decreasing cost industries would be monopolized; in Figure 20.1, they would produce Q_m and charge p_m.

How consistent is this monopoly solution with the compelling symmetry condition that all firms with the same costs must, in equilibrium, receive the same income? This condition would be satisfied if the firm producing Q_m shared its profits $p_m t v p_v$ equally with all potential firms having the cost curves AC and MC in the figure. Economists have not been attracted by such a profit-sharing solution, partly because it violates the antitrust laws in several countries, and partly because it does not appear to be empirically important (although it has not been seriously investigated. See the comments at the end of this lecture). Consequently, they have searched for other solutions, varying from stay-out pricing to economic warfare, but these all tend to violate the symmetry condition.

The theory of monopolistic competition develops a symmetric solution that does not require profit-sharing by permitting different firms with the same cost curves to produce products that are differentiated by consumers. New firms enter such a monopolistic-competitive industry to produce their own products as long as profits are available, and their entry shifts downward the demand curves of firms already in the industry. Entry would continue, and demand curves would continue to fall, until the tangency position given by point c in Figure 20.2 was reached. At that point profits are zero because average costs equal price, and no additional firms have any incentive to enter.

Although the concept of monopolistic competition captures relevant dimensions of the competition prevailing in many industries, the tangency solution has serious defects. For example, any two firms would have an

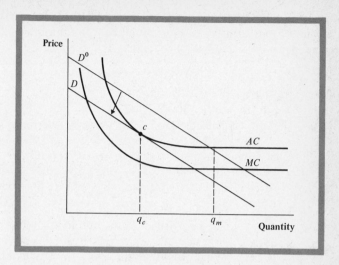

FIGURE 20.2

incentive to merge and produce more cheaply (and more profitably) the combined output q_m suitably differentiated. The pressure toward combination, unless legally or otherwise checked, would destroy the tangency solution, as well as the conclusion that firms in monopolistic-competitive industries necessarily produce on the decreasing sections of their average cost curves.

A still different solution uses the property of the tangency solution that profits are zero and yet does not assume differentiated products. It is given by point r in Figure 20.1; average costs equal price at the output Q_r, and no other firms have an incentive to enter. The difficulty with this solution is that profits appear greater at Q_m, and the firm has an incentive to move in that direction unless checked by the entry of other firms.

It has not been possible to determine empirically which solution is most relevant partly because it has been difficult to estimate monopoly profits. Since these profits fall in the category of "rents," they are allocated to good-will and other costs by diligent accountants, and thus capitalized into the market prices of firms. Not surprisingly, therefore, economists working with data generated by accountants usually find little difference between the average rates of return on capital invested in industries believed to be competitive and monopolistic.[2]

A good case study can be found in the economic history of the taxicab industry in New York City during the last 30 years. Before 1937, the industry had essentially free entry, and the price of taxi medallions was near zero. The city then began to restrict severely its issuance of new medallions, and their price has responded by rising continuously to about $30,000 in 1969. Medallion owners in the late 1930s and early 1940s undoubtedly made "monopoly" profits, but owners today receive no more than the competitive

[2] See George J. Stigler, *Capital and Rates of Return in Manufacturing Industries* (Princeton: Princeton University Press for the National Bureau of Economic Research, 1963).

rate on their labor and capital invested in the industry. They have typically paid the market price for their medallions and thus have had capitalized into their costs any monopoly profits that had developed.

PROBLEMS

20.1.   Government operation or regulation of an industry is often said to be warranted if the marginal cost curve of each potential firm were negatively inclined in the relevant region of demand. What would be the output and price in the industry if the government permitted to produce only the firm that promised to produce at the lowest price?

20.2.   What would be the effect on the output of a monopolist of a uniform *ad valorem* excise tax (a tax that is a fixed percentage of the final price)? What would be the effect on output of a progressive *ad valorem* tax (a tax that is a higher percentage of price the higher the final price)?

20.3.   If a protable fimonopoly suddenly had its money profits restricted by government regulation to an amount less than it had been earning, what would be the effect on the discrimination, nepotism, and other nonpecuniary activities of this firm? What happens to the market price of the firm? to the ratio of money earnings to market price?

20.4.   Assume that the managers of a corporation own little of the voting common stock, but effectively control all the decisions of the corporation because of the diffusion of ownership.

   a. How would the output and input decisions of this corporation compare to one in which stockholders had complete control?
   *b. How would dividend policy compare? In answering this, consider the effect of having to float additional stock periodically.

LECTURE 21

Collusion

To explain why monopolistic practices occur in some industries that apparently do not have decreasing costs, economists long ago developed a theory based on collusion. Its age can be judged from this famous statement by Adam Smith: "People of the same trade seldom meet together, even for

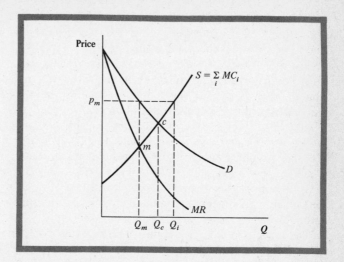

FIGURE 21.1

merriment and diversion, but the conversation ends in a conspiracy against the public, or in some contrivance to raise prices."[1] The incentive for competitive firms to collude is shown in Figure 21.1. The competitive equilibrium, given by the intersection of the industry demand and marginal cost curves (point c), clearly does not maximize the income of all firms taken together, for that requires equality between the industry marginal revenue and marginal cost curves (point m). If firms could agree to reduce total output from Q_c to Q_m, they would succeed in maximizing their income.

Since each firm separately maximizes its income, why does the competitive equilibrium fail to maximize the income of all firms taken together? The answer is that marginal revenue to each firm separately equals price whereas marginal revenue to all firms together is below price. This discrepancy is the result of external effects between firms (see the discussion of externalities in Lecture 18). Each firm lowers price ever so slightly when it produces more, which reduces the revenue of other firms. The magnitude of this reduction, and thus the difference between the monopoly and competitive solutions, depends on the difference between marginal revenue and price, which is determined by the elasticity of demand (see equation 20-2).

Since collusion, even if by merger, is the only way to internalize and thus incorporate these effects, one might expect every industry to evolve into an effectively monopolized one. But just as all firms together have a strong incentive to depart from the competitive solution, each one separately has an equally strong incentive to depart from the monopoly solution. At the monopoly price p_m, each firm considered separately would maximize its income by producing a part of Q_i rather than a part of the monopoly output Q_m, for p_m, not the MR curve, would be its marginal revenue. Since all firms

[1] *Wealth of Nations* (New York: Random House, Modern Library Edition), p. 128.

want to expand output, collusion has a tendency to break down because of "chiseling" by the members. Each firm, in effect, hopes that all others act monopolistically while it acts competitively.

For most practical purposes, economists usually have assumed either the fully competitive equilibrium at c or the fully monopolistic one at m, even though both may have shortcomings, because they have lacked a reliable general theory that also covers intermediate positions. I have developed elsewhere an analysis of crime and punishment[2] that appears to provide such a theory. Firms that violate collusive agreements can be said to commit "crimes" against the colluders; presumably, the latter try to deter such "crimes" by punishing the "criminals." The monopolistic solution results when the punishments are sufficient to deter all violations, the competitive one when punishments are completely ineffective, and various intermediate situations when punishments are partially effective.

The cost of "policing" a collusive arrangement would be lower, the smaller the number of firms[3] and customers, since it is then easier to determine what different firms are doing. Policing costs would also be lower, the less erratic the shifts by customers from one member firm to another (Why?) and the less hostile government legislation is to collusive arrangements. Violations can be effectively deterred only by punishing known violators. Some punishments, like fines, might even be profitable to collusions, but predatory-pricing, violence, intimidation, and so forth, are costly to collusions as well as to violators.

A collusion must balance its gains against its costs. Gains are negatively related to the elasticity of the industry demand curve and positively related to the elasticity of the industry marginal cost curve. If costs were large relative to gains, collusion would not pay, and the industry would remain purely competitive; if costs were relatively small, collusion would dominate and the industry would become effectively monopolistic. If both costs and gains were sizable, collusion would be profitable, and yet a significant number of violations would be permitted to occur. The price established by the collusion would take account of the violations, and would fall between the purely competitive and monopolistic prices.

In Figure 21.2, MC_a is the sum of the marginal cost curves of all firms, MC_o is the sum only of those who obey the collusion, and MC_v is the sum of those who violate it.[4] If violators act competitively and set marginal cost equal to price, the demand curve to the collusion, D_o, would be the horizontal difference between the industry demand curve D and the MC_v curve. Equilibrium is given by point i, where the curve marginal to D_o intersects MC_o;

[2] Gary Becker, "Crime and Punishment: An Economic Approach," *Journal of Political Economy*, 76 (April 1968). For a theory of oligopoly that takes the same approach, see George J. Stigler, "A Theory of Oligopoly," *Journal of Political Economy*, 72 (February 1964).
[3] This partly explains why the degree of concentration in an industry is typically used as a measure of the degree of monopoly power.
[4] Note that the identity of violators may not be known and may even change from period to period.

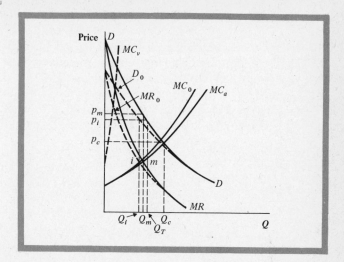

FIGURE 21.2

price equals p_i, which is less than p_m, the purely monopolistic price, and greater than p_c, the purely competitive price. The price would be closer to the monopolistic price, if violators were less important, the industry demand curve were less elastic, firms or customers were fewer in number, legislation were more favorable to collusial arguments, or fines could be more readily assessed against violators.

Traditionally, the resource misallocation caused by noncompetitive pricing is measured by the difference between the competitive and actual outputs,[5] $(Q_c - Q_t)$ in Figure 21.2, and the income misallocation by monopoly profits. The true resource misallocation would be *understated*, however, because this measure fails to include the resources spent on deterring violators, as much a social cost of monopoly as public expenditures on police are a social cost of crime. Monopoly profits have generally appeared small in different empirical studies (see Lecture 20), perhaps partly because substantial amounts have been spent on deterring violators.[6]

---

[5] Competitive output is considered ideal essentially because of the equilibrium conditions for consumers and producers. The former is given by the first equation in

$$MU/\lambda = p = MC$$

where MU is the marginal utility of a good to any consumer and λ is his marginal utility of income. The ratio measures, therefore, the money value of an additional unit of the good to all consumers. An optimal allocation of resources requires this ratio to equal the cost of producing an additional unit, as in the above equation. This is satisfied by the competitive output because $p = MC$ is the equilibrium condition for a competitive firm. A more rigorous proof can be found in most books on welfare economics.

[6] In her book *A House Is not a Home*, Polly Adler, a well-known New York madame of the 1920s, said that in spite of appearances to the contrary, her "house" and other "protected" "houses" were not very profitable because of large payoffs to the police and politicians.

PROBLEMS

21.1.   Evaluate: A cartel that maximizes the income of its members should
        distribute output among different members so as to equalize the
        average variable costs of different members.

21.2.   Security brokers who are members of the N.Y. Stock Exchange col-
        lectively set minimum commission rates to be charged customers for
        buying and selling stock. Trace the effect of this "collusion" on

        a. The amount of research on stocks "freely" provided customers.
        b. "Kick-backs" to mutual funds, insurance companies, and other
           large traders.
        c. The growth of regional (such as the Chicago) exchanges.
        d. The profitability of the brokerage business.

21.3.   Suppose all industries were competitive and in equilibrium before
        one industry was chosen *at random* to become a pure monopoly.
        The monopolist who is now the owner of that industry maximizes
        his income and presumably changes the output in the industry. How
        would the elasticity of demand for output at the monopoly equi-
        librium position compare with the average elasticity of all the com-
        petitive industries at their initial equilibrium position?

        Suppose now that the monopolist is not chosen at random, but is
        instead chosen to yield the greatest monopoly income. How would
        the elasticity in this industry before it became monopolized compare
        with the average in all industries? How would the elasticity in this
        industry at the monopoly output compare with the average
        elasticity?

LECTURE 22

Price Discrimination

We have been assuming that all consumers can buy as much as they want at
a given price. Yet monopolists sometimes find it profitable to charge different
prices to different consumers and even to the same consumer for different
quantities. Consider a monopolist with independent demand functions in
two markets and with a marginal cost function that depends only on his total
output. Clearly, his income is maximized by allocating enough output
to each market to equate the marginal revenue in each, for otherwise his
income could be increased by selling more in the market with higher
marginal revenue and less in the other market. The optimal total output

would be where both the marginal revenues equaled the common marginal cost:

$$p_1\left(1 - \frac{1}{\epsilon}\right) \equiv MR_1 = MC_{1+2} = MR_2 \equiv p_2\left(1 - \frac{1}{\epsilon_2}\right)^1 \qquad (22\text{-}1)$$

The relation between price and marginal revenue shows that the price would be higher in the market with the more inelastic demand. It is plausible that a higher price is charged in the market that is less responsive to price and a lower price in the more responsive market.

Prices differ not only between consumers, but also between different units purchased by the same consumer, as in the well-known quantity discounts. The negative slope of demand curves means that consumers are willing to pay less for an additional unit of a good the more units they are already purchasing. Therefore, if a consumer buys 10 units of a good at a fixed price of \$1 per unit, presumably the last unit is worth just about \$1 to him and each of the first nine units is worth more than \$1. A monopolistic supplier of the good could try to extract its full worth from him by charging say \$4 for the first unit, \$3.50 for a second, \$2.75 for a third, and so on.

Under certain assumptions, the full worth of a good, in the sense of the maximal amount that would be paid to avoid doing without it, is measured by the area under the demand curve for that good.[2] In Figure 22.1, the full worth of q_c is measured by the area $0Deq_c$, not by the area $0p_ceq_c$ alone. The difference between these areas, p_cDe, is called consumer's surplus and measures the gain to consumers from buying all units at the same price (p_c).

The marginal revenue to a monopolist who succeeds in extracting the entire consumer surplus would not be given by the MR curve, but by the demand curve D itself since each point on D would measure the additional revenue from selling an additional unit.[3] (Average revenue is given by the

[1] Mathematically, he maximizes

$$\Pi = TR(q_1) + TR(q_2) - TC(q_1 + q_2)$$

The first-order conditions are

$$\frac{\partial \Pi}{\partial q_i} = 0 = MR(q_i) - MC(q_1 + q_2) \qquad i = 1, 2$$

Geometrically, instead of adding the separate demand curves horizontally, he adds the separate marginal revenue curves horizontally and produces where this intersects his marginal cost curve.

[2] A full discussion can be found in W. S. Vickrey, *Microstatics* (New York: Harcourt Brace & World, 1964), pp. 66–76. Before the reader looks at this reference, he should try to show that the area under the demand curve is an exact measure of full worth for goods with zero income elasticities. (Hint: use an indifference curve diagram.)

[3] Mathematically,

$$TR(q) = \int_o^q D(v)\, dv$$

Therefore,

$$MR(q) = \frac{dTR(q)}{dq} = \frac{d}{dq}\left[\int_o^q D(v)\, dv\right] = D(q)$$

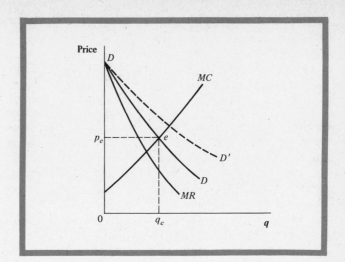

FIGURE 22.1

higher curve D'.) The equilibrium position would be at the intersection of D and the MC curve, which is also the competitive position. The paradoxical conclusion is that only monopolists who cannot fully exploit their position reduce output below the competitive level. Of course, resources are usually misallocated even by those who fully exploit their position because resources are "wasted" in suppressing competition; moreover, income may be redistributed in undesirable ways.

Price discrimination appears to increase the incomes of firms with monopoly power, yet many firms having some power hardly discriminate at all,[4] even when it is legal. A reasonable inference is that discrimination is often not profitable, and the explanation is the following: If the same good sells in different markets at price differentials that exceed the cost of "transporation," entrepreneurs would try to buy in the cheaper markets and resell at a profit in the more expensive ones. Price-discriminating firms would try to stamp out such "arbitrage" by refusing to sell in the cheaper markets to certain persons, by policing any reselling, and in various other ways. If the cost of these efforts exceeded the gain from discriminating, firms would not discriminate (witness the decline of fair-trading).

Discrimination is more likely when "policing" costs can be kept down to tolerable levels. For example, doctors and lawyers often charge higher income persons more not only because the demand for their services differs by income level, but also because income can often be easily determined, at least in a rough way. Most universities charge students on government scholarships more both because their demand is relatively inelastic and be-

---

[4] A firm is *not* said to discriminate if its prices differ because of differences in costs, due to, say, transportation or transactions size (as illustrated in Problem 22.2).

[5] Tuition for Ph.D. candidates at Columbia University was recently extended to a minimum of three years in large measure because government fellowships usually provide at least three years of support.

cause they can be distinguished from other students.[5]   Universities also discriminate by income and other criteria, and are perhaps the most blatant price discriminators in the American economy.

Movie theaters and airlines charge younger persons lower prices both because they have more elastic demand curves (since their time is less valuable, the money price is a relatively large fraction of the total price to them. Why does this mean more elastic observed demand curves?), and because age can be objectively measured, although they get many tall and well-developed eleven-year-olds. Before it was declared illegal, IBM required firms using their computers to buy punch cards from them. By charging a high price for cards, IBM used the sale of cards to "meter" the intensity of use of machines, and thereby as a device to collect higher prices from the firms that used the machines more intensively; if done directly, this would have been illegal under the Robinson-Patman Act.

PROBLEMS

22.1. Banks generally charge lower interest rates on loans to large firms than on those to small firms. Can you give

   a. An explanation based on price discrimination by size of firm?
   b. An alternative explanation based on differences in costs?
   c. If you knew the interest differential by size of firm was the same on loans made by banks in large cities and small towns, could you decide between the interpretations in 22.1a and 22.1b?

22.2. "Insane" and "unpremeditated" criminals are generally punished less severely for a given crime than are more rational, calculating criminals. Can you explain this in terms of price discrimination by society to reduce the social cost of crime?

22.3. a. Colleges and surgeons in the United States often charge wealthy customers more than poor ones. Could they be "price-discriminating" to raise their money incomes? How can colleges and surgeons have any monopoly power when there are thousands of them in the United States? Why do wealthier persons have less elastic demand curves for the services of surgeons or colleges?
   b. An alternative explanation to monopoly is that colleges and surgeons are modern "Robin Hoods" who "rob" the rich to "help" the poor. Is such an explanation consistent with (1) perfect competition in the surgeon or college industry? (2) money income maximization by surgeons or colleges?
   c. What evidence would enable you to determine whether the monopoly or Robin Hood theory was more empirically correct?

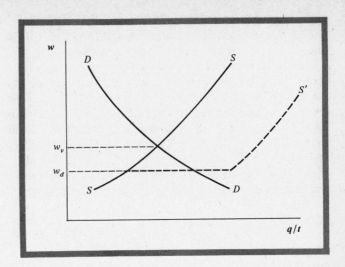

FIGURE 23.1

LECTURE 23

Non-Price Rationing

We generally assumed in the previous lectures that market prices alone are used to equilibrate different markets—if the quantity demanded exceeded the quantity supplied, prices would rise to discourage demand and encourage supply, and conversely if supply exceeded demand. Yet many other rationing mechanisms are used in the United States and even more frequently elsewhere, and this lecture analyzes their economic consequences.

The most obvious mechanism is explicit rationing of quantities, as with wartime ration coupons, quotas for oil output in Texas and oil imports from abroad, or the draft of manpower to the military. By changing the quantity demanded or supplied, explicit rationing indirectly also changes the equilibrium price, and thus automatically provides some "price control." In Figure 23.1, the draft system of acquiring manpower for the military changes the supply curve of manpower to the military from SS to SS' and the equilibrium wage from the voluntary army rate of w_v to w_d.[1] The draft permits the military to pay a lower wage and still raise the manpower it desires. The exact effect of explicit rationing on prices and quantities depends on the number of "coupons" issued, their distribution among participants, their marketability, and so forth (see Problems 23.3 and 23.4).

Non-price rationing is necessary whenever market prices are not permitted to equate supply and demand: at a price of p_c in Figure 23.2, rationing has

---

[1] Wage w_d would include the cost per recruit of running the draft system, as w_v would include the cost per recruit of running the voluntary system.

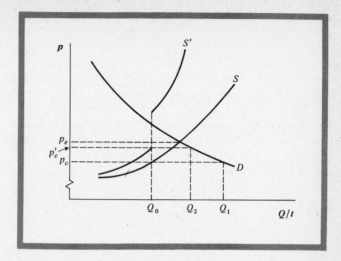

FIGURE 23.2

either to reduce the quantity demanded or to increase the quantity supplied by $Q_1 - Q_0$. There are several reasons why prices sometimes do not equate supply and demand. Most prices, in both competitive and monopolistic markets, are set for a specified period without full knowledge of the exact quantities to be demanded and supplied. An unexpected increase or decrease in demand relative to supply often is met by non-price rationing; for example, an unexpectedly heavy demand for a particular airplane flight is usually rationed on a first come–first served basis. If the relatively heavy demand (or supply) persisted, market prices would eventually be raised (or lowered) until other rationing was no longer required. The dynamic adjustment equations discussed in Lecture 19 are fundamentally based on the uncertainty of supply and demand. Governments often charge less than clearing prices for the products they sell, such as public housing or university education; apparently, they want to subsidize those demanders lucky enough to be considered acceptable.

Probably the main source of persistent and deliberate non-price rationing in the American economy, however, is government regulation of market prices. The effects of regulation on prices and quantities are really a special case of the effects of excise taxes. A well-known result states that simple excise taxes raise equilibrium prices and reduce quantities (Why?) without requiring non-price rationing. If, however, the marginal rates were discontinuous, equilibrium prices could be lowered as well as raised, and non-price rationing could be necessary. For example, assume a tax rate of 5 percent for all prices received by suppliers below or equal to p_c, and a rate of 20 percent for all prices above p_c. The supply curve in Figure 23.2 would be shifted from S to the curve S' which is discontinuous at Q_0. If the difference between the tax rates were sufficiently large, S' would be to the left of the demand curve D at all market prices less than or equal to p'_c, and to the right of D above p'_c. In other words, S' and D would not intersect, and the only equilibrium position would be a price to suppliers of p_c, a price to demanders of p'_c, a quantity of Q_0, and non-price rationing of the excess demand $Q_2 - Q_0$. (Why?) Clearly in the figure p'_c is *less* than the initial equilibrium price p_e!

Government-imposed maximum or minimum prices ("ceilings" or "floors") can be considered as discontinuous excise taxes. A maximal price of p_c is equivalent to a zero rate for all prices below or equal to p_c, and positive rates for all prices above p_c that measure the money value of the expected punishment for violating the law. If the punishment to violators were sufficiently great, the supply curve above p_c would be to the right of D, and the equilibrium would be a price of p_c, a quantity of Q_0, and "excess demand" of $Q_1 - Q_0$.[2] If the punishment were small, the new supply curve would intersect D to the left of p_e (Why?), and price control would raise prices to consumers, lower them to producers, and reduce the quantity supplied, without requiring non-price rationing. No enforcement of price ceilings may be preferable to weak enforcement, a conclusion that contradicts the presumption behind much enforcement.

Of the numerous and occasionally contradictory techniques used to ration demand and supply, perhaps the most common is past behavior: persons already in apartments are given preference under rent control, or past acreage determines current allotments under agricultural price support programs. Another common technique is queuing or first come–first served: taxicabs, theater tickets, medical services, and many other goods and services are rationed in this way when their prices are controlled. Of course, discrimination and nepotism are also widely used; the best way to get a rent-controlled apartment is to have a (friendly) relative own a controlled building. Other criteria are productivity—the least productive workers are made unemployed by minimum wage laws; income—low income persons are given preference in public housing; grades in high school—persons with high grades are favored by most colleges; collateral—borrowers with little collateral cannot receive legal loans when effective ceilings are placed on interest rates.

Each rationing technique benefits certain groups at the expense of other groups relative to their situation in a free market. Price controls are almost always rationalized, at least in part, as a desire to help the poor, yet it is remarkable how frequently they harm the poor. The difficulty intelligent laymen have in understanding this is disturbing testimony to the insights provided by even simple economic analysis.

The continuation of rent controls in New York City has been justified primarily by a desire to help poorer residents. Yet many Negro and Puerto Rican residents have been hurt by these controls because they moved to the city after controls were imposed and hence did not have "squatters'" rights to controlled apartments. Instead they have been forced to bid for apartments in less controlled markets, where "furnished," "hotel," or subdivided

[2] Work out a corresponding excise tax interpretation of minimal prices ("floors").

apartments are found. Moreover, they have seen many older, controlled buildings torn down and replaced by more expensive decontrolled ones.

There is evidence that the significant jump in minimum wages in 1957 was partly responsible for the high unemployment rates of teen-agers and Negroes in the decade after 1957. Similarly, poor persons have been hurt by the ceilings on interest rates because they have the worst collateral and thus have difficulty getting legal loans. Shut out of the legal market, they often resort to illegal loans, pay fantastic rates, and become subject to violence and other illegal methods of collection. Although the draft is supposed to be an equitable system of providing military manpower, in the United States during the last 15 years just the opposite has been true. Females are simply excluded, and married wealthier males have managed to receive educational, parent, and occupational deferments whereas poorer, single males have been drafted and paid the low wage w_d (in Figure 23.1) rather than the higher wage w_v that would be required to raise manpower voluntarily.

PROBLEMS

23.1.   Evaluate: Product A is one of the major inputs used in the production of product B. Price control is imposed on A, but not on B, at a level below the equilibrium price of A. This will cause a fall in the price of B.

23.2.   Evaluate: If effective rent control were imposed on all houses built before 1960, the demand for houses built after 1960 would be reduced.

23.3.   Suppose a maximal price is imposed in a competitive market that is below the free market equilibrium price. Assume that all demanders for this good have the same demand curve and that all have a zero income elasticity of demand. If one supplier is willing to sell all his output in the black market, and if all demanders are willing, if necessary, to buy in this market, what determines the (black market) price he can get if

   a. All demanders get an equal amount in the controlled market?
   *b. They get very different amounts in the controlled market?

23.4.   Suppose rationing is imposed and each household is given a fixed number of ration coupons that cannot be sold to another household. A certain number of coupons have to be paid out for each unit that it buys of any good (in addition, of course, to its money price), and the number of coupons paid per unit varies from good to good.

   a. If all money prices remain fixed, trace the effect of this rationing on the demand for different goods.

b. Compare the effect of an increase in the number of coupons given to any household on its demand for different goods with the effect of an increase in its money income.

*c. Could any good be both an "inferior" good with respect to an increase in money income and a "superior" good with respect to an increase in coupons, and vice versa? Why or why not?

PART THREE

Production and the Demand for Factors

chapter 7

Production by the Firm and Industry

LECTURE 24

Production Functions

The supply of goods depends directly on cost conditions, but more fundamentally on production functions and the supply of factors of production. Since production functions summarize substitution possibilities in production, they are crucial in understanding the derived demand for factors and the distribution of income between factors (the "functional" distribution of income). Production functions also describe the technology available to particular persons at a moment in time and are useful in analyzing economic development. Consequently, they are the major bridge between analyses of production, distribution, and growth.

A production function defines a relationship between inputs and useful outputs. The word "useful" is included because the law of the conservation of matter guarantees that only the form, not the amount, of matter can be changed. A production function is sometimes said to give the maximal output obtainable from given inputs; not in the sense of a physical bound, but simply under given conditions or "state of the arts." As conditions improve —as knowledge expands—the function "shifts" and a larger useful output is obtainable from the same inputs. Even at a moment in time, the functions vary from firm to firm, and, of course, from product to product as "entrepreneurial" knowledge and the nature of the product vary.

A production function can be written as

$$X = f(y_1, y_2, \ldots, y_m) \tag{24-1}$$

where X is the amount of useful output, $y_1, y_2, \ldots, y_m$ the amounts of different factors, and f describes the relationship between the two. The marginal product of any factor is defined as the change in output caused by a unit change in that factor alone, or

$$MP_i = \frac{\partial X}{\partial y_i} = \frac{\partial f(y_1, \ldots, y_m)}{\partial y_i} = f_i \tag{24-2}$$

The marginal product MP_i depends on the amounts of y_i and other factors: y_i and, say, y_2 are complements if an increase in y_2 raises MP_i; substitutes if it lowers MP_i; and independent if it has no effect on MP_i.

The average product per unit of a particular factor is defined as the ratio of total output to the quantity of that factor,

$$AP_i = \frac{X}{y_i} = \frac{f(y_1, \ldots, y_m)}{y_i} \qquad (24\text{-}3)$$

Clearly this also depends on the amounts of different factors. The mathematical relation between marginal and average quantities derived in Lecture 3 and used again in Lecture 16 also applies here:

$$MP_i = AP_i\left(1 + \frac{1}{\epsilon_{AP}}\right) \qquad (24\text{-}4)$$

where ϵ_{AP} is the elasticity of factor i with respect to average product. Consequently, marginal product is above, equal to, or below average product as average product is rising, stationary, or falling.

A production function is said to have constant returns to scale, or to be homogeneous of the first degree, if a change in all inputs by a common percentage changes output by the same percentage.[1] Marginal and average products then depend only on factor *proportions* and not on their absolute levels.[2] This convenient property is one explanation for the tremendous popularity of homogeneous production functions in the economic literature.

A production function can be graphed as a family of indifference curves or isoquants that show the difference combinations of inputs which yield a given output; Figure 24.1 graphs the isoquants for a particular function of

[1] Mathematically, f is said to be homogeneous of degree h if

$$\Gamma^h X = \Gamma^h f(y_1, y_2, \ldots, y_m) = f(\Gamma y_1, \Gamma y_2, \ldots, \Gamma y_m)$$

If $h = 1$, f is homogeneous of the first degree.

[2] If $\Gamma = 1/y_i$, then from the equation in the previous footnote with $h = 1$,

$$\frac{X}{y_i} = AP_i = f\left(\frac{y_1}{y_i}, \ldots, \frac{y_{i-1}}{y_i}, 1, \ldots, \frac{y_m}{y_i}\right) = f(R_{1i}, R_{2i}, \ldots, R_{mi})$$

where

$$R_{ji} = \frac{y_j}{y_i}$$

Since $X = y_i f(R_{1i}, \ldots, R_{mi})$,

$$MP_j = y_i \left(\frac{\partial f}{\partial R_{ji}}\right)\left(\frac{\partial R_{ji}}{\partial y_j}\right) = \frac{\partial f(R_{1i}, \ldots, R_{mi})}{\partial R_{ji}} \qquad (j \neq i)$$

Both AP and MP depend, therefore, only on factor proportions.

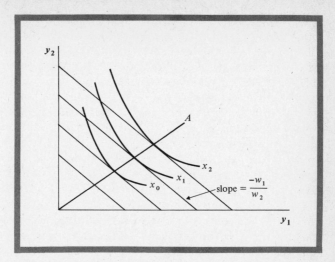

FIGURE 24.1

only two factors y_1 and y_2. Just as the slope of a consumer indifference curve equals the ratio of marginal utilities (see Lecture 11), so the slope of an isoquant equals the ratio of marginal products.[3] If a function is homogeneous of the first degree, each marginal product and thus, of course, each ratio of marginal products depends only on factor proportions.[4] Consequently, different isoquants would have the same slope along any ray from the origin (see the ray A in Figure 24.1) because factor proportions are the same along a ray.

The Cost-Minimizing Conditions

To derive the average and marginal cost functions and the way the optimal combination of factors depends on the level of output, one must know the

---

[3] The total differential of output equals

$$dX = MP_1 \, dy_1 + MP_2 \, dy_2$$

Since $dX = 0$ along a given isoquant, then

$$\frac{dy_2}{dy_1} = \text{slope} = -\frac{MP_1}{MP_2}$$

[4] This statement clearly implies that ratios of marginal products are dependent only on factor proportions for other functions as well; in fact, they are for all homogeneous functions. If a function were homogeneous of degree h, all its marginal products would be homogeneous of degree $(h - 1)$; that is,

$$MP_j = y_i{}^{h-1} \frac{\partial f(R_{1i}, R_{2i}, \ldots, R_{mi})}{\partial R_{ji}}$$

where $R_{ji} = y_j/y_i$ (prove this from the definition of homogeneous functions in footnote 1, Lecture 24). Hence

$$\frac{MP_j}{MP_k} = \left(\frac{y_i{}^{h-1}}{y_i{}^{h-1}}\right)\left(\frac{\partial f/\partial R_{ji}}{\partial f/\partial R_{ki}}\right) = \phi(R_{1i}, R_{2i}, \ldots, R_{mi})$$

factor supply functions because they determine the isocost curves—the various combinations of inputs costing the same total amount. By definition, a firm hiring in a competitive factor market can buy all it wants of a factor at the same price. The isocost curves would then be straight lines, as shown in Figure 24.1, with a slope equal to the relative factor prices (w_1/w_2).

A firm would minimize the cost of producing any output by always locating at the point on each isoquant that touched the lowest isocost curve. If isoquants were concave and isocost curves were straight lines, all the optimal positions would be at "corners" (Why?), and one of the factors would not be used. Consequently, if both were being used, the isoquants have to be convex in some regions; the optimal positions would be in these regions at the points of tangency with the isocost lines. These optimal positions imply, at least if production functions are homogeneous of the first degree, that factors tend to be complements, and that each factor has a diminishing marginal product.[5] Therefore, with production functions homogeneous of the first degree, "diminishing returns" is an implication of optimal behavior and need not be assumed a priori as a law of nature: cost-minimizing firms would not operate in any other region. "Increasing returns" would not be observed,[6] no matter how "important" it was.

Tangency between an isoquant and an isocost line means that the slope of the isoquant equals relative factor prices:

$$-\text{slope} = \frac{dy_2}{dy_1} = \frac{MP_1}{MP_2} = \frac{w_1}{w_2} \tag{24-5}$$

or

$$\frac{MP_1}{w_1} = \frac{MP_2}{w_2} \tag{24-6}$$

The cost of producing any output is minimized when the additional product of the last dollar spent on a factor is the same for all factors, perfectly analogous to a condition derived for utility maximization [see equation (11-2)].

The inverse of each ratio in equation (24-6) shows the marginal cost of changing output by changing a single factor alone.[7] At a tangency position, not only are these ratios equal to each other, but also, for small changes in output,[8] all factors are perfect substitutes at a rate of exchange equal to their

---

[5] That is,

$$\frac{\partial^2 f}{\partial y_i^2} = \frac{\partial MP_i}{\partial y_i} < 0$$

See section 1 of the Appendix for proofs.

[6] That is to say, the concave segments of isoquants would not be observed.

[7] $$MC_i = w_i \frac{\partial y_i}{\partial X} = \frac{w_i}{MP_i}$$

[8] As mentioned previously, they tend to be complements for large changes in output.

relative prices. Thus, at a tangency position, the marginal cost of a small change in a single factor alone would equal the marginal cost of small changes in all factors together. That is, equation (24-6) can be expanded to

$$\frac{MP_1}{w_1} = \frac{MP_2}{w_2} = \frac{1}{MC}\,^{9} \qquad (24\text{-}7)$$

APPENDIX

1. If a production function were homogeneous of degree h, then by Euler's theorem on homogeneous functions

$$hX = MP_1 y_1 + \cdots + MP_m y_m = \sum_{i=1}^{m} MP_i y_i\,^{10} \qquad (A\text{-}1)$$

By differentiation with respect to say y_1,

$$hMP_1 = MP_1 + MP_{11} y_1 + \sum_{i=2}^{m} MP_{i1} y_i \qquad (A\text{-}2)$$

where

$$MP_{i1} = \frac{\partial MP_i}{\partial y_1}$$

or

$$y_1 MP_{11} = (h - 1)MP_1 - \sum_{i=2}^{m} MP_{i1} y_i \qquad (A\text{-}3)$$

If $h = 1$, equation (A-3) becomes simply

$$y_1 MP_{11} = - \sum_{i=2}^{m} MP_{i1} y_i \qquad (A\text{-}4)$$

and

$$\sum_{i=2}^{m} MP_{i1} y_i \gtrless 0 \qquad \text{as} \qquad MP_{11} \lessgtr 0 \qquad (A\text{-}5)$$

In other words, an "average" factor y_j would be a complement of y_1 ($MP_{j1} > 0$) if y_1 had diminishing marginal product, a substitute if it had increasing marginal product, and independent if it had constant marginal product.

The slope of the isoquant between y_1 and y_j, with all other y_k held constant, is

$$\frac{\partial y_j}{\partial y_1} = -\frac{MP_1}{MP_j} \qquad (A\text{-}6)$$

---

[9] A mathematical proof of equation (24-7) can be found in section 2 of the Appendix.
[10] See the Appendix to Lecture 26 for a proof of this theorem when $h=1$.

Hence the rate of change in the slope is

$$\frac{\partial^2 y_j}{\partial y_1^2} = -\frac{1}{MP_j^3}(MP_{11}MP_j^2 - 2MP_{1j}MP_1MP_j + MP_{jj}MP_1^2) \qquad \text{(A-7)}$$

[Derive this by differentiating equation (A-6) with respect to y_1 and substituting equation (A-6) into the resulting expression.] The isoquant would be convex only if

$$\frac{\partial^2 y_j}{\partial y_1{}^2} > 0 \qquad \text{(A-8)}$$

or only if the term in the parentheses on the right side of equation (A-7) is negative. Now by equation (A-5), that is, if $h = 1$

$$MP_{1j} = MP_{j1} \gtrless 0 \qquad \text{as} \qquad MP_{11}, MP_{jj} \lessgtr 0 \qquad \text{(A-9)}$$

Therefore, the parentheses could be negative only if

$$MP_{1j} > 0 \qquad \text{and} \qquad MP_{11}, MP_{jj} < 0 \qquad \text{(A-10)}$$

which was to be proved.
2. Total costs are defined as

$$TC = w_1 y_1 + w_2 y_2 + \cdots + w_m y_m = \sum_{i=1}^{m} w_i y_i \qquad \text{(A-11)}$$

If TC is minimized for the given output

$$X_o = f(y_1, \ldots, y_m) \qquad \text{(A-12)}$$

the Lagrangian expression to be minimized is

$$L = \sum_{i=1}^{m} w_i y_i + \lambda[X_o - f(y_1, y_2, \ldots, y_m)] \qquad \text{(A-13)}$$

The first-order conditions are

$$\frac{\partial L}{\partial y_i} = w_i - \lambda f_i = 0$$

or

$$w_i = \lambda f_i \qquad (i = 1, \ldots, m) \qquad \text{(A-14)}$$

Hence

$$\lambda = \frac{w_i}{f_i} = \frac{w_i}{MP_i}$$

By definition,

$$MC = \frac{dTC}{dX} = w_1 \frac{dy_1}{dX} + w_2 \frac{dy_2}{dX} + \cdots + w_m \frac{dy_m}{dX} \qquad \text{(A-15)}$$

By substituting the first-order conditions into equation (A-15) one gets

$$MC = \lambda \sum_{i=1}^{m} MP_i \frac{dy_i}{dX} \qquad \text{(A-16)}$$

But

$$\frac{dX}{dX} = 1 = \sum_{i=1}^{m} MP_i \frac{dy_i}{dX} \qquad \text{(Why?)} \qquad \text{(A-17)}$$

Therefore,

$$MC = \lambda = \frac{w_i}{MP_i} \qquad \text{(A-18)}$$

PROBLEMS

24.1.　Evaluate: The law of diminishing returns is based on empirical observation.

24.2.　Evaluate: An increase in the quantity employed of each factor by *a* percent must increase output by *a* percent. Therefore, a firm must have constant returns to scale.

*24.3.　Show that if $x = f(y_1, y_2)$, where f is homogeneous of the first degree, and if the average product of one factor is increasing, the marginal product of the other one must be negative.

LECTURE 25

Cost Curves

Marginal and average costs are functions of several dimensions of output: the rate per unit time, the anticipated duration and steadiness, the accumulated volume, and perhaps others as well. In Lecture 17 we derived the effect of a change in duration on costs, and now we consider in more detail than previously the effect of a change in the rate. To avoid confusion, unless stated to the contrary, "output" refers to the rate of output, and a change in the "level" or "scale" of output refers to a change in its rate, other dimensions held constant.

If production functions were homogeneous of the first degree, cost curves and the relation between output and factor inputs take a very simple form. Since all isoquants would have the same slope along any ray, all the tangency positions would be along the same ray (see Figure 24.1) if the relative factor prices were given. The optimal factor proportions would be independent of the rate of output—a doubling of the rate would simply double all inputs. Total costs would change in proportion to and average costs would be independent of the rate of output.[1] Since the cost-minimizing marginal product of each factor would be independent of output, equation (24-7) implies that marginal cost would also be independent of output (and would equal average cost). (Why?)

If all firms in the same industry faced the same factor prices and had the same homogeneous of the first-degree production function, they would all have the same infinitely elastic marginal cost curve. If some firms were more efficient—could produce the same output with smaller inputs than other firms—their marginal cost curves would be lower than those of other firms. The most efficient firm would have "monopoly power" to the degree that its efficiency exceeded that of other firms.

Increasing and Decreasing Costs

Many cost curves encountered in the real world are not infinitely elastic: they decline at "low" rates of output as firms take advantage of the gains from specialization, and sometimes rise at "high" rates. Such cost curves are implied by some production functions that are not homogeneous of the first degree. For example, marginal and average costs would decline or increase as the degree of homogeneity was above or below unity. (Why?)

Economists have been reluctant to abandon the assumption of first-degree homogeneity partly because it is convenient analytically, and partly because the reproducibility of experiments means that if *all* factors could be increased by a common percentage, possibly including the size of the earth or the law of gravity, the rate of output would in fact increase by the same percentage. However, a natural and plausible alternative to abandoning this assumption

[1]

$$TC = \sum_{i=1}^{m} w_i y_i$$

and

$$\frac{TC}{X} = AC = \sum_{i=1}^{m} w_i \left(\frac{y_i}{X}\right)$$

where the input-output coefficients, the y_i/X, are independent of the rate of output.

about production functions is to change the assumption about factor supply conditions.

If hiring an additional unit of a factor changed its price, the cost of an additional unit, the factor marginal cost (*FMC*), would differ from its price by the additional payments to the other units employed.[2] The cost of any output would be minimized by setting the ratio of marginal products equal not to the ratio of factor prices, but to the ratio of factor marginal costs:

$$\frac{MP_i}{MP_j} = \frac{FMC_i}{FMC_j} = \frac{w_i\left(1 + \frac{1}{\epsilon_i}\right)}{w_j\left(1 + \frac{1}{\epsilon_j}\right)} \tag{25-1}$$

and

$$\frac{MP_i}{FMC_i} = \frac{1}{MC} \tag{25-2}$$

Geometrically, the slope of an isocost curve would be the ratio of factor marginal costs. (Why?) In equilibrium, it would equal the slope of an isoquant, which is the ratio of marginal products.

[2] By the formula relating marginal and average quantities:

$$FMC_i = w_i\left(1 + \frac{1}{\epsilon_i}\right)$$

where ϵ_i is the elasticity of the supply curve of the ith factor. Hence

$$FMC_i \gtrless w_i \quad \text{as} \quad \epsilon_i \gtrless 0$$

[3] Total costs,

$$TC = \sum_{i=1}^{m} w_i(y_i)y_i$$

can be minimized for the given output

$$X_o = f(y_1, y_2, \ldots, y_m)$$

by minimizing the Lagrangian expression

$$L = \sum_{i=1}^{m} w_i(y_i)y_i + \lambda[X_o - f(y_1, y_2, \ldots, y_m)]$$

The first-order conditions are

$$w_i + y_i\frac{dw_i}{dy_i} \equiv w_i\left(1 + \frac{1}{\epsilon_i}\right) = FMC_i = \lambda MP_i$$

or

$$\frac{FMC_i}{FMC_j} = \frac{w_i(1 + 1/\epsilon_i)}{w_j(1 + 1/\epsilon_j)} = \frac{MP_i}{PM_j}$$

If factor supply curves were on balance positively inclined, factor prices would tend to be positively related to the rate of output because factor quantities are positively related to output. The increase in factor prices would increase average costs, and by equation (25-2) marginal costs as well (unless factor supply elasticities increase sufficiently). Conversely, marginal and average costs would be decreasing if factor supply curves were on balance negatively inclined. There is a shift at larger outputs toward factors having relatively elastic supply curves because their marginal costs rise relatively slowly. (Why? And what happens to the equilibrium marginal products of different factors?)

Declining sections of cost curves would be interpreted, therefore, in terms of declining factor supply curves; rising sections in terms of inclining supply curves. But why, one might ask, do declining factor supply curves tend to dominate at "low" rates of outputs, and inclining supply curves at "high" outputs? Monopoly power in factor markets (called monopsony power), or specialization of certain factors to a particular industry would cause factor prices to change with output, but do not explain why they fall at "low" output and rise at "high" ones.

The cost per period of man-hour or machine-hour of work tends to decline at low rates of output, or as the number of hours worked per period increased initially because of the fixed costs of hiring and training men, installing machines, setting up men, and warming up machines.[4] These fixed costs can explain the prevalence of initially declining marginal and average costs, particularly in industries using skilled manpower and complicated equipment, because the cost of a man-hour or machine-hour of such labor and equipment would fall initially as the degree of use, or the rate of output, increased. For example, the cost of providing university education initially tends to decline with an increase in the number of students because too few students are in specialized courses in small universities to use adequately the expensive time of teachers; different retail activities are often brought under one roof, as in a department store, so that the "fixed" traveling and shopping time of customers can be "amortized" over more purchases per trip; physicians have increasingly engaged in group practice in order to spread the cost of X-ray and other expensive equipment over more patients per period and to cut down on the time "lost" each period in waiting for patients. (How does the "law of large numbers" reduce the waiting time of both physicians and patients?)

The name "entrepreneurial capacity" is given to resources supplied by owners of firms that do not have perfect substitutes among hired factors. Such resources are important primarily because only owners can protect their own interests; that is, prevent employees, suppliers, and customers from increasing their monetary and psychic income at the owner's expense. No hired factor—such as a manager, assistant, or accountant—has the same

---

[4] These fixed costs or "indivisibilities" have been traced back fundamentally to the fixed size or "indivisibility" of human beings: we are seldom below five feet tall, two feet wide, and so forth.

incentive to protect an owner's interests. Even partners often do not have proper incentives because of the "tax" on their diligence. (Why?) The larger the number of partners, the smaller the incentive provided each one.

This explains why partnerships between family members—such as the five Rothschild brothers—have been the most pervasive since each member would try to protect the interests of other members as well.[5] It also implies that the conflict of interest in large corporations between managers and owners is simply a dramatic special case, different perhaps in degree but not in kind, of the general conflict of interest between employees and owners. Managers, like other employees, have an incentive to increase their income at the expense of owner's income, especially by pilferage and the hiding of income in nonpecuniary forms—plush offices, large expense accounts, pleasure trips, and the like; managers are disciplined by owners through inventory and accounting checks, stock raids, tender offers, and other means.[6] Presumably, it is generally more difficult to discipline managers and other employees effectively as firms get larger.

A typical supply curve of entrepreneurial capacity declines initially because of the fixed cost of using the entrepreneur's own time and related resources. Eventually, it rises both because the opportunity cost of a single owner's time increases as he is forced to draw more and more on leisure and sleeping time and because additional partners and stockholders have limited incentives to protect their own and other owners' interests. Since as output expands, more entrepreneurial capacity is used, its marginal cost would eventually rise and the firm would economize on its use by hiring imperfect substitutes: managers, assistants, accountants, computers, and other inputs. The resulting increase in the quantity of hired factors per unit output (or per unit of entrepreneurial capacity) lowers their marginal products (Why?) and thus increases marginal and average costs [see equation (24-7)].[7]

To summarize, our analysis explains declining sections of cost curves by fixed costs—often related to specialization and "indivisibilities"—elastic sections by the linear homogeneity of production functions, and inclining sections by the limited capacity of owners to control the resources used in their firms. The lengths of these sections vary considerably from industry to industry: measured by the value of inputs or sales the declining section is much longer in the automotive than retail industry, and the inclining section occurs earlier in medical than in legal practice. The corporate form itself is much more important in manufacturing than in, say, services. Unfortunately,

---

[5] This is an example of the effects of interdependent preferences (see also Problem 7.4).

[6] Those who believe that the top management of giant corporations are completely immune to control by stockholders cannot explain why they do not increase their incomes many times and reduce dividends to stockholders correspondingly (see Problem 20.2). On the other hand, the importance of the corporate form—that is, of limited liability—in raising large amounts of capital is itself evidence that suppliers of equity capital fear their interests are not fully protected in large firms. In any case, if top management had complete control, they would then try to protect "their" interests against those of "their" employees.

[7] Costs inclusive of the opportunity cost of entrepreneurial capacity would increase as well as hired costs.

surprisingly little is known about why industries differ' greatly in these characteristics.

PROBLEMS

25.1.   Assume that only firms in an industry producing outputs between X_0 and X_1 continue to survive. Those producing $\leq X_0$ either go out of business or grow beyond X_0, whereas those producing $\geq X_1$ either go out of business or contract below X_1. Assume all firms maximize their incomes.

   a. If all firms have the same cost curve, can you infer anything about the shape of each one?
   b. If they have different cost curves, can you infer anything about the shape of each one?
   *c. Universities are of very different sizes. What is the implication of this analysis about the shape of their cost curves?

LECTURE 26

Technological Change

If marginal cost curves and thus supply curves were typically elastic over a substantial range of output, relative prices would respond primarily to changes in relative marginal costs, due in part to change in government regulation (see Lecture 23), other excise taxes, or factor prices. In the United States and other Western countries during the last hundred years, marginal costs have changed largely, however, because of changes in efficiency, or "productivity."

Productivity can change substantially even over five or ten years. To take an extreme example, productivity in the computer industry increased about *tenfold* between the mid-1950s and the mid-1960s.[1] Computers now calculate more rapidly, have much bigger memory capacities, and provide quicker access to the memory than they did in the fifties. This immense increase in productivity has caused an immense decrease in price: the price of a "through-put" of computer services declined about 90 percent during this period. Although the usual decade changes in productivity are much less than this, there is a strong negative relationship between the changes in price and productivity. Figure 26.1 depicts the change in price from 1954

---

[1] See Gregory C. Chow, "Technological Change and the Demand for Computers," *American Economic Review*, 56 (December 1967).

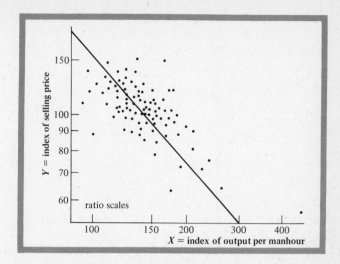

FIGURE 26.1

to 1963 for about two hundred manufacturing industries against the change in productivity, measured crudely by output per man-hour. When productivity in an industry rose by b percent more than that in the average industry, its relative price tended to fall by about b percent. In spite of the considerable errors in these data, the changes in productivity "explain" more than a third of the changes in prices.

The output of a firm can be said to depend not only on the conventional inputs of labor, capital, etc., but also on the state of a variable that we call "technology" (T):

$$X = f(y_1, \ldots, y_m; T) \tag{26-1}$$

An increase in T means an increase in the amount of X obtainable from a given set of y_i; the rate of increase can be called the marginal product of technology. The level of technology varies even among firms in the same industry because of differences in entrepreneurial ability, luck, investments in research and development, and so forth.

To examine the meaning of a change in technology in terms of costs, assume that the production function f in equation (26-1) has constant returns to scale in the y_i alone; i.e., if T were held constant, an increase in all the y_i by a common percentage would increase output by the same percentage. Then total output would be exhausted if each y_i received its marginal product:

$$X \equiv y_1\, MP_1 + y_2\, MP_2 + \cdots + y_m\, MP_m{}^2 \tag{26-2}$$

According to equation 26-2, a change in technology could have an effect on production only by changing the marginal products of the y_i. Therefore,

[2] See the Appendix for a proof of this theorem by Euler.

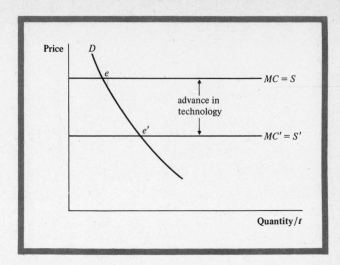

FIGURE 26.2

different kinds of technological change are defined by their different effects on these marginal products.

The combination of factors that minimizes the cost of any output must satisfy the conditions (if all factor markets are competitive):

$$MC = \frac{w_1}{MP_1} = \frac{w_2}{MP_2} = \cdots = \frac{w_m}{MP_m} \qquad (26\text{-}3)$$

(see Lecture 25). An advance in technology would increase these marginal products and thereby would reduce the y_i required to produce any output. If all the marginal products were raised by the same proportion, say 10 percent, the optimal factor *proportions* would be unchanged since only then could the ratio of marginal products continue to equal the unchanged ratio of factor prices. (Why? What do the marginal products depend on?) Marginal costs, however, would be reduced by 10 percent since all the marginal products increase by that amount (see Figure 26.2).

Technological changes that do not change the optimal factor proportions have been called "factor-neutral." Notice, though, that if production functions were not homogeneous or if factor markets were not competitive, a change in all marginal products by the same percent could change the optimal factor proportions. [Why? Consult equation (25-1).]

If some marginal products were changed more than others, the technological change is said to be biased toward the former. For example, if labor's marginal product were raised by a greater percentage than capital's, the technological advance would be biased toward labor, or "capital-saving." The reason for this description is made clear by considering equation (26-3). If a technological advance raised the marginal product of y_1 by a greater percentage than y_2, the ratio of their marginal products would no longer equal the ratio of their factor prices at the old factor proportions. The marginal product of y_2 would have to be increased by a reduction in its quantity relative to y_1. In this sense, the firm "saves" on y_2.

If all firms in an industry had the marginal cost curve MC (in Figure 26.2) before a technological advance, and MC' afterward,[3] and if the industry demand curve D were unaffected by the advance, the industry equilibrium would shift from e to e'. Output would increase and (relative) price would decrease; obviously, the increase in output would be greater the more elastic the industry demand curve was.

We pointed out earlier that the immense advance in computer technology between the mid-fifties and sixties caused an immense decline in the price of computer services. The latter apparently was responsible for almost half of the fortyfold increased use of computer services during this period.[4] To take another example, the gradual replacement of conventional fuels by atomic power in generating hydroelectric energy in recent years can be traced to technological advances. Twenty years ago the cost of using atomic power exceeded that of conventional fuels, but a series of small yet cumulative improvements have made atomic power competitive in many developed countries. Indeed, in England, where coal is expensive, atomic power is now a relatively cheap source of power, and even the United States is rapidly increasing the number of its atomic plants.

Ricardo, Mill, and other giants of nineteenth-century economics argued that agriculture was not amenable to technological developments, and expected diminishing returns in that sector to be offset by technological advances in manufacturing. Yet during the last 30 years in the United States, productivity has apparently advanced faster in agriculture than in manufacturing. Innovations like hybrid corn, mechanical tractors, new fertilizers, and new pesticides have been major contributions. The rapid improvement in agricultural productivity combined with low price and income elasticities (How does the latter enter?) have created substantial downward pressure on the relative price of agricultural goods. Governments have tried to counteract this pressure by price support programs, but these have encouraged large increases in output, which have either been stored (called the "free lunch program for rats") or discouraged by acreage restrictions. Thus technological advancement is one "cause" of the agricultural "problem" in recent decades.

The rate of technological advancement in education has apparently lagged behind that in other industries: the classroom discussion and lecture format currently used is little different from that used hundreds of years ago, although duplicating facilities, audiovisual techniques, computers, and so forth have had beneficial effects. As a consequence, the relative price of education has

---

[3] A nonneutral technological advance would reduce marginal costs by a weighted average of the increases in the different marginal products, the weights being the share of each factor in marginal costs.

[4] See Chow, *op. cit.* What do you think the other half was due to?

risen over time, which explains the great concern with the "high cost of education." One contributor to the slow rate of advance is the disregard for the students' time. Earnings forgone by spending time in school instead of at work accounts for more than half of the true total cost of college and high school education in the United States, yet they traditionally are omitted entirely from statistics on the cost of education. The consequence has been a neglect of ways to economize on students' time, such as all-year-round schooling, shorter programs, or more administrative personnel (i.e., shorter queues at registration, in libraries, and so forth).

APPENDIX

If the production function were homogeneous of the first degree,

$$X = y_1 g\left(\frac{y_2}{y_1}, \ldots, \frac{y_m}{y_1}\right) = y_1 g(R_2, \ldots, R_m) \tag{A-1}$$

where $R_i = (y_i)/(y_1)$. Therefore,

$$MP_1 = g + y_1 \sum_{i=2}^{m} g_i \frac{\partial R_i}{\partial y_1} = g + y_1 \sum_{i=2}^{m} g_i\left(\frac{-y_i}{y_1^2}\right) = g - \frac{\sum_{i=2}^{m} g_i y_i}{y_1} \tag{A-2}$$

and

$$y_1 MP_1 = y_1 g - \sum_{i=2}^{m} g_i y_i = X - \sum_{i=2}^{m} g_i y_i \tag{A-3}$$

Also,

$$MP_i = y_1 g_i \frac{1}{y_1} = g_i \quad i \neq 1 \tag{A-4}$$

and

$$y_i MP_i = y_i g_i \tag{A-5}$$

Since

$$\sum_{i=1}^{m} y_i MP_i = y_1 MP_1 + \sum_{i=2}^{m} y_i MP_i$$

from equations (A-3) and (A-5),

$$\sum_{i=1}^{m} y_i MP_i = \left(X - \sum_{i=2}^{m} g_i y_i\right) + \sum_{i=2}^{m} g_i y_i = X \tag{A-6}$$

PROBLEMS

26.1. Suppose there are many industries, all competitive, and that they all have constant costs (infinitely elastic supply curves). All experience neutral technological progress at the same rate. What happens to the relative price and output in each industry if

      a. All income elasticities equal one?
      b. These elasticities differ?
    *c. Answer 26.1a and 26.1b if the rate of neutral progress differed from industry to industry.

26.2. Suppose a firm is a monopolist and has constant costs of production. Assume that it alone experiences technological progress, and that this progress is factor-neutral. What happens to its output and relative price? What happens to its employment of labor and other factors? (Assume that its demand curve has a constant elasticity.)

26.3. Evaluate: In a competitive economy, the growth in real wages equals the growth in output per man-hour.

26.4. Evaluate: "On the empirical side some sort of increasing returns have been inferred from the very well-attested correlation between the rate of growth of productivity and the rate of growth of production between industries . . ." [F. H. Hahn and R. C. O. Matthews, "The Theory of Economic Growth: A Survey," *Economic Journal*, 74 (December 1969)].

*26.5. Since 1929, employment in the service industries has continued to grow relative to employment in the goods industries until more than half of all persons are employed in services. Yet, as far as one can tell, output of services has not grown appreciably faster than output of goods. How would you explain each of these trends? How would you reconcile them?

*LECTURE 27

Induced Technological Change

The previous lecture discussed the effect of technological change on employment, output, and prices; this one pushes the analysis one step further and asks what determines the state of technology. The question itself implies that technology is a decision variable subject to economic interpretation. Until recently the dominant view has been that new technologies or innovations are not much affected by economic incentives because they result mainly from serendipity and man's basic inquisitiveness. But the growth of large-scale and systematic research and development (R and D) activities in numerous industries, as well as the accumulating evidence on the incentives provided by Nobel, Einstein, and other prizes,[1] have encouraged the contrary view; namely, that innovations, like other activities using scarce resources, are affected by economic incentives and can be analyzed with economic principles.

Accordingly, assume each firm has a function that relates its technology during a period to E, its expenditures on R and D during the same period:

$$E = g\left(\frac{T}{T_0}\right) \tag{27-1}$$

where T_0 is its initial or base level of technology. To keep the analysis relatively simple, we assume that technological progress is not cumulative so that T reverts to T_0 whenever E falls to zero.[2]

If a firm's production function were homogeneous of the first degree in its y_i inputs, equation (26-2) states that

$$X = MP_1 y_1 + MP_2 y_2 + \cdots + MP_m y_m \tag{27-2}$$

or

$$X = a_1(MP_1^0 y_1) + \cdots + a_m(MP_m^0 y_m) \tag{27-3}$$

where, by definition,

$$a_i \equiv \frac{MP_i}{MP_i^0} \tag{27-4}$$

and MP_i^0 is the marginal product of y_i when technology equals T_0, and MP_i is the marginal product of y_i with the actual technology. If $T > T_0$, then generally $MP_i > MP_i^0$, and a_i would exceed unity. It is convenient to use the a_i to measure the effect of E on technology and to substitute them for T/T_0 in equation (27-1):

$$E = g(a_1, a_2, \ldots, a_m) \tag{27-5}$$

with presumably

$$\frac{\partial E}{\partial a_i} = g_i \geq 0$$

---

[1] See, for example, James R. Watson, *The Double Helix* (Atheneum Publishers, 1968) for a fascinating account of the secrecy and rivalry stimulated by the Nobel prize.

[2] That is, the new technology lasts only one period and $g(1) = 0$. This drastic simplification is required to avoid the timing and capitalization questions not discussed until Lecture 35.

where g_i is the marginal cost of increasing a_i. Similarly, the production function in equation (27-3) would depend on the a_i as well as y_i, and can be written as

$$X = f(y_1, y_2, \ldots, y_m; a_1, a_2, \ldots, a_m) \tag{27-6}$$

The a_i are inputs in the production of X that have a marginal price of g_i.[3]

A firm would minimize its total cost (including its expenditure on R and D) of producing any output by choosing the appropriate combinations of the conventional inputs (the y_i) and the technology inputs (the a_i). As usual, the optimality condition is that the marginal productivity of the last dollar spent on any input must be the same for all inputs:

$$\frac{1}{MC} = \frac{\partial f/\partial y_1}{w_1} = \cdots = \frac{\partial f/\partial y_m}{w_m} = \frac{\partial f/\partial a_1}{g_1} = \cdots = \frac{\partial f/\partial a_m}{g_m} \tag{27-7}[4]$$

where w_i is the price of y_i. These equations indicate that technology is not a free good, and imply that the level of technology could be "too" high, i.e., its cost could be excessive compared to what could be achieved by spending the same amount on conventional inputs. From equations (27-2) and (27-3),

$$\frac{\partial f}{\partial y_i} = MP_i \quad \text{and} \quad \frac{\partial f}{\partial a_i} = MP_i^0 y_i \tag{27-8}$$

[3] The production function given by (27-6) or (27-3) is homogeneous of the first degree not only in the y_i alone, but also in the a_i alone. (Why?) What is the degree of homogeneity with respect to changes in both the a_i and y_i? Under what conditions would the firm still be in a competitive industry?

[4] Mathematically, the problem is to minimize

$$TC = \sum_{i=1}^{m} w_i y_i + E$$

subject to

$$X_0 = f(y_1, \ldots, y_m; a_1, \ldots, a_m)$$

and

$$E = g(a_1, \ldots, a_m)$$

Forming the Lagrangian

$$L = \sum_{i=1}^{m} w_i y_i + g(a_1, \ldots, a_m) + \lambda[X_0 - f(y_1, \ldots, y_m; a_1, \ldots, a_m)]$$

and differentiating with respect to the y_i and a_i, the first-order conditions are

$$w_i = \lambda \frac{\partial f}{\partial y_i} \quad \text{and} \quad g_i = \lambda \frac{\partial f}{\partial a_i}$$

where λ is marginal cost.

hence equation (27-7) can be expressed as

$$\frac{MP_1}{w_1} = \cdots = \frac{MP_m}{w_m} = \frac{MP_1^0 y_1}{g_1} = \cdots = \frac{MP_m^0 y_m}{g_m} \qquad (27\text{-}9)$$

The resulting optimal a_i can be determined from equation (27-9) to be

$$a_i \equiv \frac{MP_i}{MP_i^0} = \frac{w_i y_i}{g_i} \qquad (27\text{-}10)$$

That is, the optimal marginal productivity function of y_i relative to its base level would equal the ratio of the total expenditure on y_i to the marginal cost of improving its productivity. The technological improvement would be factor-neutral (all the a_i the same by the definition of neutrality in Lecture 26) if, and only if, all the marginal improvement costs were proportional to these expenditures[5]; the improvement would be directed toward (away from) those factors with low (high) marginal-improvement costs relative to their total expenditures. Notice that the direction of the improvement is determined by factor expenditures, not by factor prices, as often alleged[6]; indeed, a factor's total expenditure would be negatively related to factor price only if the elasticity of substitution between factors exceeded unity. (See Lecture 29 for a discussion of the elasticity of substitution.)

The optimal expenditure on R and D can be shown geometrically if there were only two direct factors of production, y_1 and y_2. Figure 27.1 plots a family of concave "isocost" curves that show the various combinations of a_1 and a_2 achievable with given amounts of E. The slope of these curves is the ratio of the marginal costs of a_1 and a_2.[7] The series of straight-line "isoquants" depicts the various combinations of a_1 and a_2 that can produce a given rate of output, holding y_1 and y_2 constant.[8] The slope of these isoquants, $MP_1^0 y_1 / MP_2^0 y_2$ (Why?), is the ratio of the contributions to output of a_1

---

[5] By equation (27-10), $a_i = a_j$ only if

$$\frac{w_i y_i}{g_i} = \frac{w_j y_j}{g_j}$$

[6] For example, the eminent British economic historian H. Habakkuk argued that technological progress in the nineteenth century was more labor-saving (capital-using) in the United States than in Great Britain because wage rates were higher in the former. See his *American and British Technology of the Nineteenth Century* (Cambridge, England: Cambridge University Press, 1962).

[7] If $E = g(a_1, a_2)$, then

$$dE = 0 = g_1 \, da_1 + g_2 \, da_2$$

and

$$\frac{da_2}{da_1} = -\frac{g_1}{g_2}$$

[8] The isoquants are straight lines because if y_1 and y_2 are constant, MP_1^0 and MP_2^0 are also constant; then equation (27-3) would define a linear relation between X and a_1 and a_2.

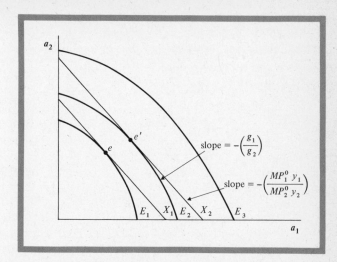

FIGURE 27.1

and a_2. Hence the point of tangency between an isoquant and an isocost curve gives the minimum cost of achieving a given output, holding y_1 and y_2 constant. More complete equilibrium conditions, which also determine the optimal y_i, are given in equation (27-9).

It is clear from the figure that an increase in output would increase the optimal expenditure on R and D. For an increase in output would shift the relevant isoquant outward, and thus shift the tangency position to a higher isocost curve from point e to e'. A similar conclusion follows from equation (27-10). (Why?) The incentive to invest in R and D is greater at larger outputs essentially because a given increase in the marginal productivity functions would apply over more units of the y inputs at larger outputs. Therefore, the empirical observation that large firms invest more in R and D than small firms need not be explained by differential access to funds or monopoly power, for it follows directly from the basic theory of R and D investment.

Equations (27-1) and (27-5) relate technology in a firm to its own expenditures on R and D; a relevant modification would be to suppose that R and D expenditures by one firm increases the technology in others, particularly those in the same industry. These benefits to other firms provide the justification for a system that awards firms exclusive ownership rights, say through patents, over their innovations. Since a firm's expenditures on R and D are positively related to its rate of output (see above), the level of technology available to all firms in an industry would tend to be positively related to industry R and D and industry output. Lecture 18 shows that such effects of industry output on a firm's costs make the industry supply curve more elastic than that of a typical firm. Indeed, even if the latter were positively inclined, the former could be negatively inclined (a situation defined as increasing returns to scale for the industry) if the effects of one firm on another were sufficiently powerful.

   This analysis helps reconcile two apparently conflicting interpretations of the secular improvement in productivity in countries like the United States: one stresses the development of new technologies, the other increasing returns to industry scale. In our analysis, these interpretations are complementary rather than in conflict, and the increasing returns are consistent with competition.

   Some caution is prudent, however, in accepting the basic supposition that R and D expenditures by one firm reduce the costs of other firms. Firms introducing innovations are alleged to be forced to share their knowledge with competitors through the bidding away of employees who are privy to their secrets. This may well be a common practice, but if employees benefit from access to salable information about secrets,[9] they would be willing to work more cheaply than otherwise. If so, innovating firms would be able to hire labor more cheaply than other firms, and this would at least partly offset the loss from having to disclose one's knowledge to competitors. For example, research assistants work for the National Bureau of Economic Research more cheaply because the knowledge they acquire about empirical techniques can be used later to obtain better paying jobs elsewhere. Similarly, top fashion designers (perhaps inadvertently) sell many of their most expensive designs to firms planning to copy them; the high prices paid partly measure the gains from copying and mass producing these designs.

PROBLEMS

27.1.   A well-known argument concludes that, in the absence of a patent system or similar legislation, there would be underinvestment in the production of new knowledge and technology.

      a. What is the argument?
     *b. Do you consider it valid?

*27.2.   Another well-known argument concludes that there is overinvestment in the production of knowledge due to "wasteful duplication" of investment. For example, Linus Pauling invested much effort in arriving at the structure of DNA, but the Cambridge group discovered it first.

      Assume the existence of a patent or other prize (e.g., Nobel) that is awarded to those succeeding first. Does competition in the production of knowledge imply overinvestment? How does the probability of succeeding first enter into the analysis?

---

[9] Employees might not benefit from access to secrets because competition between them could reduce the market price of their information to zero.

chapter 8

Demand for Factors

LECTURE 28

Derived Demand for Factors of Production

The lectures on marginal cost, production functions, and technology have many implications about the demand for factors of production. In the next few lectures we examine systematically this "derived" factor demand, ultimately derived, that is, from the demand for final products (in turn derived, as in Lecture 10, from the demand for household-produced commodities). Derived demand analysis can be used to show the effects on factor prices and uses of changes in product markets—in excise taxes, production functions, or the amount of competition—and of changes in factor supply conditions—an increased stock of capital or labor, the development of strong trade unions, or reduced subsidies to graduate education in the sciences. We begin by analyzing the derived demand of a single firm and proceed to the derived demand of an industry and a country.

A firm maximizes its income when

$$MR = MC = \frac{FMC_1}{MP_1} = \frac{FMC_2}{MP_2} = \cdots = \frac{FMC_m}{MP_m} \qquad (28\text{-}1)$$

(see Lectures 20 and 25), where MR and MC are marginal revenue and marginal cost, FMC_i is the cost of an additional unit of the ith factor, and MP_i is its marginal product. Hence

$$FMC_i = (MR)(MP_i) \qquad (28\text{-}2)$$

or the marginal cost of a factor would equal the value of its marginal product. A firm hires more of factors costing less than the revenue they add, and less of those costing more until the equilibrium condition in equation (28-2) is satisfied for all factors. Since the marginal revenue of firms selling in competitive markets equals the product price, and the factor marginal costs of

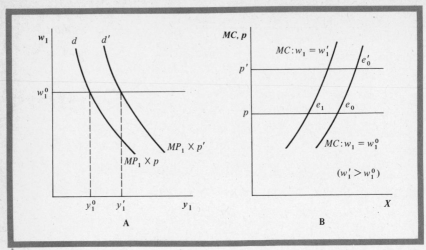

FIGURE 28.1

those buying in competitive markets equals the factor prices, equation (28-2) is the familiar

$$w_i = (p)(MP_i) \tag{28-3}$$

for firms in both competitive product and factor markets.

Fixed Quantities of Other Factors

The demand for a particular factor, say y_1, can be readily derived if the quantities of all other factors used in the firm were fixed, and if the firm were competitive in both the product and y_1 markets. Equation (28-3) would hold for y_1, but neither equation (28-2) nor (28-3) is applicable to the other factors because their marginal costs would be infinite at their fixed amounts. The firm's demand curve for y_1, the curve showing the relation between w_1 and the quantity demanded of y_1, would be completely determined by equation (28-3).[1] If w_1 were reduced by a given percentage, y_1 would have to increase by an amount sufficient to reduce MP_1 by the same percentage: y_1 must be increased to reduce MP_1 because of diminishing marginal productivity.[2]

---

[1] That is, the single equation

$$w_1 = p \frac{\partial f(y_1, y_2, \ldots, y_m)}{\partial y_1}$$

is sufficient to determine the relation between y_1 and w_1 if p and $y_2, \ldots, y_m$ are constant.

[2] To maximize income, not only must factor marginal costs equal the value of marginal product but also the former must rise faster or fall slower than the latter. If factor and product prices were constant, this implies diminishing marginal productivity. (Why? Also see Lecture 24.)

In other words, the derived demand curve for y_1 must be negatively inclined; indeed, with fixed amounts of other inputs, it would simply be the marginal productivity curve of y_1 converted into monetary units through multiplication by the product price (see panel A of Figure 28.1).

Panel B looks at the process shown in panel A from a different point of view. Since marginal cost equals the ratio of w_1 to MP_1, the MC curve rises because MP_1 diminishes as more y_1 is used, i.e., as more output is produced. An increase in w_1 would raise the MC curve by the same percent and shift the equilibrium output to the left, from e_0 to e_1, by an amount directly related to the elasticity of the MP_1 curve. (Why?) An increase in the product price would increase the equilibrium output, from e_0 to e'_0, and thus also the demand curve for y_1, from d to d' in panel A. An increase in the input of other factors would tend to raise MP_1 because factors tend to be complements (see the proof in Lecture 24). The rise in MP_1 would shift both the MC curve and the derived demand curve to the right, thereby increasing both output and the quantity of y_1 used.

Fixed Prices of Other Factors

If the prices rather than quantities of other factors were given at different points along each derived demand curve, equation (28-3) would give the equilibrium condition for all factors. A reduction in w_1 would, as before, increase the quantity demanded of y_1; therefore, the marginal products and thus the demand curves of other factors would also increase. (Why?) This would, in turn, increase the marginal product of y_1 and thus the quantity demanded of y_1, which would further increase the marginal products of other factors, and so on. This process continues until equation (28-3) is again satisfied for all factors. The derived demand curve for y_1 with fixed prices of other factors is more elastic than its marginal product curve because the quantities of other (complementary) factors would be increased along with y_1 at lower values of w_1.

Figure 28.2 plots several marginal productivity curves of y_1. An increase in the input of other factors raises the marginal productivity of y_1 and thus shifts its MP curve to the right because factors tend to be complements. The figure also plots a derived demand curve for y_1 that holds the prices of other factors constant; it is a locus of points along different MP curves because the quantity demanded of other factors would be different at different values of w_1. In particular, it is more elastic than an MP curve because more of the other factors are demanded at lower values of w_1.

The total effect of a change in w_1 on the amount demanded of a factor can be decomposed into expansion and substitution effects that are analogous to the income and substitution effects in consumer theory. A reduction in w_1 would lower the marginal cost curve, and thereby increase the equilibrium output, which would also generally increase the demand curves for all factors. A reduction in w_1 also encourages a substitution of the cheaper y_1 for other

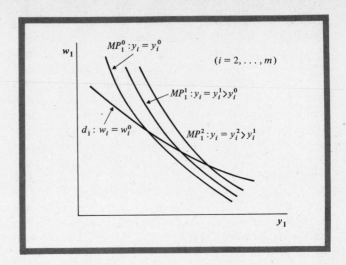

FIGURE 28.2

factors in the production of any given output. The derived demand curve
for y_1 is necessarily negatively inclined because both the expansion and
substitution effects increase the amount demanded of y_1 at lower values
of w_1. We have shown that the amount demanded of other factors would
also increase; therefore, although the substitution effect decreases the demand
for other factors, the expansion effect *must* be more powerful.

PROBLEMS

28.1. Evaluate: The marginal productivity theory of wages is wrong
because it neglects the effect of unions and other institutions on
wages.

28.2. Evaluate: Unskilled laborers receive relatively low wages because
their productivity is low.

28.3. Evaluate: In a monopsonistic labor market the imposition of a
minimum wage above the market wage *must* increase employment.

28.4. Evaluate: In a monopsonistic industry, real wages will not grow
even if there is technological progress in the industry.

28.5. Assume that y_1 is an "inferior" factor of production, i.e., the
production function for a good X is such that an increase in X
would *reduce* the quantity of y_1 used. Can the derived demand
curve for y_1 by a competitive firm producing X be positively inclined?
Hint: What is the effect of a decline in the unit price of y_1 on the
marginal cost curve and thus on output?

*28.6. Can a rise in the wage rate of a factor *increase* the "profits" or
residual incomes of employers in a particular industry initially?
Permanently? Why or why not?

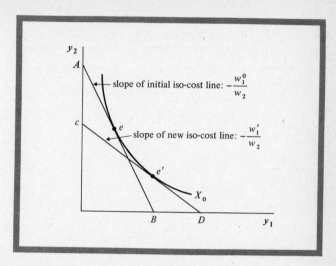

FIGURE 29.1

*28.7.   Suppose that workers in a competitive labor market become union-ized. Assume that the union sets a wage rate and that firms buy whatever (union) labor they want at that rate. What wage rate is set by the union and how many labor units are employed if the union is controlled by a "racketeer" who wants to maximize his own money income? He is "paid" by employers a wage rate for each unit of labor he supplies and he "pays" union members a (possibly different) rate for each unit of their labor that he uses.

LECTURE 29

Substitution Between Factors

The expansion and substitution effects, especially the latter, are now con-sidered in more detail. An increase or decrease in w_1 shifts the marginal cost curve upward or downward by a percentage equal to the share of y_1 in marginal cost.[1] Therefore, a given percentage change in w_1 has a smaller effect on output—a smaller expansion effect—the smaller is the share of y_1 in marginal cost.[2]

The pure substitution between y_1 and other factors induced by a change in w_1 is shown in Figure 29.1. A fall in w_1 shifts the minimal cost of producing X_0 from the point of tangency e toward y_1 and away from y_2 to a new point

---

[1] See section 1 of the Appendix for a proof.
[2] Similarly, a change in the price of a good has an income effect in the Slutsky equation [equation (8-3)] that is smaller, the smaller the fraction of the consumer's budget spent on that good.

of tangency e'. The increase in y_1 and decrease in y_2 is inversely related to the curvature (not slope) of the production isoquant. For example, if the isoquant were a straight line, the minimal cost position would shift to the y_1 axis. (Why?) On the other hand, if the isoquant formed a right angle at e, the minimal cost position would be unchanged.

A widely used measure of curvature is the percentage change in factor proportions required to change the slope of an isoquant by 1 percent:

$$\sigma = \frac{d(y_2/y_1)}{d(\text{slope})} \cdot \frac{(\text{slope})}{(y_2/y_1)} \tag{29-1}$$

where σ is called the elasticity of substitution. Since the slope equals the ratio of marginal products (see Lecture 24), σ can be written as

$$\sigma = \frac{d(y_2/y_1)}{d(MP_1/MP_2)} \cdot \frac{(MP_1/MP_2)}{(y_2/y_1)} \tag{29-2}$$

The convexity of isoquants implies that σ cannot be negative: its numerator and denominator cannot move in opposite directions. (Why?) The elasticity of substitution is zero if an isoquant forms a right angle (Why?), unity in the Cobb-Douglas production function

$$X = ky_1^a y_2^{1-a} \tag{29-3}$$

and infinity for straight-line isoquants. (Why?) The "ease" of factor substitution is essentially *defined* by the size of σ.

The definition in equation (29-2) is not useful in empirical studies because marginal products seldom have been measured directly, although a few indirect "econometric" estimates have been developed in recent years. If, however, a cost-minimizing firm were buying factors in competitive markets, or more generally, in markets having the same supply elasticity for each

---

[3] The marginal product of y_1 would then be

$$MP_1 = ka\left(\frac{y_2}{y_1}\right)^{1-a}$$

and

$$MP_2 = k(1-a)\left(\frac{y_1}{y_2}\right)^{a}$$

or

$$\frac{MP_1}{MP_2} = \left(\frac{a}{1-a}\right)\left(\frac{y_2}{y_1}\right)$$

Hence

$$\frac{(MP_1/MP_2)}{(y_2/y_1)} = \frac{a}{1-a}$$

and

$$\frac{d(y_2/y_1)}{d(MP_1/MP_2)} = \frac{1-a}{a}$$

Therefore,

$$\sigma = \left(\frac{1-a}{a}\right)\left(\frac{a}{1-a}\right) = 1$$

factor, the equilibrium ratio of marginal products would equal the ratio of factor prices,[4] and the latter could be substituted in the definition of σ to give

$$\sigma = \frac{d(y_2/y_1)}{d(w_1/w_2)} \cdot \frac{(w_1/w_2)}{(y_2/y_1)} = \frac{d(y_2/y_1)}{d(w_1/w_2)} \cdot \frac{w_1 y_1}{w_2 y_2} \qquad (29\text{-}4)$$

The elasticity σ would measure the extent to which a firm moves along a given isoquant as relative factor prices change and is itself measured by the effect of a change in relative factor prices on the shares of different factors in total cost.[5] For example, if the ratio of y_2 to y_1 were reduced by the same percentage as the ratio of w_2 to w_1 increased, the share of y_1 in total cost would be unchanged, and σ would equal unity; if the relative quantities were reduced by a greater percentage than the relative prices increased, the share of y_1 would increase, and σ would exceed unity.

Data on factor shares in costs and on factor prices have been used in practically all the elasticities of substitution estimated in recent years. Usually the substitution between aggregate labor and capital in broadly defined industries, such as all manufacturing or textiles, has been considered, although sometimes the substitution between more narrowly defined factors in more specific industries has been considered. The estimates almost always are well above zero, thus ruling out fixed proportions or fixed input-output coefficients, at least at the level of aggregation studied. Very few have exceeded 1.5 or fallen below 0.5, and to some economists a central tendency of unity is evident. To others, the elasticity of substitution at least between broadly defined labor and capital is less than unity because labor's share in national income has risen over long periods of time as countries have developed despite the growth in wage rates relative to the user price of capital, and labor currently receives a greater share in developed than in undeveloped countries. Such evidence may also be consistent, however, with elasticities equal to or above unity because the quality of labor—its education, training, health, and so forth (see Lectures 35 and 36)—increases with development and tends to raise labor's share, or because technological change may have been "capital saving" (see Lecture 26).

[4] A firm would minimize costs only if

$$\frac{MP_1}{MP_2} = \frac{FMC_1}{FMC_2} = \frac{w_1(1 + 1/\epsilon_1)}{w_2(1 + 1/\epsilon_2)}$$

where ϵ_1 and ϵ_2 are the elasticities of the supply curves of y_1 and y_2 (see Lecture 25). If $\epsilon_1 = \epsilon_2$, then

$$\frac{MP_1}{MP_2} = \frac{w_1}{w_2}$$

[5] See section 2 of the Appendix for a proof.

APPENDIX

1. Since

$$TC = \sum_{i=1}^{m} w_i y_i$$

then

$$\frac{dTC}{dw_1} = y_1 + \sum_{i=1}^{m} w_i \frac{dy_i}{dw_1} \tag{A-1}$$

Also

$$\frac{dX}{dw_1} = \sum_{i=1}^{m} MP_i \frac{dy_i}{dw_1} \tag{A-2}$$

by the total differential formula. If the effect of a change in w_1 on costs is to be evaluated at a fixed X,

$$\frac{dX}{dw_1} = 0 = \sum_{i=1}^{m} MP_i \frac{dy_i}{dw_1} \tag{A-3}$$

The cost-minimizing condition is that

$$MP_i = \lambda w_i$$

where $1/\lambda$ equals marginal cost (see the Appendix to Lecture 24). Substituting this into equation (A-3), we get

$$\sum_{i=1}^{m} w_i \frac{dy_i}{dw_1} = 0$$

Consequently, equation (A-1) becomes simply

$$\frac{dTC}{dw_1} = y_1$$

Therefore,

$$\frac{d\left(\frac{dTC}{dw_1}\right)}{dX} = \frac{dy_1}{dX} \tag{A-4}$$

Since

$$\frac{d\left(\frac{dTC}{dw_1}\right)}{dX} = \frac{d\left(\frac{dTC}{dX}\right)}{dw_1} = \frac{dMC}{dw_1}$$

by the irrelevance of the order of differentiation, then by equation (A-4)

$$\frac{w_1}{MC}\frac{dMC}{dw_1} = w_1\frac{\left(\dfrac{dy_1}{dX}\right)}{MC} = s_1' \tag{A-5}$$

where s_1' is the share of y_1 in marginal cost. (Why?)

2. Since

$$\frac{s_1}{s_2} = \frac{w_1 y_1}{w_2 y_2} \tag{A-6}$$

where s_1 and s_2 are the shares of y_1 and y_2 in total cost, then

$$\frac{d(s_1/s_2)}{d(w_1/w_2)} = \frac{y_1}{y_2} + \frac{w_1}{w_2}\frac{d(y_1/y_2)}{d(w_1/w_2)} \tag{A-7}$$

$$= \frac{y_1}{y_2}(1 - \sigma) \tag{A-8}$$

by the definition of σ in (29-4).

Hence

$$\frac{d(s_1/s_2)}{d(w_1/w_2)} \gtreqless 0 \quad \text{as} \quad \sigma \lesseqgtr 1 \tag{A-9}$$

PROBLEMS

*29.1.   Suppose there are two industries, X_1 and X_2, that use two factors, y_1 and y_2. Factor prices are given to each industry and both exhibit constant returns to scale. X_1 is more y_1-intensive than X_2, but the elasticity of substitution between y_1 and y_2 is greater in X_2 than in X_1. What is the effect of a rise in the price of y_1 on

        a. Output in X_1 compared to X_2?
        b. y_1-intensity in X_1 compared to X_2?

*29.2.   Evaluate: The elasticity of demand for labor by a competitive industry cannot be less than α times the elasticity of substitution between labor and "all other factors of production" in that industry, where α represents the fraction of total costs accounted for by other factors.

LECTURE 30

Substitution Between Industries: A Numerical Example

An important cause of differences between derived demand curves for an
economy and for a firm or industry is the difference in the supply conditions
of other factors. Firms and even small industries have elastic supply curves
for most factors because large quantities of these factors can be attracted
from the many other firms and industries. This is why the prices of other
factors can generally be assumed constant at all points along the derived
demand curve for a particular factor by a firm or even a small industry. A
closed economy, on the other hand, has nowhere else to turn, and can increase
its supply of factors only over time by investments in physical and human
capital, reproduction being included in the latter.[1] The lower elasticities
of factor supply to an economy make the derived demand curve for a particular factor by an economy less elastic than those by single firms or industries.
(Why? See Lecture 28.)

However, derived demand curves by an economy incorporate substitutions
among industries as well as among and within firms in the same industry,
and interindustry substitutions increase the elasticities of an economy's
derived demand curves. To bring this effect out clearly, a simple numerical
model of the economy is developed in this lecture. We isolate substitutions
between industries by assuming away any substitution within industries.
Thus we assume that all firms in an industry use factors in the same fixed
proportion, which can be taken as the industry proportion. Factor supply
curves to the economy, not to a particular industry, are assumed to be
completely inelastic at all factor prices above a particular level, and completely elastic at that level, w_1^0 in Figure 30.1. At w_1^0, all units of y_1 are indifferent between working and remaining "idle" (for labor inputs that means
using their time in nonmarket activities). If the economy's derived demand
curve intersected the supply curve in the elastic section, as D does, some
units would be employed at a price of w_1^0 whereas others would be voluntarily
"idle" or "unemployed" (and equally well off). If the demand and supply
curves intersected in the vertical section, as at e, all units would be employed
at a price above w_1^0.

A Single Industry

Assume initially only a single industry X_1 that requires one unit each of
y_1 and y_2 to produce one unit of output. The marginal cost of each firm

---

[1] The long-run supply of labor to an economy in the classical growth models was supposed to
be infinitely elastic at the "subsistence" wage.

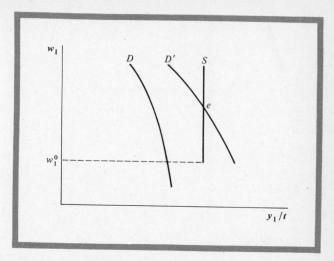

FIGURE 30.1

and thus of the industry would equal $w_1 + w_2$; this would equal the price of X_1 if the industry were in competitive equilibrium:

$$w_1 + w_2 = p_1 \tag{30-1}$$

or

$$w_1' + w_2' = 1 \tag{30-2}$$

where w_1' and w_2' are the prices of y_1 and y_2 measured in units of X_1.

For simplicity, let the supply curve of y_2 be completely elastic when $w_2' = 0$ for $0 \le y_2 < 300$, and completely inelastic at 300 units. If fewer than 300 units of y_1 were available, some y_2 would have to be unemployed. (Why?) Therefore, its equilibrium price would be zero. Equation (30-2) immediately implies that $w_1' = 1$. Put differently, if $y_1 < 300$, an additional unit of y_1 has a marginal product equal to a unit of X_1 because a unit of y_2 would be freely available to help produce a unit of X_1. Similarly, if $y_1 > 300$, an additional y_1 has a zero marginal product because all the y_2 would be employed, and no X_1 could be produced by y_1 alone. Hence, $w_1' = 0$ and $w_2' = 1$. Finally, if $y_1 = 300$, its marginal product would be indeterminate between zero and unity: a decrease in y_1 would decrease output by the same amount, and an increase would have no effect on output.

These results are summarized in the derived demand curve D_1 shown in Figure 30.2. It is infinitely elastic at $w_1' = 1$ as long as $y_1 < 300$, infinitely elastic at $w_1' = 0$ for $y_1 > 300$, and indeterminate between these limits at $y_1 = 300$. Clearly, derived demand curves are negatively inclined, although in a rather extreme form, even with fixed proportions and only one industry. If the supply curve of y_1 were $S_1 = 250$, and if $y_2 = 300$, the equilibrium value of w_1' (at e_0) would be unity, and 50 units of y_2 would be "structurally" unemployed; a shift of S_1 to the right to $S_1' = 400$ would move the equilibrium price of y_1 down the "negatively inclined" demand curve to the lower price $w_1' = 0$ (at e_0'), and 100 units of y_1 would now be "structurally" unemployed.

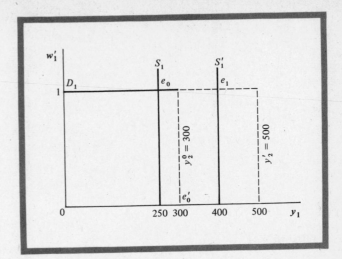

FIGURE 30.2

If the supply of y_2 shifted to the right, say to 500 units, the elastic section of D_1 at $w'_1 = 1$ would be extended to the right, and the intersection with S'_1 would be raised to e_1. As expected, an increase in the supply of other factors "shifts" the derived demand curve for y_1 to the right, and raises its equilibrium price.

Two Industries

Let us add a second industry X_2 that also uses factors in fixed proportions, but let the amount of y_2 needed per unit of y_1 be greater in X_2 than in X_1. To be concrete, assume that one unit of y_1 and two units of y_2 are needed to produce one unit of X_2. If the total supply of y_2 were still fixed at 300 units, some y_2 would be "structurally" unemployed whenever $y_1 < 150$, and some y_1 would be "structurally" unemployed whenever $y_1 > 300$. (Why?) What happens between these limits depends not only on "technology," but also on the demand functions for X_1 and X_2.

The market demand function for each good can be written as

$$X_i = D^i\left(\frac{p_i}{p}, \frac{I}{p}\right) \qquad i = 1, 2 \tag{30-3}$$

where I is income and p is the price level. If each good had a unitary income elasticity, the demand for X_1 relative to X_2 would be independent of I and p (Why?), and could be written as

$$\frac{X_1}{X_2} = R\left(\frac{p_1}{p_2}\right) \tag{30-4}$$

The negative slope of demand curves implies that an increase in p_1 relative to p_2 would lower X_1 and raise X_2, or

$$\frac{d(X_1/X_2)}{d(p_1/p_2)} = R' < 0 \tag{30-5}$$

For the present we assume that R has the simple form

$$R\left(\frac{p_1}{p_2}\right) = \left(\frac{p_1}{p_2}\right)^{-1} \tag{30-6}$$

If both industries were in competitive equilibrium, marginal costs would equal product prices; if both industries hired in the same factor markets, factor prices would be the same in both, and the equilibrium conditions can be written as

$$MC_1 = w_1 + w_2 = p_1$$
$$MC_2 = w_1 + 2w_2 = p_2$$

or

$$w_1' + w_2' = 1$$
$$w_1' + 2w_2' = p_2/p_1 \tag{30-7}$$

where w_1, w_2, p_1, and p_2 are measured in dollar units, and w_1', w_2', and p_2/p_1, are measured in units of X_1. If $y_1 < 150$, necessarily $w_2' = 0$, and thus $w_1 = 1$, $p_1 = p_2$, and $X_1 = X_2$. For example, if $y_1 = 130$, all 300 units of y_2 could not be employed even if only the y_2-intensive good X_2 were produced. Competition among the y_2 for the limited employment opportunities would reduce their wage rate to zero; then the cost of producing X_1 and X_2 and thus their prices would be the same since each product uses one unit of y_1 for each unit of output. Conditions (29-4) and (29-6) imply that equal quantities of X_1 and X_2 would be demanded if their prices were the same. Since $y_1 = 130$, $X_1 + X_2$ must equal 130, or $X_1 = X_2 = 65$. The demand for y_2 equals $2X_2 + X_1 = 195$; if 300 units are available, 105 would be unemployed, 40 due to "structure"—i.e., 40 would be unemployed even if only X_2 were produced—and the remainder due to demand. With the demand conditions assumed, some y_2 would be unemployed as long as $y_1 < 200$. (Why?) However, when $y_1 \geq 150$, none of the unemployment of y_2 would be due to structure, for all 300 units could be employed if the output of X_2 were sufficiently large relative to X_1.

If $y_1 > 200$, w_2' would be above zero and w_1' below unity, for otherwise the demand for y_2 would exceed its supply[2] and upward pressure would be

[2] For example, if $y_1 = 250$, and if $w_2' = 0$ and $w_1' = 1$, then $X_1 = X_2 = 125$ (if the y_1 market were in equilibrium), and 375 units of y_2 would be demanded, 75 more than the 300 available.

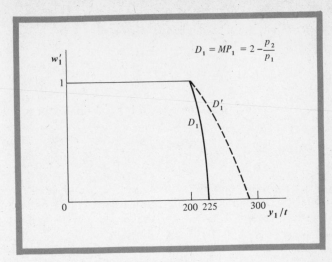

FIGURE 30.3

exerted on w_2'. An increase in w_2' would increase p_2 relative to p_1 [by equation (30-7)], and thereby reduce the demand for y_2 since the y_2-intensive good, X_2, would decline relative to X_1. The increase in w_2', p_2, and X_1, and decrease in w_1', p_1, and X_2 would continue until supply and demand were equalized in all the goods and factor markets.

Since the quantities supplied of both factors are fixed, the economy's derived demand curve for a factor would equal that factor's economy-wide marginal productivity curve. The economy-wide marginal product of, say, y_1 can be defined as the value of the total change in output when y_1 changes by a unit. If both factors were fully employed, an increase in y_1 by one unit would reduce w_1'/w_2' and p_1/p_2 sufficiently to stimulate an increase in X_1 and reduction in X_2 that maintained full employment. This implies that X_2 would have to be reduced by one unit and X_1 increased by two units. (Why?) The marginal product of y_1, measured in X_1 units (since the price of X_1 is the numeraire), would then be

$$MP_1 = \frac{2p_1 - p_2}{p_1} = 2 - \frac{p_2}{p_1} \qquad (30\text{-}8)$$

Figure 30.3 plots the marginal product curve of y_1. As long as both factors are fully employed, it continues to fall as y_1 increases because p_1 would continue to fall and p_2 continue to increase in order to stimulate the needed expansion of X_1 and contraction of X_2. Put differently, the marginal product of

---

[3] If equations (30-7) are solved for w_1' and w_2', one gets

$$w_1' = 2 - \left(\frac{p_2}{p_1}\right) = MP_1$$

$$w_2' = \left(\frac{p_2}{p_1}\right) - 1 = MP_2 \quad \text{(Why?)}$$

In competitive equilibrium, the wage rate of each factor must equal its marginal product.

y_1 falls because y_1-intensive goods must be substituted for y_2-intensive goods as y_1 increases. When $y_1 \leq 200$, $w'_2 = 0$, $p_2 = p_1$, and $MP_1 = 2 - 1 = 1$; when $y_1 \geq 225$, $w'_2 = 1$, $p_1 = 1/2 = p_2$ (Why?), and $MP_1 = 2 - 2 = 0$; when $200 < y_1 < 225$, both factors are fully employed, and $0 < MP_1 < 1$. The marginal product curve declines very rapidly from unity to zero with only a $12\frac{1}{2}$ percent increase in y_1.

PROBLEMS

30.1.   The British government proposed a tax on firms that would be proportional to the number of persons employed by each firm. The rate of tax per employee would be higher to firms in service industries than to those in manufacturing.
What would happen to:

    a. The amount of overtime worked?
    b. British exports?
   *c. Under what conditions would employment in service industries *increase relative* to employment in manufacturing?

LECTURE 31

Substitution Between Industries: A General Model

Although the qualitative conclusions of the last lecture continue to hold with more general assumptions about factor intensities and the elasticities of substitution between factors and products, the quantitative conclusions are seriously affected. This lecture examines the effects of generalizing the model.

The greater the differences in factor proportions between industries, the more easily an economy could accommodate different supplies of factors (Why?); therefore, the greater would be the range in factor supplies that is consistent with full employment of all factors. In particular, suppose X_1 still required $1y_1$ and $1y_2$ for one unit of output, but X_2 required $1y_1$ and ky_2, where $k \geq 1$. Then given y_2, both factors would be fully employed over a larger range of y_1, the larger k.[1] For example, if k were 4 rather than the 2 assumed in deriving D_1 in Figure 30.3, if $y_2 = 300$, and if demand conditions were given by equation (30-6), full employment of both factors would occur when $120 \leq y_1 \leq 187.5$, a range of 56 percent, instead of the $12\frac{1}{2}$ percent range in D_1.

The greater the elasticity of substitution in consumption between products, the smaller the change in product prices required to induce a given change

---

[1] See the Appendix for a proof of this and other statements in the lecture.

in outputs. (Why?) Therefore, the effect of a given change in factor supply on factor prices would be smaller; in other words, the derived demand curves would be more elastic. For example, if the elasticity of substitution between X_1 and X_2 equaled 3 rather than unity, the derived demand curve for y_1 would be D_1' rather than D_1 in Figure 30.3: the former is higher, more elastic, and has a greater full employment interval.

If factor proportions were variable within each industry, the optimal proportion would change as factor prices changed. A decline in the relative price of y_1 not only stimulates an expansion of y_1-intensive industries relative to others,[2] but also greater y_1-intensity in each industry. Therefore, the greater the elasticity of substitution between factors within industries, the more elastic are the derived demand curves for factors and the greater is the range in factor supplies consistent with full employment. Indeed, if factor proportions were continuously variable in each industry, and if positive quantities of each factor were required in each industry, all factor prices would be positive and all factors fully employed, regardless of factor supplies. (Why?)

The system of equilibrium conditions in the factor and product markets would usually be sufficient to determine a unique set of factor and product prices for any number of factors and products. An increase in their number would not significantly affect the derived demand curve for a particular factor unless accompanied by a change in the average elasticity of substitution between products or in the other variables discussed in this lecture.

APPENDIX

1. If two industries used each of two factors in fixed proportions, without any loss in generality we can choose the units of measuring y_1, y_2, X_1, and X_2 so that $1y_1$ plus $1y_2$ produces $1X_1$, and $1y_1$ plus ky_2 produces $1X_2$. Assuming that X_2 is the relatively y_2-intensive product, we have $k > 1$. The total amount demanded of each factor can be written as

$$X_1 + X_2 \leq y_1^0 \qquad\qquad\qquad \text{(A-1)}$$

$$X_1 + kX_2 \leq y_2^0$$

where y_1^0 and y_2^0 are the factor endowments. Equality would hold if an endowment were fully employed; otherwise, the price of that factor would be zero, and some units would be unemployed.

---

[2] Industry X_1 is said to be uniformly more y_1-intensive than X_2 if X_1 uses more y_1 relative to y_2 than X_2 at all factor prices, that is, if

$$\frac{y_{11}}{y_{12}} > \frac{y_{21}}{y_{22}} \qquad \text{for all } \frac{w_1}{w_2}$$

where y_{12} is the amount of y_2 used in X_1, and so forth.

Marginal cost would equal price in competitive equilibrium:

$$MC_1 = w_1 + w_2 = p_1$$
$$MC_2 = w_1 + kw_2 = p_2$$

$$(A-2)$$

Once p_1 and p_2 are known, both factor prices are uniquely determined.[3] Equation (A-2) can be written as

$$w_1' + w_2' = 1$$
$$w_1' + kw_2' = \frac{p_2}{p_1}$$

$$(A-3)$$

The relative demand function is assumed to have a constant elasticity form:

$$\frac{X_1}{X_2} = a\left(\frac{p_2}{p_1}\right)^{\sigma}$$

$$(A-4)$$

where σ is the elasticity of substitution between X_1 and X_2. For simplicity, a is set equal to unity.

2. If y_1 were sufficiently small relative to y_2^0, some units of y_2 would be unemployed and $w_2' = 0$. Then by equations (A-3) and (A-4), $w_1' = 1$, $p_2 = p_1$, and $X_1 = X_2$. The minimal value of y_1 that would fully employ all y_2 (or the maximal value of y_1 that would leave any y_2 unemployed) can be found by substituting $X_1 = X_2$ into equation (A-1) with the inequality signs omitted, and solving:

$$2X_1 = y_1^{\min}$$
$$(k + 1)X_1 = (k + 1)\frac{y_1^{\min}}{2} = y_2^0$$

or

$$y_1^{\min} = \frac{2}{(k + 1)}y_2^0$$

$$(A-5)$$

This value would be smaller the larger is k (the difference in factor intensities between X_1 and X_2).

If y_1 were sufficiently large relative to y_2^0, some units of y_1 would be unemployed, and $w_1' = 0$. Then $w_2' = 1$, $p_1 = (1/k)p_2$, and $X_1 = k^{\sigma}X_2$. The maximal value of y_1 consistent with its full employment is given by

$$(k^{\sigma} + 1)X_2 = y_1^{\max}$$
$$(k^{\sigma} + k)X_2 = \frac{(k^{\sigma} + k)y_1^{\max}}{(k^{\sigma}+1)} = y_2^0$$

---

[3] This is the essence of the factor-price equalization theorem in international trade theory. See P. A. Samuelson, "International Factor-Price Equalization Once Again," *Economic Journal*, 59 (June 1949).

or

$$y_1^{\max} = \frac{k^\sigma + 1}{k^\sigma + k} y_2^0 \tag{A-6}$$

This value is also smaller the larger is k, unless σ is large (how large?).

The relative length of the interval during which both factors are fully employed can be found by taking the ratio of $y_1^{\max}$ to $y_1^{\min}$:

$$\frac{y_1^{\max}}{y_1^{\min}} = \frac{(k + 1)(k^\sigma + 1)}{2(k^\sigma + k)} \tag{A-7}$$

This ratio is larger, the larger k or σ. [Show this by differentiating equation (A-7) with respect to k and σ.]

3. The elasticity of the derived demand curve for y_1 is defined as

$$E_1 = -\frac{w_1'}{y_1} \frac{\partial y_1}{\partial w_1'} \tag{A-8}$$

We now prove that

$$\partial E_1 / \partial \sigma \geq 0 \tag{A-9}$$

that is, an increase in the elasticity of substitution in consumption would tend to increase the elasticity of derived demand. We can decompose E into

$$E_1 = \epsilon_1 \psi_1 \tag{A-10}$$

with

$$\epsilon_1 = -\frac{\partial R}{\partial w_1'} \frac{w_1'}{R}$$

and

$$\psi_1 = \frac{\partial y_1}{\partial R} \frac{R}{y_1} \tag{A-11}$$

where

$$R \equiv \frac{X_1}{X_2}$$

Therefore, since $\partial \psi_1 / \partial \sigma \equiv 0$,

$$\frac{\partial E_1}{\partial \sigma} = \frac{\partial \epsilon_1}{\partial \sigma} \psi_1 \tag{A-12}$$

The sign of $\partial E_1 / \partial \sigma$ is the same as the sign of $\partial \epsilon_1 / \partial \sigma$ because $\psi_1 \geq 0$.[4]

[4] Assuming full employment and solving equation (A-1), we get

$$X_2 = \frac{y_2^0 - y_1^0}{k - 1}$$

$$X_1 = \frac{ky_1^0 - y_2^0}{k - 1}$$

According to equations (A-3) and (A-4),

$$w_1' = \frac{1}{k-1}(k - R^{1/\sigma}) \tag{A-13}$$

Consequently,

$$\frac{\partial w_1'}{\partial R} = -\frac{1}{\sigma(k-1)} R^{1/\sigma - 1}$$

or

$$\frac{\partial R}{\partial w_1'} = -\sigma(k-1)R^{1-1/\sigma} \tag{A-14}$$

Hence

$$\epsilon_1 = \sigma(k-1)R^{-1/\sigma}\left(\frac{k}{k-1} - \frac{1}{k-1}R^{1/\sigma}\right) = \sigma(kR^{-1/\sigma} - 1) \tag{A-15}$$

and

$$\frac{\partial \epsilon_1}{\partial \sigma} = kR^{-1/\sigma} + \frac{\sigma k}{(-\sigma^2)} R^{-1/\sigma} \log_e\left(\frac{1}{R}\right) - 1$$
$$= kR^{-1/\sigma}\left(1 + \frac{\log_e R}{\sigma}\right) - 1 \tag{A-16}$$

Since $w_1' \geq 0$, equation (A-13) implies that

$$kR^{-1/\sigma} \geq 1 \quad \text{(Why?)} \tag{A-17}$$

Also,

$$\log_e R \geq 0 \tag{A-18}$$

since $X_1 \geq X_2$. (Why?) Therefore, equations (A-17) and (A-18) together imply that

$$\frac{\partial \epsilon_1}{\partial \sigma} \geq 0 \tag{A-19}$$

Therefore,

$$R = \frac{X_1}{X_2} = \frac{ky_1^0 - y_2^0}{y_2^0 - y_1^0}$$

Hence

$$\frac{\partial R}{\partial y_1^0} > 0 \quad \text{with} \quad k > 1$$

4. If m factors produce n goods with variable coefficients of production, the appropriate generalizations of equations (A-1) and (A-3) are

$$
\begin{aligned}
a_{11}X_1 + a_{12}X_2 + \cdots + a_{1n}X_n &\le y_1^0 \\
\vdots \qquad\quad \vdots \qquad\qquad\quad \vdots \qquad\quad \vdots & \\
a_{m1}X_1 + a_{m2}X_2 + \cdots + a_{mn}X_n &\le y_m^0
\end{aligned}
\tag{A-20}
$$

and

$$
\begin{aligned}
a_{11}w_1' + a_{21}w_2' + \cdots + a_{m1}w_m' &= p_1/p_1 = 1 \\
\vdots \qquad\quad \vdots \qquad\qquad\quad \vdots \qquad\quad \vdots & \\
a_{1n}w_1' + a_{2n}w_2' + \cdots + a_{mn}w_m' &= p_n/p_1
\end{aligned}
\tag{A-21}
$$

where all production functions are assumed to be homogeneous of the first degree, and a_{ij} measures the amount of y_i used to produce a unit of X_j. These input-output coefficients are not constants, but depend on the w_i'. Equations (A-20) and (A-21) give $(m + n)$ equations[5] in the $(m + 2n - 1)$ unknowns: $w_1', \ldots, w_m'; X_1, \ldots, X_n$; and the $p_2/p_1, \ldots, p_n/p_1$ (the y_i endowments are assumed to be given). If $n - 1$ *relative* demand functions are also given:

$$
\begin{aligned}
\frac{X_2}{X_1} &= R_2\!\left(\frac{p_2}{p_1}, \frac{p_3}{p_1}, \ldots, \frac{p_n}{p_1}\right) \\
\vdots \qquad & \\
\frac{X_n}{X_1} &= R_n\!\left(\frac{p_2}{p_1}, \frac{p_3}{p_1}, \ldots, \frac{p_n}{p_1}\right)
\end{aligned}
\tag{A-22}
$$

there would be $(m + 2n - 1)$ equations to determine the $(m + 2n - 1)$ unknowns.

PROBLEMS

31.1.   Let there be two industries, X_1 and X_2, and two factors, y_1 and y_2. Factors are used in fixed proportions: $1y_1$ and $1y_2$ produce $1X_1$ whereas $1y_1$ and $2y_2$ produce $1X_2$. Assume that y_2 is fixed at 400 units and y_1 at 300. Solve for p_1/p_2, w_1', w_2', X_1, and X_2 where $w_1' = w_1/p_1$, and so forth, given that the demand function is

---

[5] If one of the factors, say y_i, were unemployed, the endowment of y_i would not be a binding constraint since

$$
a_{i1}X_1 + a_{i2}X_2 + \cdots + a_{in}X_n < y_i^0
$$

Unemployment of y_i implies, however, that

$$
w_i' = 0
\tag{A-20'}
$$

and that is a binding equation or constraint.

a. $X_1/X_2 = 5/4(p_1/p_2)^{-1}$, or

b. $X_1/X_2 = 5/4(p_1/p_2)^{-2}$.

c. Find the effect in both 31.1a and 31.1b if a minimum wage of $w_1' = 0.8$ were imposed by the government. What happens to the employment of y_1 and to the "wage bill" paid to y_1 and y_2? How does this differ between 31.1a and 31.1b?

d. Suppose that the minimum wage were imposed only in the X_2 industry, the X_1 industry being "exempt." What happens to w_1' and w_2', the outputs X_1 and X_2, their prices, and so forth?

e. Suppose that technological change occurs in X_1 that reduces the inputs of both y_1 and y_2 per unit output by $1/10$. What happens, with demand given by 31.1a and 31.1b, to the variables in the system?

f. Suppose that y_1 becomes unionized and maximizes its wage bill. What is its optimal wage rate (with demand given by 31.1a and 31.1b)?

31.2. Suppose that there are two countries, A and B; two goods; and two factors, labor and capital. The production function for each good is the same in both countries, and is homogeneous of the first degree. A certain amount of labor is assumed to migrate from A to B. Find the effect of this on the prices of labor and capital services in both A and B if

a. There is initially no trade in goods between A and B.

*b. There is initially free trade between A and B that equalized the price of labor and capital in both countries.

PART FOUR

Supply of Factors
of Production

chapter 9

Human Capital

LECTURE 32

Land, Labor, and Capital

We have only casually discussed the determinants of the quantity supplied of different factors of production to an economy or to its various subdivisions. The supply of factors is one of the most difficult and unsettled topics in economic theory although progress has been rapid during the last 15 years. Consequently, our lectures on factor supply will be closer to the frontier of current research than were the lectures on the supply and demand of final products, production functions, and derived factor demand because these topics have been better worked out for a longer period.

The classical economists presumed three basic factors of production: land, labor, and capital (called the "holy trilogy of economics" by Frank Knight) according to their presumed supply responses to prices. Land was assumed to be endowed by "nature" with "original and indestructible properties" (to use David Ricardo's term) that were unresponsive to changes in the price of land. The supply of labor, on the other hand, was assumed to be regulated by the forces of misery, vice, and virtue. If wage rates rose above the "subsistence" level, the supply of labor would readily increase both because births would be increased by earlier marriages and less abstinence while married and because deaths from disease and starvation would decrease. The elasticity of labor was, therefore, presumed to be high. The elasticity of the supply of physical capital was considered to be between those of labor and land although closer to the former.

These distinctions were not valid even in the nineteenth century, and today they are extremely misleading. Although the physical size of the earth has been fixed and indestructible (trips to outer space have begun to change this!), the economic supply of land has been greatly changed by man's efforts. For example, much of the land in the Netherlands was under water a few hundred years ago and became available only through large-scale drainage programs. Similarly, irrigation programs have greatly increased the agricultural land in

159

Israel and other dry parts of the world. Mankind has also cleared forests, drilled oil wells on the bottoms of seas, built tall buildings, and so forth. Economists now recognize these developments by treating land simply as a "produced" durable factor of production, that is, as one kind of capital.

Increasingly, labor too is treated as capital, human capital. This is in recognition of the small part of wages and salaries in advanced economies that is attributable to "raw" human labor, and the correspondingly large part that is attributable to investment in humans: education, on-the-job training, health, and so forth. The analysis of human capital, however, has not simply merged into a general analysis of capital because some of the determinants of the supply of human capital are unique.

Our discussion of human capital tries to answer three related questions. What determines the number of human beings, i.e., the total available man-hours? the division of this total between "work" and "leisure," or more accurately, between the market and nonmarket sectors? and the division among various kinds of work and leisure? In other words, we discuss the determinants of population, labor force participation, and "occupational" choice.

Population

In a closed economy, the growth in population is completely determined by birth and death rates. In developed countries birth control techniques are widely disseminated, and birth rates are largely determined by socioeconomic variables rather than physiological capacities. Since children provide pleasure to their parents, and since parents in developed countries make large outlays on their children, economists analyze family formation in developed countries primarily in terms of the framework provided by consumption theory. In particular, family size is said to be determined by the incomes of parents, by the cost of raising children relative to the cost of "other" commodities, and by preferences.

An increase in income, with preferences and prices held constant, would increase both the number of children and the amount spent on each child (their "quality"), for children are not an "inferior" good. The increase in quality would be large compared to the increase in quantity (or numbers) if the effect of income on the demand for children were similar to that observed for other goods (see the discussion in Lecture 7). An increase in income does appear to increase slightly family size in the United States and perhaps elsewhere,[1] and to increase substantially expenditures on the education[2] and other measures of the quality of (or the amount spent on) children.

[1] See Becker, "An Economic Analysis of Fertility," in *Demographic and Economic Changes in Developed Countries* (Princeton, N.J.: Princeton University Press for the National Bureau of Economic Research, 1957) and Stanley Friedlander and Morris Silver, "A Quantitative Study of the Determinants of Fertility Behavior," *Demography*, Vol. 4, No. 1, 1967.

[2] See Robert Michael, *The Effect of Education on Efficiency in Consumption* (unpublished Ph.D. dissertation, Columbia University, 1969).

The classical economists expected a much greater response of family size to changes in incomes because they took essentially a Malthusian approach. They expected a rise in income above the subsistence level to reduce sharply the age of marriage and perhaps also the abstinence while married. The development and diffusion of effective mechanical methods of birth control greatly reduced the need to rely on delayed marriage and abstinence, which partly explains why we no longer expect family size to respond greatly to a change in income.

Several empirical observations confirm the expected negative relation between family size and the cost of children. Families are larger in rural than in urban areas primarily because children are cheaper in the former: food and housing are obviously cheaper, and children can readily help with farm chores. The value of the time spent by parents, especially mothers, is an important cost of raising children, and women with more expensive time do tend to have fewer children.[3] An increase in education in the United States and elsewhere appears to lower family size, but nobody has yet provided a satisfactory explanation.

Economists have said little about the determinants of mortality, except to repeat the Malthusian observation that poverty can contribute to mortality through its effects on disease and starvation. In the last few years, however, under the impetus of the expanding interest in human resources, economists have begun to analyze seriously the determinants of mortality, and less extreme manifestations of ill-health. According to one promising approach, the stock of health is "produced" by combining medical care, exercise, proper diet, environmental variables, and other inputs in household production functions (see Lecture 10 for a discussion of these functions). The demand for health, including life itself, is not absolute, but along with the demand for other commodities is determined by prices, incomes, productivity, and preferences. Cigarettes are smoked and rich food eaten even though health may be reduced because the costs and benefits of health are balanced against those of other commodities.

In this approach, education reduces mortality and otherwise increases health because it raises the productivity of the household production functions. (How does this work itself out? Again see Lecture 10.) An increase in income appears to *increase* mortality and generally reduce health in the United States,[4] contrary to the Malthusian presumption. Health, including life itself, may be an "inferior" commodity in rich countries, but I am inclined to believe that the "pure" effect of income on health is positive and that the measured effect has been biased by an unmeasured positive correlation between the true price of health and income.[5]

---

[3] See Jacob Mincer, "Market Prices, Opportunity Costs, and Income Effects," in *Measurement, in Economics*, C. Christ, ed. (Stanford University Press, 1963).

[4] See Victor Fuchs, *Some Economic Aspects of Mortality in the United States* (Mimeographed, National Bureau of Economic Research, 1965), and Michael Grossman, *The Demand for Health: A Theoretical and Empirical Investigation* (unpublished Ph.D. dissertation, Columbia University, 1970).

[5] See Grossman, *op. cit.*, for an extensive discussion of this possibility.

PROBLEMS

32.1.   Evaluate: The secular increase in educational expenditures on chil-
        dren increased the cost of children and thus was partly responsible
        for the decline in birth rates over time.

LECTURE 33

Labor Force Participation

Once the population level is determined, the total hours of labor available
are also determined; for example, 1,000 persons have 168,000 hours available
each week. These can be devoted either to activities that provide monetary
payment in return—called market or work activities—or to activities that
directly provide utility—called nonmarket or consumption activities. If t_w
is the total time spent at work and t_c the total spent at consumption, then
necessarily

$$t_w + t_c \equiv t \tag{33-1}$$

where t is the total time available per week (or month, year).

Time not spent working has usually been called "leisure" time, but includes many activities, such as child-rearing, housecleaning, preparation of
income tax statements, and sleeping that are not ordinarily considered part
of leisure. We include them all under consumption time, and assume, following Lecture 10, that each person produces the commodities entering his preference function by combining consumption time and purchased goods:

$$Z_i = f_i(x_i, t_i) \qquad i = 1, \ldots, m \tag{33-2}$$

(environmental variables are ignored), with

$$U = U(Z_1, \ldots, Z_m) \tag{33-3}$$

$$\sum_{i=1}^{m} t_i = t_c \tag{33-4}$$

and

$$\sum_{i=1}^{m} p_i x_i = I \tag{33-5}$$

where I is money income. By definition

$$I = w t_w + v \tag{33-6}$$

where w is the average wage rate and v is property income. If Z_k were pure contemplation, then $Z_k \equiv t_k$.

The cost of producing each Z_i is minimized only if the ratio of the marginal products of goods and time equals the "real" wage rate (Why?):

$$\frac{\partial f_i}{\partial x_i} \bigg/ \frac{\partial f_i}{\partial t_i} = \frac{MP_{x_i}}{MP_{t_i}} = \frac{p_i}{w} \qquad i = 1, \ldots, m \qquad (33\text{-}7)$$

The combination of commodities is optimal only if the marginal utility of each commodity is proportional to its "shadow" price (Why)?:

$$\frac{\partial U}{\partial Z_i} \bigg/ \frac{\partial U}{\partial Z_j} = \frac{MU_i}{MU_j} = \frac{\pi_i}{\pi_j} = \frac{p_i \dfrac{dx_i}{dZ_i} + w \dfrac{dt_i}{dZ_i}}{p_j \dfrac{dx_j}{dZ_j} + w \dfrac{dt_j}{dZ_j}} \qquad (33\text{-}8)$$

(Why is π_i the "shadow" price of Z_i? See Lecture 10.)

An increase in property income without a change in wage rates would not change the optimal combination of goods and time [if household production functions are homogeneous (Why?)] but would increase the quantities of different commodities consumed. Since this would generally increase the total amount of time (and goods) used in commodity production, time spent at work would decline: by equation (33-1), the change in t_w must be equal and opposite to the change in t_c.

An increase in the wage rate compensated by a decline in property income would, by the definition of compensated, have no effect on total opportunities, but would have two substitution effects. Goods would be substituted for time in the production of each commodity (Why?), and goods-intensive commodities would be substituted for time-intensive ones in consumption. (Why? What happens to the shadow prices of different commodities?) [1] Both substitutions reduce the total time spent in consumption and, therefore, increase the time spent at work.

These results are shown graphically in Figure 33.1, where the vertical axis measures the wage rate, and the horizontal axis measures working hours to the right of the origin and consuming hours to the left. Each supply curve holds real income constant; [2] each supply curve of hours worked is positively

---

[1] Time and goods intensities are defined by their shares in production costs:

$$s_i = w \frac{dt_i}{dZ_i} \bigg/ \pi_i$$

and

$$1 - s_i = p_i \frac{dx_i}{dZ_i} \bigg/ \pi_i$$

[2] Real income is measured by S/π, where S is money "full" income defined as

$$\sum_{i=1}^{m} p_i x_i + w t_c$$

(see Lecture 10), and π is an average of the π_i.

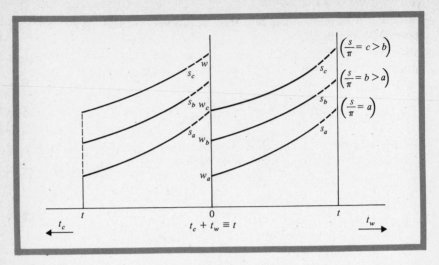

FIGURE 33.1

inclined because of the substitution effects toward work induced by a rise in the wage. The corresponding supply curve of hours consumed is, of course, negatively inclined: The sum of hours worked and consumed equals the fixed total available. An increase in real income shifts the supply curve of hours worked and of hours consumed to the left by equal amounts. An uncompensated rise in the wage rate—say due to technological progress in the market sector—would induce substitution effects toward, and income effects away from, hours worked, the net result depending on their strengths. The large secular decline in hours worked—increase in hours consumed—as countries have developed is considered evidence of strong income effects.[3]

Since wage rates differ greatly among individuals, market supply curves can relate the aggregate hours worked (or consumed) to the average wage rate, if the distribution of relative wages as well as real income were held constant along a given curve. A compensated rise in the average wage would induce persons already in the labor force to work more hours, and might also induce some of those outside the labor force to enter. For example, if the real income of the person shown in Figure 33.1 equaled a, he would enter the labor force only if his wage rate exceeded w_a. In the United States, much of the secular increase in the labor force participation of women is apparently explained by the increase in their wages as wages generally have risen.[4]

A rise in real income, wage rates held constant, would induce all persons in the labor force to work fewer hours and might induce some to drop out entirely. For example, a rise in his real income from a to b would induce the

[3] What are some alternative explanations? A couple are given in Becker, "A Theory of the Allocation of Time," *Economic Journal* (September 1965).

[4] See Jacob Mincer, "Labor Force Participation," in *International Encyclopedia of the Social Sciences*, Vol. 8 (New York: Macmillan, 1968).

person shown in the figure to drop out if his wage rate were between w_a and w_b. Much of the secular decline in the labor force participation of the young and the old—groups with lower wage rates—is apparently explained by the secular growth in incomes.[5]

PROBLEMS

33.1.   Evaluate: A rise in a man's income would cause his wife to place a higher price on an hour of her time if, and only if, she is *not* in the labor force.

[5] See Mincer, *ibid.*

LECTURE 34

Nonmarket Activities

Time devoted to consumption helps produce recreation, sleep, eating, child-rearing, housekeeping, and the like. We have seen that a rise in the wage rate induces a substitution toward less time-intensive and more goods-in-tensive methods in the production of each commodity. For example, wives work less than their husbands and spend more time in producing household activities partly because their time is usually cheaper. A rise in the relative market value of their time would reduce the time they spend at household activities and increase the time they spend at work *relative* to the time spent at household activities and work by their husbands.

Or consider the problem of how to travel between two cities. Some modes, such as buses, use the traveler's time more and his goods less than do other modes, such as planes. Consequently, the incentive to travel by goods-intensive modes is greater for persons with higher earnings; air travelers, for example, do have relatively high earnings.[1] Some research indicates that supersonic air travel would be worth while to develop if a considerable fraction of long-distance travelers would choose supersonic travel at a price 30 or 40 percent above that for conventional jet travel. The crucial variable in assessing potential demand is the value different travelers place on a reduction in travel time; widely divergent assessments have been advanced because of differences in the value of time assumed.

[1] See Reuben Gronau, *The Value of Time in Passenger Transportation: The Demand for Air Travel* (New York: Columbia University Press for the National Bureau of Economic Research, 1970).

Occupational Choice

Total hours worked is the sum of the hours spent at market activities—those providing monetary earnings—and each of these activities (as distinct from nonmarket activities) will be called an "occupation." What determines the allocation of time to different occupations, and why do some provide higher earnings than others? These are the main questions to be answered in this and the two succeeding lectures.

Assume that occupations A_1 and A_2 pay the wage rates w_1 and w_2 to each person for each hour of work supplied, and that there are no training or other entrance requirements. If neither occupation provided any direct utility or disutility—that is, in the formal language of the last lecture, if working time did not also help produce commodities entering preferences—all working time would be supplied to the occupation paying the higher wage rate. Both A_1 and A_2 could attract persons only if $w_1 = w_2$, and then everyone would be indifferent between them.

A more complicated situation arises when one or both occupations also provide utility or disutility, that is, when working time also helps produce useful commodities. Some working time would be supplied to the lower paying occupation if the difference in earnings were offset by a difference in utility. For example, some college graduates give up higher earnings in business to enter the ministry because of the satisfaction they receive from spiritual work; undertakers are paid well to offset the discomfort people feel when dealing with cadavers; or workers helping to construct the top floors of skyscrapers are paid well because of the real or imagined risks involved.[2]

A person would continue to increase the time allocated to A_1 as long as the difference in wage rates, $w_1 - w_2$, exceeded the monetary equivalent of the difference in marginal utilities. The distribution of time between A_1 and A_2 would be optimal when the wage differential exactly equaled the marginal utility differential,[3] and changes in the wage differential or in real income would change the optimal distribution. Consider Figure 34.1, where the vertical axis measures the absolute difference in real wage rates and the horizontal one the time supplied to A_1 by a single person. Absolute rather than relative wage differences provide the appropriate generalization of Figure 33.1 since there the market wage rate is, in effect, the *absolute* difference between it and the zero wage rate in the nonmarket sector.

Each supply curve gives the relation between the time allocated to A_1 and the wage rate differential when real income is held constant. These curves are positively inclined because an increase in the wage differential, Δw, lowers

[2] Most of these workers used to be drawn from a single tribe of American Indians.
[3] That is, when

$$w_1 - w_2 = \frac{1}{\lambda}(MU_2 - MU_1)$$

where MU_1 and MU_2 are the marginal utilities of the time in A_1 and A_2, and $1/\lambda$ is the monetary equivalent of a marginal unit of utility. This intuitively plausible result (Why?) is derived in the Appendix.

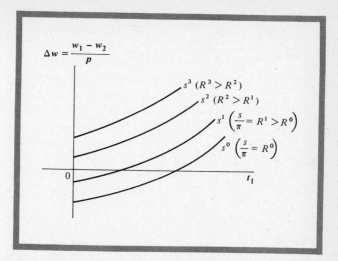

$$\Delta w = \frac{w_1 - w_2}{p}$$

$s^3 \ (R^3 > R^2)$

$s^2 \ (R^2 > R^1)$

$s^1 \left(\frac{s}{\pi} = R^1 > R^0\right)$

$s^0 \left(\frac{s}{\pi} = R^0\right)$

0

t_1

FIGURE 34.1

the relative cost of "consuming" A_1 and, therefore, induces a substitution toward A_1 and away from A_2. (What determines the elasticity of response?) The marginal utility of t_2 exceeds that of t_1 at all points along s^2 and s^3. (Why?) The opposite holds along s^0 and s^1 for smaller values of t_1. An increase in real income cannot increase the supply of time to all activities because the total is fixed.[4] It can only reallocate the time among activities; the figure implicitly assumes that t_1 is adversely affected. (Why is this implicit?)

If each person's supply curve were independent of the supply curves of others, the market supply curve would simply be the horizontal sum of the individual curves. Its elasticity would depend, however, on the distribution of entry points into A_1 as well as on the elasticities of the individual curves. Since the market supply curve (shown in Figure 34.2) has a concave kink each time a person enters A_1, it would be elastic in any interval if many new entrants are in that interval. The greater the dispersion in entry points, the

[4] Since

$$t_1 + t_2 + t_c = t$$

where t_c is the time at nonmarket activities, then

$$\frac{\partial t_1}{\partial S} + \frac{\partial t_2}{\partial S} + \frac{\partial t_c}{\partial S} = 0$$

or

$$k_1\eta_1 + k_2\eta_2 + k_c\eta_c = 0$$

where

$$k_i = \frac{t_i}{t} \qquad i = 1, 2, c$$

and

$$\eta_i = \frac{\partial t_i}{\partial S}\cdot\frac{S}{t_i}$$

A weighted average of the income elasticities of demand for different uses of time must add up to zero, the weights being the fraction of the total time spent in an activity. Contrast this result with the one derived for goods (see Lecture 4). Why are they different?

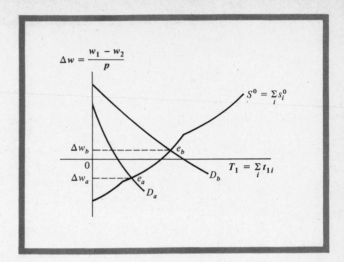

FIGURE 34.2

fewer contained in any interval around the average entry point, hence the smaller market elasticity in that interval. Since a person's entry point is completely determined by his income and preferences, the market elasticity would be inversely related to the dispersion in incomes and preferences.

The equilibrium wage differential and supply of time to A_1 are given by point e_a in Figure 34.2 if S^0 and D_a are the market supply and demand curves.[5] Only persons with preference for A_1 enter A_1 since Δw_a is negative. An increase in demand to D_b would raise the equilibrium wage differential to the positive level Δw_b, and significantly increase the time supplied to A_1. Persons already in A_1 would substitute further toward A_1, and those having entry points between Δw_b and Δw_a would now enter. The increased demand increases the consumers' surplus or "rents" of persons with preference for A_1 via the increase in Δw because a preference for A_1 is a scarce "resource." (Derive the supply curves and equilibrium differentials when everyone has the same preference.) It thus "pays to be different" if wage rates are determined by the market mechanism.

A fruitful application of this analysis is to the controversy over recruitment of military manpower. If military pay were increased sufficiently to recruit all men voluntarily, only those with relatively strong preference for military service would enter; a draft or lottery, on the other hand, inevitably catches some persons with a strong dislike for military service—as the present discontent among young persons dramatically illustrates. A voluntary army would be very expensive (in terms of explicit budget costs only!) for the present-day United States if the supply curve of volunteers were inelastic in the

---

[5] Demand curves as well as supply curves in Figure 34.2 have been drawn as functions of absolute wage differentials, even though the analysis in Lectures 28 and 29 implies that derived demand curves are functions of relative differentials. One way around this difficulty is to assume that Δw changes because of changes in w_1 alone so that absolute and relative differentials move in the same direction and by well-defined amounts.

vicinity of current military pay, for increased pay would then primarily increase the "rents" of persons already volunteering. Recent[6] empirical investigations indicate, however, that the supply of volunteers is quite responsive to the level of pay, as is the length of time served by volunteers through reenlistments. Of course, the large armed forces of today are considerably more expensive to raise voluntarily than were the tiny peacetime forces of earlier days. Indeed, an excessive number of persons used to volunteer during business recessions even at the low military pay rates. (Why?)

APPENDIX

Let t_1 and t_2 measure the time spent by a person at work activities A_1 and A_2, and assume that working time contributes, perhaps negatively, to his production of commodities. Then we have

$$U = U(Z_1, Z_2, Z_3) \tag{A-1}$$

with

$$
\begin{aligned}
Z_1 &= f_1(t_1, x_1) \\
Z_2 &= f_2(t_2, x_2) \\
Z_3 &= f_3(t_c, x_3)
\end{aligned}
\tag{A-2}
$$

and

$$
\begin{aligned}
t_1 + t_2 + t_c &\equiv t \\
p_1 x_1 + p_2 x_2 + p_3 x_3 &= w_1 t_1 + w_2 t_2 + V
\end{aligned}
\tag{A-3}
$$

where the x_i are the inputs of goods, t_c is the time spent at nonmarket activities, the f_i are his "household" production functions, and w_1 and w_2 are the wage rates in A_1 and A_2 respectively. If the Lagrangian expression

$$
L = U(Z_1, Z_2, Z_3) - \lambda\left[\sum_{i=1}^{3} p_i x_i - (w_1 t_1 + w_2 t_2 + V)\right]
$$
$$
- \mu(t_1 + t_2 + t_c - t) \tag{A-4}
$$

is formed and maximized with respect to the input of goods and time, the equilibrium conditions for the allocation of time are

$$
\frac{\partial U}{\partial t_1} = U_1 f_{11} = -\lambda w_1 + \mu
$$

$$
\frac{\partial U}{\partial t_2} = U_2 f_{22} = -\lambda w_2 + \mu \tag{A-5}
$$

$$
\frac{\partial U}{\partial t_c} = U_3 f_{3c} = \mu
$$

---

[6] See Walter Y. Oi, "The Economic Cost of the Draft," *American Economic Review*, 57 (May 1967) and Anthony C. Fisher, "The Cost of the Draft and the Cost of Ending the Draft," *American Economic Review*, 59 (June 1969).

where

$$U_1 = \frac{\partial U}{\partial Z_1}$$

$$f_{11} = \frac{\partial f_1}{\partial t_1}, \text{ and so forth}$$

λ = marginal utility of money income

μ = marginal utility of time

By substitution for μ one gets

$$\lambda w_1 = \frac{\partial U}{\partial t_c} - \frac{\partial U}{\partial t_1}$$

$$\lambda w_2 = \frac{\partial U}{\partial t_c} - \frac{\partial U}{\partial t_2}$$

(A-6)

Equations (A-6) show that the marginal utility of working time could be positive—work could be pleasant—as long as the marginal utility were less than the marginal utility of nonmarket or consumption time. Indeed, whether work is pleasant or irksome cannot even be ascertained from observed behavior and is thus a meaningless, although frequently discussed, question. Only the *difference* between the marginal utilities of consumption time and work (relative, of course, to the marginal utility of goods) is knowable.

Equations (A-6) immediately imply that

$$w_1 - w_2 = \frac{1}{\lambda}\left(\frac{\partial U}{\partial t_2} - \frac{\partial U}{\partial t_1}\right)$$

(A-7)

Any difference in wage rates must be compensated by the monetary equivalent of the difference in psychic income or marginal utility. It follows that if $\partial U/\partial t_1 = \partial U/\partial t_2 = 0$, individuals would spend time in both A_1 and A_2 only when

$$w_1 = w_2$$

(A-8)

Since

$$\lambda = \frac{\left(\frac{\partial U}{\partial x_1}\right)}{p_1} = \frac{\left(\frac{\partial U}{\partial x_2}\right)}{p_2} = \frac{\left(\frac{\partial U}{\partial x_3}\right)}{p_3} \text{ (Why?)}$$

(A-9)

by substitution for λ in (A-7),

$$\frac{w_1 - w_2}{p_i} = \frac{\left(\frac{\partial U}{\partial t_2}\right) - \left(\frac{\partial U}{\partial t_1}\right)}{\left(\frac{\partial U}{\partial x_i}\right)} \qquad i = 1, 2, 3$$

(A-10)

PROBLEMS

34.1.   Evaluate: If there are only two occupations in the economy, A_1 and A_2, and if real wages in each change by the same proportion, so that the ratio of wages in A_1 to wages in A_2 remains constant, the labor supplied to A_1 would be unchanged.

34.2.   Suppose that two occupations use persons of the same skill and ability. One occupation (g_1) provides stable employment throughout the year whereas the other (g_2) has a known period of seasonal unemployment.

   a. Would the wage rate in g_2 be higher than that in g_1? Why or why not?

   b. Would annual income in g_2 be higher than that in g_1? Why or why not?

   Suppose that an unemployment compensation system pays all unemployed persons (including those seasonally unemployed) a certain amount for each week of unemployment. What is the effect of this on:

   c. The wage rate in g_2 relative to g_1?
   d. The number of persons seasonally unemployed?

34.3.   (The Economics of Accidents) Suppose that accidents to workers of a given skill are more likely in industry B than in A (assume, for simplicity, no accidents in A).

   a. If workers were not compensated for any of their time lost or other costs to them of accidents (they bear the "liability"), what determines the wage rate in B compared to A? The total earnings of each person in B compared to A?

   b. If a system of workmen's compensation were introduced so that employers were fully responsible for any costs suffered by their employees, how would this affect wages and earnings in both industries?

   *c. If, instead, a system of "fault liability" were introduced, so that employers have to compensate workers only if the workers were not "responsible" (at "fault") for their accidents, how would this affect wages and earnings?

   d. If the accident rate in B increased, how would this affect the labor-capital ratio and output in this industry?

34.4.   Suppose that a union is formed to control fully the supply of a particular kind of labor in what was a competitive labor market. The union sets a wage rate and firms hire their desired amount of labor at that rate. What rate should the union set if it wants to maximize the economic welfare of union members as a whole? Assume that all union members have identical supply curves of man-hours to the labor market.

a. Would this differ from the rate that maximized the wage bill? If so, how?

b. Would it differ from the rate that maximized employment? How?

*c. Now assume that the union controls only part of this labor supply. How would the optimal wage rate depend on the fraction of workers that are unionized? Assume that nonunion workers receive the same wage rate as union workers, they are employed in firms that produce the same product as unionized firms, and the market demand curve for workers and the supply curves of union and nonunion workers have constant elasticities.

34.5. Suppose that recruitment of all persons to the military is by a completely voluntary process.

a. What military income would have to be paid to recruit 1/5 of the eligible population? Assume that the distribution in this group of their *real* civilian alternatives is log-normal, with a median equal to $3,500 per year, and with a standard deviation of the log of their alternatives equal to the log of 3,500. Hint: The median of the logs of a distribution equal the log of the median.

b. By how much would military pay have to change if recruitment changed to 3/5 of the group? to 5/6? to 1/20?

*34.6. Suppose that involuntary first termers were recruited by a completely random lottery of all eligible 24-year-olds. By "eligible" I mean physically fit males who had not previously enlisted. Work out some general principles that determine whether or not a person would enlist at an earlier age. Assume that enlistees serve longer than draftees, but otherwise receive the same treatment.

*34.7. Consider two occupations A and B. No training is required in either. A is, however, a risky occupation that offers a probability distribution of earnings whereas B offers a fixed amount with certainty. Suppose a person maximizes expected utility.

a. Under what conditions would he specialize in one occupation?

b. Under what conditions would he put some time into both?

c. Can this explain why many criminals engage part time in criminal activities, and part time in legal ones?

LECTURE 35

Investment in Training

The last lecture assumed that working time was divided between several occupations, yet there is considerable specialization by people in a single occupation. A person is not usually both a doctor and a dentist, a sociologist and a plumber, or a machinist and a mason. The basic reason for the discrepancy between the theory in the last lecture and actual behavior is our assumption that hourly wage rates are independent of the time, including education and other training time, allocated to each occupation. If these rates were positively related to the time previously spent training for and in an occupation, specialization would be encouraged, for the total amount earned would rise at an increasing rate with the total time devoted to an occupation.

A simple source of specialization to one job during any day is the time "wasted" getting to and from work, setting up tools and other equipment, and cleaning up afterward. A person holding two jobs in the same day "wastes" more time than does someone working equally long at a single job. The most important source, however, is the education and training that enhances competence in an occupation. The amount of schooling by doctors, lawyers, or physicists is well known, but important too is the informal on-the-job training acquired in many occupations. Specializing in one (or at most a few) occupations reduces the total amount of time that persons "waste" in training.

An emphasis on training helps reconcile another discrepancy between the theory in the last lecture and actual behavior. That theory implies [see equation (A-7) in Lecture 34] that unpleasant occupations are forced to pay higher wage rates to compensate entrants for the unpleasantness. When the amount invested in training is held constant, unpleasant jobs do pay more. When the amount invested differs significantly, however, this is no longer true: doctors, engineers, and carpenters, for example, are paid much more than common laborers, domestic servants, and janitors, and at least all writers on social problems agree that the former are the more pleasant occupations. The positive relation between earnings and the amount invested in training can be explained by introducing the cost of training, along with differences in opportunities and abilities.

Analytically, the optimal allocation of time between two occupations A_1 and A_2 would depend not only on the current wage rate differential but also on the influence of the current allocation on subsequent differentials. By allocating most of his current working time to A_1, one might convert negative existing differentials into sizable positive differentials at later ages. In general, the whole lifetime stream of possible earnings would have to be considered in deciding on the optimal allocation at each age. The analysis can be greatly simplified, however, without any real loss of substance, by assuming that these "time dependencies" are sufficiently strong to induce complete specialization in a single occupation. The problem is then reduced to deciding whether the stream of earnings obtained by specializing completely in A_1 is preferred to the stream obtained by specializing in A_2.

The value of an earnings stream is not simply the sum of earnings at different ages because $1,000 in 1980 can no more be added to say $4,000 in 1975 than three apples can be added to five shirts. Apples and shirts are made comparable through multiplication of quantities by prices that measure the number of apples considered equivalent to one shirt. Similarly, dollars in year i can be made comparable to dollars in year j through multiplication by a price that measures the number of dollars in year j considered equivalent to a dollar in year i. A stream of earnings in different years would be converted into its equivalent in earnings in a single year, and the relative value of different streams would be determined from their earnings-equivalent in the same year, just as the relative cost of different baskets of goods is determined from their shirt, Cadillac, or dollar-equivalents.

If a_i were the value in 1970 dollars of a dollar i years later, the earnings stream $E_0, E_1, \ldots, E_n$ would be equivalent to

$$V_0 = E_0 + a_1 E_1 + \cdots + a_n E_n \qquad (35\text{-}1)$$

1970 dollars, or to

$$V_5 = \frac{V_0}{a_5} = \frac{E_0}{a_5} + \frac{a_1}{a_5} E_1 + \cdots + E_5 + \cdots + \frac{a_n}{a_5} E_n \qquad (35\text{-}2)$$

1975 dollars, since a_8/a_5 must be the value in 1975 dollars of a dollar in 1978, and so forth. (Why? How does "arbitrage" insure that this is so?)[1] Therefore, if one earnings stream were equivalent to more 1970 dollars than another stream, it would also be equivalent to more dollars in any other year,[2] and can be said unambiguously to be worth more.

Consider a person in 1970 choosing between the earnings stream $E_{01}, \ldots,$ E_{n1} in A_1 and $E_{02}, \ldots, E_{n2}$ in A_2. If the nonmonetary aspects of both occupations were the same, he would be guided solely by monetary worth, and would choose that stream with the greater value in say 1970 dollars, where the value in 1970 dollars is called "the present value" of an earnings stream. Maximization of the present value of earnings or income is a natural generalization

---

[1] A 1978 dollar is worth a_8 1970 dollars, and the latter is worth a_8/a_5 1975 dollars. If $1/a_{85}$ is the value of a 1975 dollar in 1978, then $\frac{a_8/a_5}{a_{85}}$ is the value of a_8/a_5 1975 dollars in 1978. If $\frac{a_8}{a_5} \cdot \frac{1}{a_{85}}$ exceeded unity, a person could become a millionaire by continuing to convert 1978 dollars first into 1970 dollars, then into 1975 dollars, and then back into 1978 dollars. Similarly, if this ratio were less than unity, he could become a millionaire by converting 1975 dollars first into 1970 dollars, then into 1978 dollars, and then back into 1975 dollars. To rule out such arbitrage profits, it is necessary that

$$\frac{a_8/a_5}{a_{85}} = 1$$

or

$$a_{85} = \frac{a_8}{a_5}$$

[2] That is, if $V_0 > V_0'$, then

$$V_i = \frac{1}{a_i} V_0 > V_i' = \frac{1}{a_i} V_0'$$

of the maximization of current earnings or income under stationary conditions. He would choose A_1, A_2 or be indifferent between them as

$$V_{10} = E_{10} + a_1 E_{11} + \cdots + a_n E_{1n} \gtreqless V_{20}$$
$$= E_{20} + a_1 E_{21} + \cdots + a_n E_{2n} \qquad (35\text{-}3)$$

or as

$$(E_{10} - E_{20}) + a_1(E_{11} - E_{21}) + \cdots + a_n(E_{1n} - E_{2n}) \gtreqless 0 \qquad (35\text{-}4)$$

This condition can be given a simple interpretation if A_1 required training during the initial year only, and if A_2 required no training. If E_{10} were net of the outlays on tuition and other direct costs of training, the total cost of training can be defined as

$$C = E_{20} - E_{10} \qquad (35\text{-}5)$$

C would equal the sum of direct outlays and the earnings forgone by spending time training in A_1 rather than earning in A_2. Forgone earnings are a major part of the cost of most training programs—they account for more than half of the total cost of college education in the United States.

The absolute earnings differential in year i between A_1 and A_2 can be interpreted as the return in year i on the training undertaken in the initial year. If the return were the same in all years,

$$\Delta E_i = (E_{1i} - E_{2i}) = \Delta E \qquad i = 1, \ldots, n \qquad (35\text{-}6)$$

and the condition in equation (35-4) could be written more revealingly as

$$\Delta E(a_1 + \cdots + a_n) \equiv \Delta E(R) \gtreqless C \qquad (35\text{-}7)$$

where R is the present value of a dollar a year for n years. (Why?) Condition (35-7) says that training is undertaken if, and only if, the present value of all the returns, given by $\Delta E(R)$, were at least as large as the cost.

The earnings differential that would exactly compensate for the cost of training is given by

$$\Delta E^* = \frac{C}{R} = rC \qquad (35\text{-}8)$$

where $r \equiv 1/R$. (What interpretation can you give to r? It will be discussed in the following lecture.) The compensating differential would increase if either costs or the value of current dollars relative to future ones increased. Panel A of Figure 35.1 gives the supply curves to A_1 of a single person, panel B the market supply curves of a group of identical persons. The discontinuity

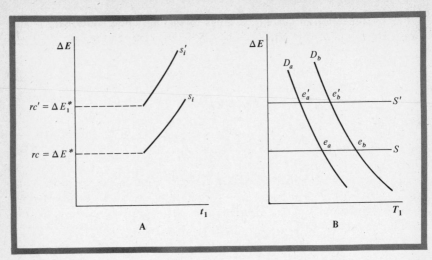

FIGURE 35.1

in an individual supply curve at the compensating differential is not notice-able in a market curve. An increase in the demand for A_1 from D_a to D_b would increase the number of persons choosing A_1, but would not change the equilib-rium earnings differential. On the other hand, an increase in the cost of training from C to C' would increase the equilibrium differential, and decrease the number choosing A_1 (compare e_a and e_a' or e_b and e_b').

PROBLEMS

35.1. Evaluate: The typical male college graduate in the United States gains $100,000 from going to college since the sum of his lifetime earnings exceeds the sum of the lifetime earnings of a typical high school graudate by $100,000.

35.2. Evaluate: Wages of unskilled workers are lower in India than in the United States because there are relatively more unskilled workers in India than in the United States.

35.3. Evaluate: There is underinvestment in on-the-job training because employers have little incentive to provide training for workers who will leave to take better paying jobs.

35.4. Evaluate: New York City pays $600 a year extra salary to teachers who enter the system with a fifth year of training. No one does this, unless he is required to, because teachers are not as interested in money income as other persons.

35.5. Evaluate: The incentive to invest in on-the-job training is generally greater for men than women because the former participate much more in the labor force.

*35.6. Consider two mutually exclusive occupations, y_1 and y_2. There is no risk in y_1 or y_2, no investment required to enter either, and some nonpecuniary aspects to y_2. A group of homogeneous persons has to allocate itself between these occupations. What is the effect on the fraction entering y_1 of

   a. A strictly proportional tax on current money income?
   b. A highly progressive tax on current money income? Distinguish between nonpecuniary income and nonpecuniary costs in your answers.

LECTURE 36

Differences in Abilities and Opportunities

The cost of training can explain why earnings and skill are positively related, but the formulation presented in the previous lecture is not fully satisfactory because it implies that differences in earnings between occupations exactly offset differences in training costs, that the present value of earnings net of these costs is the same in all occupations. Yet a widely shared belief based on an increasing amount of evidence is that the present value of earnings and training are positively related. This relation is generally explained by assuming that some persons have more ability or better opportunities than others.

Ability in the market sector can be defined either by the earnings attained with a given investment in training, or equivalently, by the investment required to attain given earnings. A definition in terms of earnings or investment costs is oriented toward results and does not prejudge whether the main determinants of ability are IQ, motivation, imagination, will power, or the many other measures frequently mentioned.

If C_j were the cost of the investment in training needed by the jth person to enter A_1, his compensating differential would be

$$\Delta E_j^* = \frac{C_j}{R} = rC_j \qquad j = 1, \ldots, \ell \qquad (36\text{-}1)$$

where E and r are still assumed to be the same for everyone. The compensating differential would be directly proportional to the investment required, i.e., inversely proportional to the level of ability. The market supply curve to A_1 would be positively inclined, as in Figure 36.1, because less able persons must receive greater compensation to induce them to enter A_1. Each person, upon entering, imparts a horizontal kink to the market supply curve; the distribution of these entry kinks is determined by the distribution of abilities.

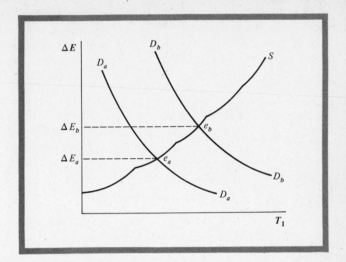

FIGURE 36.1

If D_a were the demand curve for A_1, the equilibrium earnings differential would be ΔE_a. All persons with compensating differentials less than ΔE_a choose A_1 because the present value of their earnings is greater in A_1; all those with compensating differentials greater than ΔE_a choose A_2 because the present value of their earnings is greater in A_2. If earnings in A_2 are the same for everyone, persons choosing A_1 receive the higher present value of earnings; in other words, they receive "rent" or returns on their superior ability that are consistent with full equilibrium and equal opportunity. An increase in demand to D_b would increase the equilibrium earnings differential and thus the rents to superior ability, and encourage less able persons also to enter A_1.

Differences in compensating differentials between individuals also result from differences in their opportunities. A trade union, like the electricians' union or even the American Medical Association, that raises the earnings of its members by restricting their numbers (see Problem 34.4) improves the opportunities of persons fortunate enough to gain membership partly at the expense of other persons. A country, like the United States, that raises the earnings of its citizens by restricting immigration from elsewhere improves the opportunities of persons fortunate enough to be born there partly at the expense of those born elsewhere.

We want to discuss mainly the unequal opportunities to children resulting from the unequal distribution of parents' wealth. Their wealth is crucial because of the legal restrictions on indentured labor contracts and other transactions that suggest the sale of human beings rather than simply the short-term rental of labor services. The higher earnings expected from an investment in training is poor collateral on loans to cover the costs of training because lenders could not gain control of the human capital resulting from training if borrowers forfeited on their obligations. Wealthier families can supply their own funds to pay for training and thereby circumvent the commercial market whereas poorer families are forced to rely on scholarships and low levels of consumption before and during the training period.

Stated in formal language, the premiums on present dollars relative to future dollars (measured by r) are greater for poorer persons and others who cannot readily obtain resources to invest in training. If r_j were the premium for the jth person, his compensating differential would be

$$\Delta E_j^* = r_j C \quad j = 1, \ldots, \ell \tag{36-2}$$

where ability and thus C is assumed to be the same for everyone. The market supply curve to A_1 would be positively inclined, as in Figure 36.1, because persons with better opportunities have lower entry points; the distribution of these points is determined by the distribution of opportunities. The present value of earnings to a person choosing A_1 would exceed that to a person choosing A_2 if each converted future into present dollars with their own premiums. (Why?) The present value of earnings is usually said to be greater in the more skilled occupations because the premiums usually used to discount earnings are more appropriate to persons entering these occupations. (What would the comparisons look like if premiums more appropriate to persons entering the less skilled occupations were used?)

The Distribution of Earnings

Let us define the equalizing discount on future dollars (R^*), or the equalizing premium on present dollars (r^*), for the jth person as the discount or premium that equates the present value of his actual earnings differential with his investment in training. If ΔE_j is his earnings differential (assumed to be the same in all years), and C_j his investment, then by definition

$$\Delta E_j = \frac{C_j}{R_j^*} = r_j^* C_j \tag{36-3}$$

or

$$E_{j1} = E_{j2} + r_j^* C_j \tag{36-4}$$

where E_{j2} would be his earnings if he did not invest and E_{j1} would be his earnings if he did. Equation (36-3) or (36-4) is the fundamental equation in the vast recent literature on investment in human capital.

These equations have been used to measure the gain from investing in different occupations and education levels, to explain why earnings rise at a decreasing rate with age[1] or why younger persons invest more in themselves than older ones, and to interpret numerous other important findings.[2] We

---

[1] The mathematics of age-earnings profiles are presented in section 1 of the Appendix.
[2] Many applications can be found in Gary S. Becker, *Human Capital* (New York: Columbia University Press for National Bureau of Economic Research, 1964). Also see T. W. Schultz, *The Economic Value of Education* (New York: Columbia University Press, 1963).

briefly discuss here the role of human capital in the personal distribution of earnings, a subject of considerable social interest.

Section 2 of the Appendix shows that if training fully occupied j's "working" time for m_j years—for example, 12 years of schooling—equation (36-4) can be written as

$$E_{j1} = E_{j2} + r_j^* C_j = E_{j2}(1 + r_j^*)^{m_j} \qquad (36\text{-}5)$$

Taking the natural logarithm of both sides, we get

$$\log E_{j1} \gtrsim \log E_{j2} + m_j r_j^* \qquad (36\text{-}6)$$

since

$$\log (1 + r_j^*) \gtrsim r_j^* \qquad (36\text{-}7)$$

if r_j^* is not large. If $\log E_{j2}$, m_j, and r_j^* are uncorrelated with each other, then by a well-known formula[3]

$$\sigma^2_{\log E_{j1}} = \sigma^2_{\log E_{j2}} + \bar{r}^{*2}\sigma^2_{m_j} + \bar{m}^2\sigma^2_{r_j^*} + \sigma^2_{m_j}\sigma^2_{r_j^*} \qquad (36\text{-}8)$$

where σ^2 is the measure of dispersion called the variance, $\bar{m}$ is the average years of training in the population, and $\bar{r}^*$ is the average compensating premium.

The variance in the logarithm of earnings, a commonly used measure of dispersion or inequality in earnings, is positively related to the average level and to the inequality (or dispersion) in years of training and in compensating premiums. Much of the observed differences in inequality between states and regions of the United States, regions of Canada, and even rich and poor countries is apparently explained by differences in the average compensating premium and in the inequality in years of schooling.[4] There is little empirical evidence on the effect of the inequality in compensating premiums although an increase in the average amount of training apparently does increase inequality.[5]

APPENDIX

1. The net earnings of a person in the initial period is defined as

$$E_{10} = E_{20} - C_0 \qquad (A\text{-}1)$$

---

[3] The variance of the product of two uncorrelated random variables x and y is
$$\sigma^2(xy) = \bar{y}^2\sigma^2(x) + \bar{x}^2\sigma^2(y) + \sigma^2(y)\sigma^2(x)$$
where $\bar{y}$ and $\bar{x}$ are the means of y and x.

[4] See Barry R. Chiswick, *Human Capital and the Personal Distribution of Income by Region* (unpublished Ph.D. dissertation, Columbia University, 1967).

[5] See Barry R. Chiswick, "The Average Level of Schooling and the Intra-Regional Inequality of Income: A Clarification," *American Economic Review*, 58 (June 1968).

where C_0 is his investment in training during this period, and E_{20} his earnings if he did not invest. Similarly, his net earnings in period 1 can be defined as

$$E_{11} = E_{21} + r_0^* C_0 - C_1 \qquad \text{(A-2)}$$

where C_1 is his investment during period 1, and $E_{21} + r_0^* C_0$ would be his earnings if he did not invest during this period, where r_0^* is the compensating premium on C_0 [see the discussion of equation (36-4)]. In a like manner,

$$E_{12} = E_{22} + r_0^* C_0 + r_1^* C_1 - C_2 \qquad \text{(A-3)}$$

where r_1^* is the compensating premium on C_1; more generally,

$$E_{1m} = E_{2m} + \sum_{i=0}^{m-1} r_i^* C_i - C_m \qquad \text{(A-4)}$$

If we assume for simplicity that $r_0^* = r_1^* = \cdots = r^*$, and $E_{21} = E_{22} = \cdots = E_2$, equation (A-4) can be written as

$$E_{1m} = E_2 + r^* \sum_{i=0}^{m-1} C_i - C_m \qquad \text{(A-5)}$$

Since the theory of investment in human capital implies that the incentive to invest declines with age (Why?), at least eventually the amount spent on investing would also decline with age:

$$\Delta C_i \equiv C_i - C_{i-1} \leq 0 \qquad \text{(A-6)}$$

Therefore, by equation (A-5),

$$\Delta E_i \equiv E_{1i} - E_{1i-1} = r^* C_{i-1} - \Delta C_i > 0 \qquad \text{(A-7)}$$

that is, earnings would rise with age as long as, and only as long as, the investment process continued. The "overtaking age"[6] is defined by

$$E_{1h} = E_2$$

or by the definition of E_{ih} in equation (A-5)

$$r^* \sum_{i=0}^{h-1} C_i = C_h \qquad \text{(A-8)}$$

---

[6] I owe this concept to Jacob Mincer.

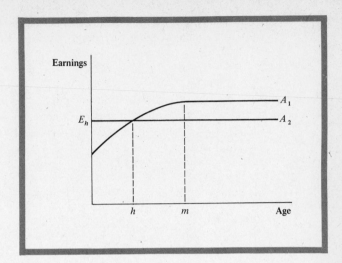

FIGURE 36.2

Since by equation (A-6) $C_i \geq C_h$, $i = 0, \ldots h - 1$,

$$r^* h C_h \leq C_h \text{ (Why?)} \tag{A-9}$$

or

$$h \leq \frac{1}{r^*} \tag{A-10}$$

If A_1 and A_2 in Figure 36.2 are the life cycle profiles of earnings in A_1 and A_2, earnings in A_1 would overtake earnings in A_2 at age h. If r^* were at least 0.10, as seems to be generally true, earnings of skilled persons would overtake those of unskilled persons early in their working lifetimes.

The rate of increase in earnings would decelerate if

$$\Delta^2 E_i = \Delta E_i - \Delta E_{i-1} = r^* \Delta C_{i-1} - \Delta^2 C_i \leq 0 \tag{A-11}$$

If

$$\Delta^2 C_i \geq 0 \tag{A-12}$$

equation (A-11) must hold since $\Delta C_{i-1} \leq 0$; equation (A-11) would hold even if equation (A-12) did not as long as

$$r^* \Delta C_{i-1} \leq \Delta^2 C_i = \Delta C_i - \Delta C_{i-1}$$

or

$$(1 + r^*) \Delta C_{i-1} \leq \Delta C_i \tag{A-13}$$

2. If all potential earnings were invested in each of the first m periods and none after that, costs would be

$$C_k = E_2 + r^* \sum_{i=0}^{k-1} C_i \qquad k = 0, \ldots, m - 1 \tag{A-14}$$

and

$$C_k = 0 \qquad k = m, \ldots, n \tag{A-15}$$

Net earnings would be

$$E_{1k} = 0 \qquad k = 0, \ldots, m - 1 \tag{A-16}$$

and

$$
\begin{aligned}
E_{1k} &= E_2 + r^* \sum_{i=0}^{m-1} C_i \qquad k = m, \ldots, n \\
&= E_2 + r^*[E_2 + E_2(1 + r^*) + E_2(1 + r^*)^2 + \cdots + E_2(1 + r^*)^{m-1}] \\
&= E_2 \left\{ 1 + r^* \left[\frac{1 - (1 + r^*)^m}{-r^*} \right] \right\} \tag{A-17}
\end{aligned}
$$

by the formula for the sum of a geometric series. By division and subtraction then,

$$E_{1k} = E_2(1 + r^*)^m \qquad k = m, \ldots, n \tag{A-18}$$

PROBLEMS

36.1. Evaluate: Negroes would have less education than whites even if all schools admitted them on the same terms as whites.

36.2. Evaluate: Evidence that ability has little effect on earnings is that persons with IQs over 120 do not earn much more than persons with IQs between 90 and 120.

*36.3. Do you agree that the inequality in earnings in any country is primarily the result of inequality in ability? What kinds of evidence would support your answer?

chapter 10

Accumulation of Capital over Time

LECTURE 37

Consumption and Savings

The rates of exchange between future and present dollars—the a_i introduced in Lecture 35—are presumably determined by the supply and demand functions for present and future goods in the same way that the rates of exchange between apples and pears or British pounds and French francs are determined by the supply and demand functions for apples and pears or pounds and francs. Yet the exchange between present and future goods merits more explicit attention than does the exchange between most other goods, just as economists pay elaborate attention to the exchange between domestic and foreign goods. Since future and present goods are physically the same "thing," differing only in dating, the rate of change over time in the supply of goods—economic growth in other words—is a meaningful and important question.

Moreover, the demand for capital goods, bonds, equities, and other stocks that are valued for the stream of monetary and psychic income yielded can only be understood by considering the exchange between goods at different dates. Let me point out here that a "flow" has the dimensions of a rate of quantity *per* unit time, as a rate of $600 billion of income per year or 40 man-hours per week; a "stock" has the dimensions of quantity *at* a moment in time, as $40 billion of currency on April 10, 1969, or 200 million persons in September 1968. Stocks are the source of all flows, as the populations of persons and equipment are the source of the man-hours and machine-hours supplied each week. Close attention to the dimensions of variables helps avoid many errors in economics, especially in capital theory.

The lectures on demand (see Chapter 3) ignored the dating of consumption. This defect is now remedied, and preferences at any moment in time are assumed to depend not only on current consumption but also on planned future consumption:

$$U = U(Z_{01}, \ldots, Z_{0m}, Z_{11}, \ldots, Z_{1m}, \ldots, Z_{n1}, \ldots, Z_{nm}) \qquad (37\text{-}1)$$

where U is the present utility, Z_{ij} is the planned consumption of the jth commodity in period i, and n is the length of the planning horizon. The partial derivative

$$\frac{\partial U}{\partial Z_{ij}} = MU_{1j} \qquad (37\text{-}2)$$

measures the change in utility from a planned change by one unit in the consumption of commodity j in period i. To simplify the exposition without any loss in generality, only the aggregate of consumption during each period, called C_i, will be considered:

$$U = U(C_0, C_1, \ldots, C_n) \qquad (37\text{-}3)$$

More significantly, C_i is interpreted as an aggregate rate of consumption of goods rather than of the commodities produced with goods and time.[1]

Lecture 35 shows how the optimal earnings stream is determined from the large number of streams available to a household. Define the income in each period as the sum of the optimal earnings and the given receipts from the ownership of property and from other sources. If the amount spent on consumption in a period had to equal the income available in the same period, then

$$C_i = \frac{I_i}{p_i} \qquad i = 0, \ldots, n \qquad (37\text{-}4)$$

where I is the income in period i, p_i is the price of a unit of C_i, and the allocation of consumption over time would be trivially easy. The main purpose of the a_i is to permit an exchange between consumption at different times so that consumption at any time is not rigidly tied to income of the same time. For example, by reducing expenditures on consumption in the initial period by one dollar, $1/a_1$ additional dollars could be spent on C_1, or $1/a_2$ additional dollars on C_2, and so forth. Any combination of expenditures would be feasible as long as their present value did not exceed the present value of receipts:

$$p_0 C_0 + a_1 p_1 C_1 + \cdots + a_n p_n C_n = I_0 + a_1 I_1 + \cdots + a_n I_n = V_0 \quad (37\text{-}5)$$

where V_0 is a household's wealth. The market price of "futures" reflected in the a_i transforms the rigidity of equation (37-4) into the flexible present value formulation given by equation (37-5).

Each household is assumed to maximize the utility function given by equation (37-3) subject to the budget constraint given by equation (37-5). The

---

[1] See the Appendix to Lecture 38 for a treatment in terms of commodities.

formulation is now identical to the usual formulation of consumer choice since the C_i can be interpreted simply as different goods, V_0 as total resources, and $a_i p_i$ as the set of prices. Consequently, all the results of consumer theory are applicable to choices over time. For example, the optimal consumption plan equalizes the marginal utility of the last present dollar spent in each period:

$$\frac{\partial U}{\partial C_i} \Big/ a_i p_i \equiv \frac{MU_i}{a_i p_i} = \frac{MU_j}{a_j p_j} \qquad \text{all } i \text{ and } j$$

or

$$\frac{MU_i}{MU_j} = \frac{a_i p_i{}^2}{a_j p_j} \qquad\qquad (37\text{-}6)$$

The term on the right side of equation (37-6) is the number of units of C_j that can be exchanged for a unit of C_i. (Why?)[3] In equilibrium, this must equal the rate of exchange in utility between C_i and C_j. Notice that the relative prices of goods, p_i/p_j, and dollars, a_i/a_j, enter symmetrically: If a rise in the price of goods between i and j (i.e., p_i/p_j) were offset by an equal percentage fall in the value of dollars between i and j (i.e., a_i/a_j), the "real" terms of trade between these periods would be unaffected.[4]

The theorem on negatively inclined demand curves implies that a compensated[5] decrease in $a_i p_i$ would increase C_i and reduce the other C_j as a whole. Similarly, an increase in wealth would tend to increase all the C_i since a weighted average of their wealth elasticities must add up to unity.[6] Figure

---

[2] Mathematically, one maximizes the Lagrangian

$$L = U(C_0, \ldots, C_n) - \mu\left(\sum_{i=0}^{n} a_i p_i C_i - V_0\right)$$

The first-order conditions are

$$\frac{\partial L}{\partial C_i} = 0 = MU_i - a_i p_i \mu$$

or

$$\frac{MU_i}{a_i p_i} = \mu$$

where μ is the marginal utility of wealth.

[3] A unit of C_i is worth p_i dollars in period i, which can be exchanged for $(a_i/a_j)p_i$ dollars in j; the latter can buy $a_i p_i/a_j p_j$ units of C_j.

[4] This is the crux of the distinction between "real" and "monetary" interest rates.

[5] One holding the level of utility or "apparent" opportunities constant (see Lecture 7).

[6] Since

$$\sum_{i=0}^{n} a_i p_i C_i = V_0$$

then

$$\sum a_i p_i \frac{\partial C_i}{\partial V_0} = 1$$

or

$$\sum s_i \mu_0 = 1$$

where

$$s_i = \frac{a_i p_i C_i}{V_0}$$

and

$$\mu_0 = \frac{V_0}{C_j} \frac{\partial C_i}{\partial V_0}$$

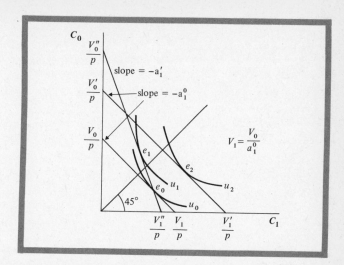

FIGURE 37.1

37.1 plots C_1 along the horizontal axis and C_0 along the vertical one, and assumes, for simplicity, that C_0 and C_1 are the only commodities, and $p_1 = p_0 = p$. A rise in a_1 compensated by a decrease in incomes that made the budget line pass through the initial position e_0 would shift the equilibrium position to e_1, or toward C_0 and away from C_1. (Why?) A rise in incomes would shift the budget line outward, and the equilibrium position from e_0 to e_2. This figure clearly shows why each person enters the occupation that maximizes the present value of his earnings: In this way he maximizes utility.

The demand curves for C_0 are shown in panel A of Figure 37.2. Their elasticity is inversely related to the curvature of the indifference curves of Figure 37.1, i.e., directly related to the ease of substituting C_1 for C_0. An increase in real wealth shifts the demand curve to the right, unless C_0 is an inferior good, the size of the shift depending on the wealth elasticity of demand for C_0. The latter, in turn, is determined by the slopes of the indifference curves along a given ray from the origin. If the slopes were the same, all wealth elasticities would equal unity; if they were larger (in absolute value) at higher indifference levels, C_0 would have an elasticity less than unity. (Why? What would be the elasticity of C_1?) Keynes' second "law" of consumption, that the marginal propensity is less than the average propensity to consume, assumes, therefore, that the indifference curves between present and future consumption are more "biased" toward future consumption at higher preference levels.

The consumption function portrayed in Figure 37.2 can be written algebraically as

$$C_0 = f(1/a_1, V) \tag{37-7}$$

where V is taken as real wealth. The preceding analysis suggests $\partial C_0/\partial(1/a) < 0$, and generally $0 < \partial C_0/\partial V < 1$.

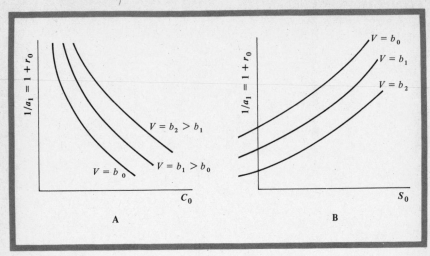

FIGURE 37.2

If the price of current consumption is taken as the numeraire and set equal to unity, current savings can be defined simply as the difference between current income and consumption:

$$S_0 = I_0 - C_0 \tag{37-8}$$

The demand curves for S_0 shown in panel B are inversely related to those for C_0 because S_0 is defined to be inversely related to C_0; for example, an increase in $1/a_1$ would reduce C_0 and increase S_0. However, an increase in real wealth due to an equal percentage increase in income in all periods would increase S_0 as well as C_0, if the wealth elasticity of C_0 were not much above unity.[7] Equation (37-8) shows that S_0, unlike C_0, also depends on current income even when prices and wealth are held constant. Indeed, an increase in current income alone would increase S_0 by the same amount. This is the essence of the distinction between "transitory" and "permanent" income used to ex-

[7] By definition,

$$\frac{\partial S_0}{\partial I_0} > 0 \quad \text{if} \quad \frac{\partial C_0}{\partial I_0} < 1$$

By assumption,

$$\frac{\partial I_0}{I_0} = \frac{\partial V}{V}$$

Therefore,

$$\frac{\partial S}{\partial V} > 0 \quad \text{if} \quad \frac{\partial C_0}{\partial V} \cdot \frac{V}{I_0} < 1$$

or if

$$\mu_0 = \frac{\partial C_0}{\partial V} \cdot \frac{V}{C_0} < \frac{I_0}{C_0}$$

plain observed differences in savings,[8] and indicates why savings is considered a "residual." The savings function can be written algebraically as

$$S_0 = g\left(\frac{1}{a_1}, V, I_0\right)$$

with

$$\frac{\partial S_0}{\partial \left(\frac{1}{a_1}\right)} > 0 \qquad -1 < \frac{\partial S_0}{\partial V} < 0 \ (\text{Why?}) \qquad \frac{\partial S_0}{\partial I_0} = 1 \qquad (37\text{-}9)^{[9]}$$

Savings and consumption are usually related to interest rates, the percentage premiums on present dollars. Since the current period's interest rate is inversely related to a_1 according to the formula

$$1 + r_0 = \frac{1}{a_1} \tag{37-10}$$

the relations between C_0, S_0, and $1/a_1$ in Figure 37.2 and equations (37-7) and (37-9) are essentially the usual ones with the interest rate.

Although the consumption and savings functions given by equations (37-7) and (37-9) have been derived for a single future period, they can easily be generalized to many periods. Either all the prices of future dollars in terms of present ones can be explicitly introduced into these functions with the conditions

$$\frac{\partial C_0}{\partial (1/a)_i} < 0 \qquad \frac{\partial S_0}{\partial (1/a)_i} > 0 \qquad i = 1, \ldots, n \tag{37-11}$$

or these prices can be reduced to a single parameter by assuming that the price of dollars in period i in terms of dollars in $i - 1$ is the same for all i. This assumption implies that

$$\frac{a_i}{a_{i-1}} = a_1 \qquad (\text{Why?}) \tag{37-12}$$

---

[8] See especially Milton Friedman, *A Theory of the Consumption Function* (Princeton University Press for the National Bureau of Economic Research, 1957). "Permanent" income can be defined as the yield on wealth, or

$$I_p^0 = r_0 V_0$$

where r_0 is defined in equation (37-10).

[9] Footnote 7, Lecture 37, indicates that if V and I_0 increase by the same percentage, S_0 would also increase unless the wealth elasticity of C_0 were sufficiently larger than unity.

Consequently,

$$a_i = a_1^i \qquad i = 0,\dots, n^{10} \text{ (Why?)} \qquad (37\text{-}13)$$

The two n derivatives given by (37-11) would reduce to the two derivatives given by equations (37-7) and (37-9).

The qualitative properties of the demand functions derived for a single household hold also for the market if the a_i are interpreted as the average prices facing different households, and V as the average real wealth. (Why?) The market elasticity is determined, however, by the distribution of entry points and any interdependencies among preferences (see Lectures 8 and 34) as well as by the average household elasticity.

PROBLEMS

37.1.   Suppose that a person expects his income to remain at a constant level indefinitely into the future. If he would save a positive amount out of current income at a zero interest rate, what can you say about his time preference for the present compared to the future?

37.2.   Evaluate: Households have time preference for the present because it is known that an additional unit of current consumption would raise their utility more than an additional unit of consumption at some future date.

37.3.   How would an increase in the rate of growth of income with age affect the optimal consumption path? The optimal savings path? Make explicit any assumptions about "time preference" or future prices.

*37.4. Several economists have argued that an increase in the rate of population growth would increase the fraction of income saved (because of the desire to save for retirement). Analyze the effects on the aggregate savings ratio of an increase in the rate of population growth. Assume that this increase has no effect on per capita incomes, future prices, or wage rates. Also assume that there is an increase in the number of people at age j compared to age i, where $j < i$.

---

[10] Since

$$a_1 = \frac{1}{1 + r_0}$$

then

$$a_i = \frac{1}{(1 + r_0)\, i}$$

LECTURE 38

The Rate of Growth in Consumption

The rate of growth in consumption between the current period and a single future one is inversely related to a_1 (or positively related to the interest rate) because an (compensated) increase in a_1 would raise C_0 and lower C_1. The rate of growth also depends on two parameters of indifference curves: "time preference" and the elasticity of substitution between C_0 and C_1. Time preference measures whether an increase in current consumption increases utility by a greater amount than an equal increase in future consumption. Of course, diminishing marginal rate of substitution implies that the marginal utilities of current and future consumption change systematically as the level of consumption changes. The shape of indifference curves can be isolated from a movement along them by defining time preference by the marginal utilities when present and future consumption are equal. Geometrically, this is equivalent to defining it by the slope of an indifference curve along the 45° line in a figure like 37.1. Preference is said to be for the present, future, or neither ("neutrality") as the slope is less than, greater than, or equal to unity.[1] Of course, all the slopes need not be the same along the 45° line; indeed, many persons believe that preference for the present is stronger at "low" levels of consumption.

Preference for the present reduces the rate of growth in consumption whereas preference for the future does the opposite. For example, if $a_1 = 1$, i.e., if future dollars are as valuable as present ones, consumption necessarily falls over time if the present is preferred, and rises if the future is preferred. (Why?)[2] Alleged differences in preference for the present[3] have been used to

[1] Since

$$- \text{slope} = \frac{MU_1}{MU_0}$$

$$- \text{slope} \lesseqgtr 1 \quad \text{as} \quad MU_0 \gtreqless MU_1$$

[2] In equilibrium,

$$a_1 = \frac{MU_1}{MU_0}$$

If $a_1 = 1$,

$$\frac{MU_1}{MU_0} = 1$$

Since preference for the present means that

$$\frac{MU_1}{MU_0} < 1 \quad \text{when} \quad C_0 = C_1$$

then by diminishing marginal rate of substitution,

$$\frac{MU_1}{MU_0} = 1 \quad \text{only when} \quad C_0 > C_1$$

[3] Preference for the present is sometimes called "impatience with the future" or "telescoped time calculations."

explain why poorer children drop out of school more than richer children (but see our discussion in Lecture 26), why some persons save relatively large fractions of their income, and even why some countries grow more rapidly than others.

If $a_1 < 1$ and preferences were time neutral, consumption would grow over time at a rate that depends on how rapidly the slope of an indifference curve declines as future consumption increases relative to present consumption—in other words, on σ, the elasticity of substitution between present and future consumption.[4] The larger σ, the more rapidly consumption grows for any given value of $a_1 < 1$.

To show explicitly the combined influence of a_1, time preference, and σ on the rate of growth in consumption, assume that the ratio of marginal utilities can be written simply as

$$\frac{MU_1}{MU_0} = \alpha \left(\frac{C_0}{C_1}\right)^{1/\sigma}{}^5 \tag{38-1}$$

where α is a measure of time preference. (Why? Also what is the implied wealth elasticity of demand for C_o and C_1?) Since the equilibrium ratio of marginal utilities equals a_1,

$$a_1 = \alpha \left(\frac{C_0}{C_1}\right)^{1/\sigma} \tag{38-2}$$

or

$$\frac{C_1}{C_0} = \left(\frac{1}{\alpha}\right)^{-\sigma} a^{-\sigma} \tag{38-3}$$

Then

$$\log \frac{C_1}{C_0} \equiv \log 1 + g \eqsim g = \sigma \log \alpha - \sigma \log a_1 \tag{38-4}$$

or

$$g = \sigma r_0 - \sigma t_0 = \sigma(r_0 - t_0) \tag{38-5}$$

where g is the rate of growth in consumption, and t_0 measures the preference

---

[4] By definition

$$\sigma = \frac{d\left(\frac{C_0}{C_1}\right) \frac{C_1}{C_0}}{d\left(\frac{MU_1}{MU_0}\right) \frac{MU_0}{MU_1}} \qquad \text{along } U = U_0$$

[5] This form can be derived from the utility function

$$U = (b_0 C_0^{-\beta} + \alpha b_0 C_1^{-\beta})^{-1/\beta}$$

where β is a constant and $\sigma = 1/(1 + \beta)$.

for the present.[6] Consumption would grow over time if r_0 exceeded t_0; its rate of growth would be larger, the greater the difference between r_0 and t_0, and the greater σ.

Equation (38-5) can be generalized to many periods if the ratio of adjacent marginal utilities can be written as

$$\frac{MU_i}{MU_{i-1}} = \alpha_{i-1}\left(\frac{C_{i-1}}{C_i}\right)^{1/\sigma_i - 1}{}^7 \qquad \text{all } i \qquad (38\text{-}6)$$

where α_{i-1} measures the time preference and σ_{i-1} the elasticity of substitution between C_{i-1} and C_i. Then

$$\log \frac{C_i}{C_{i-1}} \approx g_{i-1} \approx \sigma_{i-1}(r_{i-1} - t_{i-1}) \qquad (38\text{-}7)$$

Consumption would grow at a constant rate if the elasticity of substitution, time preference, and interest rate did not change over time; it would tend to grow at a declining rate if, for example, the interest rate declined over time. (This conclusion is used in Lecture 40.)

APPENDIX

Assume that the commodities consumed in each period are produced according to

$$C_i = f_i(x_i, t_{c_i}) \qquad (A\text{-}1)$$

where $i = 0, \ldots, n$ are different time periods. The inputs are subject to the constraints

$$t_{c_i} + t_{w_i} = t \qquad i = 0, \ldots, n \qquad (A\text{-}2)$$

[6] If
$$\alpha = 1 - t_0$$
then
$$\log \alpha \approx -t_0$$
Since
$$a_1 = \frac{1}{1 + r_0}$$
$$\log a_1 = -\log(1 + r_0) \approx -r_0$$
Therefore,
$$\sigma \log \alpha - \sigma \log a_1 \approx \sigma r_0 - \sigma t_0$$

The term α was introduced to measure time preference: $\alpha \gtreqless 1$ implies the time preference is for the future, present, or neither. By the definition of t_0, $t_0 \lesseqgtr 0$ as $\alpha \gtreqless 1$. Therefore, $t_0 \lesseqgtr 0$ implies the time preference is for the future, present, or neither.

[7] That is, we assume that the utility function is "separable" (see the discussion in Problems 11.1 and 11.2).

where t_{ci} and t_{wi} are the time spent at consumption and work in the ith period, and

$$\sum_{i=0}^{n} a_i p_i x_i = \sum_{i=0}^{n} a_i I_i \tag{A-3}$$

where the x_i are assumed to be nondurable goods. If the set of wage rates w_i were given, the time constraints could be substituted into the goods constraint to get

$$\sum_{i=0}^{n} (a_i p_i) x_i + \sum_{i=0}^{n} (a_i w_i) t_{c_i} = \sum_{i=0}^{n} (a_i w_i) t + u_i \tag{A-4}$$

where u_i is property income in period i. If the utility function is maximized subject to equations (A-1) and (A-4), the commodity equilibrium conditions are

$$\frac{MU_i}{MU_{i-1}} = \frac{\pi_i}{\pi_{i-1}} \equiv \frac{a_i p_i \dfrac{dx_i}{dC_i} + a_i w_i \dfrac{dt_{c_i}}{dC_i}}{a_{i-1} p_{i-1} \dfrac{dx_{i-1}}{dC_{i-1}} + a_{i-1} w_{i-1} \dfrac{dt_{c_{i-1}}}{dC_{i-1}}} \tag{A-5}$$

The cost minimizing conditions for x_i and t_{c_i} are the usual

$$\frac{MP_{x_i}}{MP_{t_{c_i}}} = \frac{p_i}{w_i} \qquad i = 0, \ldots, n \tag{A-6}$$

and are independent of the a_i.

The implications of this model have been fully worked out elsewhere[8]; here we illustrate them with an example. Assume that $p_i = p_{i-1}$, $a_i = a_{1i}$, and that the ratio of marginal utilities is given by equation (38-6). If the real wage rate is denoted by $w_i^* = w_i/p_i = w_i/p_{i-1}$, equation (A-5) could be written as

$$\alpha_{i-1} \left(\frac{C_{i-1}}{C_i}\right)^{1/\sigma_{i-1}} = a_i D_{i-1} \tag{A-7}$$

with

$$D_{i-1} = \frac{\dfrac{dx_i}{dC_i} + w_i^* \dfrac{dt_{c_i}}{dC_i}}{\dfrac{dx_{i-1}}{dC_{i-1}} + w_{i-1}^* \dfrac{dt_{c_{i-1}}}{dC_{i-1}}} \tag{A-8}$$

[8] See Gilbert Ghez, *A Theory of Life Cycle Consumption* (unpublished Ph.D. dissertation, Columbia University, 1970).

Therefore,

$$\log \frac{C_i}{C_{i-1}} \approxeq g_{i-1} = -\sigma_{i-1} \log a_1 + \sigma_{i-1} \log \alpha_{i-1} - \sigma_{i-1} \log D_{i-1}$$

or

$$g_{i-1} \approxeq \sigma_{i-1}(r_{i-1} - t_{i-1}) - \sigma_{i-1} \log D_{i-1} \qquad \text{(A-9)}$$

Even if $t_{i-1} = r_{i-1}$, g_{i-1} would not be zero unless $w_i = w_{i-1}$ since

$$D_{i-1} \gtrless 1 \qquad \text{as} \qquad w_i \gtrless w_{i-1} \qquad \text{(A-10)}$$

[Can the reader prove this? Use equation (A-6) and the formula for a total differential.] The C_i would fall over time when the wage rate was rising because a rising wage rate increases the cost of future consumption relative to present consumption; i.e., increases the cost of C_j relative to C_i (not of x_j relative to x_i), where $j > i$.

PROBLEMS

38.1. If a utility function were of the form

$$U = b \sum_{i=0}^{n} C_i$$

      a. What is the elasticity of substitution between different periods' consumption?

      b. If the rate of interest were positive, what would be the planned consumption path?

38.2. If a utility function were

$$U = C_0{}^{b_0} C_1{}^{b_1}, \ldots, C_n{}^{b_n}$$

and the rate of interest were positive, what would be the planned consumption path?

38.3. Assume that a person at time zero has the utility function

$$U = b_0 f(x_0, l_0) + b_1 f(x_1, l_1) + b_2 f(x_2, l_2) + \cdots + b_n f(x_n, l_n)$$

where x_i are the goods consumed in the ith period, l_i is the "leisure" in the ith period, the b_i are constants and $f(x_i, l_i)$ is the same function in each period (assume that f is homogeneous of a degree less than one).

a. How would you define neutral time preference?

b. If he has neutral time preference, if his wage rates are the same in all periods, and if the interest rate were zero in all periods, in what periods would the planned values of x and l reach their maximum? How would your answer be changed if the interest rate were positive in all periods?

*c. If all interest rates were zero, how would your answer to 38.3b be changed if the wage rate were known to rise for a number of periods and then fall until the last period?

*38.4. There are two significant aspects of mortality conditions: the expected lifespan and the coefficient of variation around this expectation. What is the effect on savings of

a. An increased expected lifespan and no change in the variance, so that the coefficient of variation declines?

b. A reduced variance with no change in the expected length?

c. Over time in the United States, the expected span has increased and the variance has decreased. What would be the net effect on savings of these changes?

*LECTURE 39

The Determination of Interest Rates

Previous lectures on product prices and factor (service) prices indicate that no matter what the institutional arrangement or how complicated the inter-dependencies, the determination of these prices can be analyzed within a supply-demand framework. It is a reasonable presumption that the prices of future dollars in terms of present dollars—the a_i—or the premiums on present dollars—the r_i—are determined in the same way; that is, by the intersection of demand curves for consumer goods with appropriate supply curves.

The supply of consumer goods is assumed to be related to the input of labor and capital by the production function

$$C = f(k, l) \qquad\qquad (39\text{-}1)$$

where f = a production function that is homogeneous of the first degree
  k = the input of capital services
  l = the input of labor services

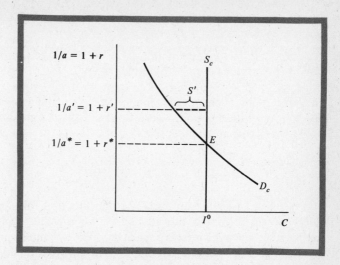

FIGURE 39.1

We assume that the flow of capital services is proportional to the stock of capital, K; thus the production function could be written with K instead of k. If K and l, the only factors, never wore out and could not be increased, all the units of K and l would be used to produce consumer goods—assuming full employment—and the quantity initially produced or supplied would equal

$$C_0 = f(K_0, l_0) = I^0 \tag{39-2}$$

where K_0 and l_0 are the initial quantities of labor and capital (at time t_0), and I^0 is initial income. The supply curve of consumption would be completely inelastic. Income would not change over time if f did not change since K and l are fixed at their initial values; therefore, all the supply curves of consumer goods for times $0, 1, \ldots, n$ could be written simply as

$$C_i = I^0 \qquad i = 0, \ldots, n \tag{39-3}$$

Figure 39-1 plots the inelastic supply curve of C given by equation (39-3) and the demand curve corresponding to the appropriate level of wealth. The equilibrium position is at E, where households consume the amount of C being supplied. Since the latter equals income, the desired rate of savings (S) over any period would be zero. (Why?)

The forces pushing a and r toward their equilibrium values a^* and r^* can be examined by considering a price a' below a^*: the demand for C at a' would be less than I^0, the difference equaling desired savings, S'. Savings can only be used to purchase capital goods since labor is nontransferable, financial assets, like bonds or currency, are ruled out, and consumer goods are assumed to be nondurable. If P is the price of a unit of capital stock measured in terms of forgone consumption for one period, then S' of savings over one period could purchase

$$\Delta K' = \frac{S'}{P'} \qquad (39\text{-}4)$$

units of capital. Each unit of capital provides a claim to w_k units of consumption in every future period, where w_k equals the marginal product of capital if factor markets are competitive:

$$w_K = \frac{\partial f(K_0, \ell_0)}{\partial K} \qquad (39\text{-}5)$$

Any one household can exchange consumption for some of the capital stock owned by others, but all households together cannot increase their capital stock since the total is fixed at K_0. The attempt to purchase $\Delta K'_0$ units more than are in existence can only bid up the price of capital as households compete for the existent supply. A higher price discourages savings and encourages consumption because the amount of current consumption that must be given up for future consumption is increased. (Why?) As long as desired savings were positive, the demand for capital would exceed its supply, and the price of capital would have to be higher. At P^*, where $S = 0$, the demand for capital equals K_0, and the demand for C equals I^0.

The relation between P^* and r^*, which are alternative ways to express the equilibrium premium on present consumption, can easily be derived. The present value of the income stream yielded by a unit of capital stock is

$$V \equiv a_1 w_k + a_2 w_k + \cdots + a_n w_k \qquad (39\text{-}6)$$

If $a^i = a_i = \dfrac{1}{(1 + r)^i}$, equation (39-6) can be written as

$$
\begin{aligned}
V &= w_k(a + a^2 + \cdots + a^n) \equiv w_k \left[\frac{a}{1 - a}(1 - a^n) \right] \\
&\equiv w_k \left(\frac{1}{1 + r} + \frac{1}{(1 + r)^2} + \cdots + \frac{1}{(1 + r)^n} \right) \equiv \frac{w_k}{r} \left(1 - \frac{1}{(1 + r)^n} \right)
\end{aligned} \qquad (39\text{-}7)
$$

In equilibrium, the price or worth of a unit of capital must equal the present value of the income stream yielded. (Why?)

$$P \equiv V \equiv w_k \left[\frac{a}{1 - a}(1 - a^n) \right] \equiv \frac{w_k}{r} \left[1 - \frac{1}{(1 + r)^n} \right] \qquad (39\text{-}8)$$

Therefore, P^* is essentially inversely proportional to r^*,[1] with w_k, the marginal product of capital, being the factor of proportionality.

---

[1] If n is large and $r > 0$, $1/(1 + r)^n \gtrless 0$, and $V \gtrless w_k/r$.

The equilibrium rate of interest is completely determined by time preference (if there is no investment permitted) if all households are identical. Since each household's as well as aggregate consumption would then be constant over time [see equation (39-3)], equation (38-5) implies that

$$r^* = t \qquad (39\text{-}9)$$

where t measures the degree of preference for the present. A decrease in t would shift the demand curves for C downward in Figure 39.1 (Why?), and thereby reduce r^* and raise P^*. Notice that zero or negative interest rates are not ruled out,[2] and occur if preferences are either time neutral or favor the future.

A once and for all advance in the technology of producing consumer goods that increases income to I' would increase the equilibrium level of consumption to

$$C_i = I' \qquad i = 0, \ldots, n \qquad (39\text{-}10)$$

Since C_i would still be constant over time, the interest rate would still be determined by time preference. If t were the same at I' as at I^0—that is, if the wealth elasticity of demand for C equaled unity—r^* would be unchanged; if t were smaller at I'—if the wealth elasticity for C were less than unity—r^* would be *reduced*. The effect on P^* depends on the effect of the technological advance on w_k (the marginal product of capital) as well as on r^*. If w_k rose by the same percentage as income, and if r^* were unaffected, P^* would also rise by the same percentage. (Why?)

If anticipated continuing technological advance increased the income from *given* capital and labor at the rate of g percent per period, consumption would also grow at this rate. Equation (38-7) indicates that the equilibrium rate of interest would then depend on the rate of technological advance (i.e., the rate of growth of the endowment), and the elasticity of substitution in consumption (Why are they relevant?) as well as time preference:

$$r^* = \frac{g}{\sigma} + t \qquad (39\text{-}11)$$

Either an increase in g or a decrease in σ would increase r^*.[3] Try to show this equilibrium graphically; plot current consumption along one axis and a single period of future consumption along the other. If savings are not possible, where must the equilibrium position be? Then what determines the equilibrium interest rate?

---

[2] Nonpositive rates cause difficulties if the time horizon were infinitely long, for equation (39-7) indicates that the price of capital would be infinite (in terms of current consumption) if $r \leq 0$ and $n = \infty$.

[3] Try to work out the effect on P^* if w_k also rose at g percent per period.

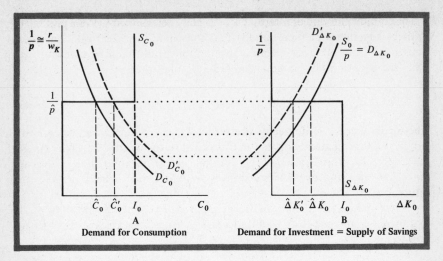

FIGURE 39.2

The Rate of Investment = Savings

Let us drop the assumption of a fixed capital stock (no savings or production of capital) and assume instead that capital can be produced in a competitive capital-goods industry according to the relation

$$\Delta K = h(K_k, l_k) \tag{39-12}$$

where h is homogeneous of the first degree, and K_k and l_k are the rates of input of capital and labor into this industry (we still assume that capital does not wear out). If the consumer and capital-goods industries purchased l and K in the same competitive markets and if both industries always used the same factor proportions, the supply curve in each industry would be infinitely elastic until all the l and K were used in that industry. (Why?) It would then become completely inelastic (see the supply curves labeled S_{C_0} in panel A of Figure 39.2 and $S_{\Delta K_0}$ in panel B). The price of capital goods along the infinitely elastic section, $\hat{P}$ in the figure, equals the number of consumer goods that could have been produced with the labor and capital that are used to produce one capital good.

The current rate of consumption, given by C_0, is determined by the intersection of the supply and demand curves for consumption; similarly the current rate of savings (measured in investment units)[4] is determined by the intersection of the supply and demand curves for investment. The price of

---

[4] Since the rate of current savings supplied, S_0, has been shown to be positively related to r and thus to $(1/P)$, the demand for investment goods, (S_0/P), must also be positively related to $(1/P)$. Since the vertical axis in panel B is $(1/P)$, the demand curve is positively sloped while the supply curve is negatively sloped.

capital goods is determined only by the opportunity cost of producing capital goods, as long as equilibrium occurs in the infinitely elastic sections of the investment or consumption curve. Demand conditions, i.e., preferences, then determine the distribution of total income between consumption and savings.[5] An increase in the preference for the present shifts the demand curve to the right to D'_{C_0} in panel A and to the left to $D'_{\Delta K_0}$ in panel B, thereby raising consumption to $\hat{C}_0$ and lowering investment to $\Delta K'_0$.

Once $\hat{P}$ is determined, the rate of interest is given by equation (39-8); therefore it also is determined by opportunity costs (if $S_0 > 0$). The interest rate measures the productivity of "roundabout" methods—that is, the total command over consumption yielded by a capital good—and would be positive if roundabout methods were more "productive" than direct methods; that is to say, if the consumption forgone to produce a unit of capital were less than the total command over consumption of that unit during the relevant time horizon.[6]

A once-and-for-all equal improvement in the technology of producing consumer and capital goods would not change the equilibrium price of capital since the number of consumer goods forgone to produce one capital good would be unchanged. According to equation (39-8), however, the interest rate would increase by approximately the same percentage as the marginal product of capital did. Therefore, an equal improvement in technology would increase the productivity of "roundabout" methods. The absolute amount of savings would increase if only because wealth increased,[7] but even the fraction of income saved would tend to increase because of the increase in interest rates.

PROBLEMS

39.1. Evaluate: If interest rates decline relative to wage rates, the demand for capital would increase relative to the demand for labor.

39.2. Evaluate: The internal rate of return on an investment is equal to the rate of interest at which funds can be borrowed.

39.3. Evaluate: A decline in the price of labor would cause an equal percentage decline in the price of all capital goods since labor is used to produce these goods.

---

[5] If different factor proportions were used in the consumer and capital goods industries, the supply curve of investment would be negatively related to $1/P$ (Why?); then the price of capital goods would be determined by time preference as well as opportunity costs.

[6] According to equation (39-7)

$$\hat{P} \equiv \frac{w_k}{(1 + \hat{r})} + \frac{w_k}{(1 + \hat{r})^2} + \cdots + \frac{w_k}{(1 + \hat{r})^n} \qquad (39\text{-}7')$$

If

$$\hat{P} < w_k + w_k + \cdots + w_k = nw_k$$

equation (39-7') can hold only if $\hat{r} > 0$.

[7] If endowed income increased by the same percentage in all periods, current savings would increase if the product of the average propensity to consume out of current income and the wealth elasticity of current consumption was less than unity (see footnote 7, Lecture 37).

*LECTURE 40

Growth Paths

Since each unit of capital is assumed to last forever, the capital stock necessarily grows as long as some capital is produced. The stock K_0 available in the initial period grows to $K_1 = K_0 + \hat{\Delta}K_0$ at the beginning of period one, where $\hat{\Delta}K_0$ units are produced during the initial period. A growth in the capital stock, with no change in the stock of labor or in the production function, raises the marginal product of labor and lowers the marginal product of capital. (Why?) The productivity of roundabout methods and thus the interest rate would be reduced by the reduction in the marginal product of capital because the opportunity cost of producing capital goods would be unchanged (if the consumer and capital-goods industries use factors in the same proportions).[1]

Therefore, an accumulation of capital would not change the supply curve of investment, but would shift the demand curve for investment to the left because of the reduction in the interest rate: In Figure 40.1, the demand curve shifts from S_0/P to S_1/P, and investment from $\hat{\Delta}K_0$ to $\hat{\Delta}K_1$. The further growth in the capital stock in period 1 from K_1 to

$$K_2 = K_1 + \hat{\Delta}K_1 = K_0 + \hat{\Delta}K_0 + \hat{\Delta}K_1 \tag{40-1}$$

lowers the marginal product of capital, the interest rate, the demand curve for investment, and the amount invested still further.

This process continues until the demand and supply curves for investment intersect on the vertical axis. At that point, the stock of capital, the interest rate, and the marginal productivities are constant because nothing is invested. This long-run equilibrium interest rate is determined solely by the degree of preference for the present. [Why? See equation (39-9).] Income would grow at a decreasing rate (even if the fraction of income saved—and invested—remained the same over time[2]) and would stop growing when the capital stock stopped growing.

Total income in a number of countries has grown continually for over a century; one way to rationalize such persistent growth is to drop the assumption that the stock of labor is fixed and assume instead an exogenously determined growth rate of n percent per period. If capital grew initially at a rate greater than n,[3] the marginal product of capital and hence the interest rate would fall. (Why?) Even if the fraction of income saved and invested remained the same over time, the rate of growth of capital would decline, essentially because income would grow less rapidly than capital.[4] The growth in capital would decline even faster if the fraction of income saved declined,

---

[1] See section 1 of the Appendix to this lecture.

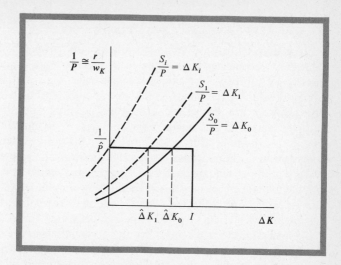

FIGURE 40.1

say because the decline in interest rates reduced the incentive to save. The growth in capital would continue to decline until it grew at the same rate as labor. Thereafter, as long as the fraction of income saved remained constant, the interest rate and the marginal products of labor and capital would be constant; since income, labor, and capital would all grow at the same rate (n), per capita income would also be constant.

A few countries like the United States and Sweden have not only experienced persistent growth in total income but also more or less persistent growth in per capita income and in the capital-labor ratio. The model of capital and labor accumulation just set out is only of limited help, therefore, in understanding growth in such countries[5] and needs to be significantly modified.

One modification is to introduce continual progress in the technology of producing consumer and capital goods. Technological progress increases the output from given inputs, which is almost the same thing as an increase in income per capita. We showed in the previous lecture that technological progress encourages saving and investment. The positive effect of progress on investment could offset the negative effect of capital accumulation, the result possibly being a steady rate of investment and a continual increase in the capital-labor ratio.[6] Progress in technology is sometimes related to the accumulation of capital, as when new technologies are "embodied" in new capital goods, or when investments in scientists, engineers, economists, and

[2] For a proof see section 2 of the Appendix.
[3] That is, if $\Delta K_0 / K_0 > n$.
[4] See section 3 of the Appendix for a mathematical proof.
[5] It is of considerable help, however, in understanding the many countries that have not experienced persistent growth in per capita incomes.
[6] See section 4 of the Appendix for a proof.

other human capital stimulate the development of new ideas and technologies.

A second modification retains the distinction between human and physical capital stressed earlier (see Lecture 32). Some evidence indicates that physical capital is a substitute for raw or conventional labor and a complement for human capital. Let us make the extreme assumption that physical capital and raw labor are perfect substitutes, and let the composite of the two, call it the "physical-labor" factor, be a complement for human capital. Then if the rate of growth of "physical-labor" were the same as the rate of growth of human capital, the marginal productivity of and the rate of return on each factor would not change over time. Aggregate income as well as income per unit of raw labor (i.e., per head) would grow indefinitely at the same rate as human capital and "physical-labor" as long as raw labor did not grow and the fraction of income invested remained constant. (Why?)[7]

These last four lectures provide only the essentials of the modern approach to capital theory. They can fairly readily be expanded to incorporate: (1) Depreciation of the capital stock so that some output of the capital-goods industry just replaces capital wearing out. (2) Positively inclined supply curves of consumption and investment because different factor proportions are used in the consumer and capital-goods industries. [Interest rates would then be determined by time preference as well as by the productivity of roundabout methods. (Why?)] (3) A positive response of the supply of labor to changes in wage rates along the lines analyzed in Lectures 32 and 33. (4) Financial assets, like cash balances or bonds, with only an indirect claim to real resources, and held according to the principles set out in the recently developed asset-portfolio theory.

A more important defect is the absence of any explicit consideration of the uncertainty surrounding future wage rates and other prices, production functions, preference functions, factor supplies, and so forth. The expectations of a household or firm and thus their consumption and investment plans may be significantly altered over time as additional evidence accumulates. The incorporation of uncertainty into the theory of capital is left for the brilliant reader to develop.

APPENDIX

1. Since the consumer and capital-goods industries and the factor markets are all assumed to be competitive, the price of a unit of capital, P, would equal

$$P = \frac{AC^K}{AC^C} = \frac{MC^K}{MC^C} = \frac{MP_\ell^C}{MP_\ell^K} = \frac{MP_K^C}{MP_K^K} \qquad \text{(Why?)} \qquad \text{(A-1)}$$

[7] See section 5 of the Appendix for a proof.

where AC^K is average cost in the capital-goods industry, MP_ℓ^K is the marginal product of labor in this industry, and so forth. Since the optimal factor proportions are assumed to be identical

$$\frac{\ell_K}{K_K} = \frac{\ell_C}{K_C} \tag{A-2}$$

then

$$\frac{MP_\ell^K \ell_K}{MP_K^K K_K} = \frac{MP_\ell^C \ell_C}{MP_K^C K_C} \tag{A-3}$$

or the same share of output must go to labor (and capital) in both industries. This can be true for every (ℓ_K/K_K) only if

$$MP_\ell^K = \alpha MP_\ell^C$$

$$MP_K^K = \alpha MP_K^C \qquad \text{whenever} \quad \frac{\ell_C}{K_C} = \frac{\ell_K}{K_K} \tag{A-4}$$

where α is a constant. In other words, the production function in the capital-goods industry differs from that in the consumption-goods industry by a multiplicative constant (α). Hence by equation (A-1), $P = 1/\alpha$ and is also a constant.

2. By definition, output or income measured in units of current consumption would equal

$$I = C + P(\Delta K) = f(\ell_C, K_C) + P \cdot g(\ell_K, K_K) \tag{A-5}$$

Since P is a constant measuring the consumption forgone per unit of capital produced, $P \cdot g(l_k, K_k)$ measures the total consumption forgone; therefore,

$$I = f(\ell_C, K_C) + P \cdot g(\ell_K, K_K) = f(\ell_0, K) = P \cdot g(\ell_0, K) \tag{A-6}$$

where

$$\ell_C + \ell_K = \ell_0 \qquad \text{and} \qquad K_C + K_K = K \tag{A-7}$$

By differentiation of $f(\ell_0, K)$,

$$q = \frac{dI}{I} = \frac{\partial f}{\partial K} \frac{dK}{I} = MP_K^C \frac{dK}{I} \tag{A-8}$$

If q can be shown to decline over time when a constant fraction of income goes into the production of capital, q must decline when this fraction declines. Let

$$P(dK) = sI \tag{A-9}$$

where s is a constant: The amount saved (invested) is a constant fraction of income. Then

$$dq = \frac{s}{P} MP_{KK}^C dK = \left(\frac{s}{P}\right)^2 IMP_{KK}^C < 0 \qquad \text{(A-10)}$$

by diminishing marginal productivity, so that the rate of growth of income declines over time.

3. By equations (A-6) and (A-9)

$$m = \frac{dK}{K} = \frac{sg(\ell, K)}{K} \qquad \text{(A-11)}$$

Since g is assumed to be homogeneous of the first degree,

$$g(\ell, K) = K \cdot h\left(\frac{\ell}{K}\right) \qquad \text{(A-12)}$$

or

$$m = s \cdot h\left(\frac{\ell}{K}\right) \qquad \text{(A-13)}$$

where

$$\frac{dh}{d\left(\frac{\ell}{K}\right)} = h' \equiv \frac{\partial g}{\partial \ell} \equiv MP_\ell > 0$$

Therefore,

$$dm = sh' \frac{d\ell}{K} + sh'\left(\frac{-\ell}{K^2}\right) dK$$

$$\qquad \text{(A-14)}$$

$$= sh' \frac{\ell}{K} n - sh' \frac{\ell}{K} m$$

$$= sh' \frac{\ell}{K} (n - m) \qquad \text{(A-15)}$$

where $n = d\ell/\ell$. Thus

$$dm \gtreqless 0 \qquad \text{as} \qquad n \gtreqless m \qquad \text{(A-16)}$$

4. We preserve all the assumptions of section 3 except that the production function is written as

$$g(\ell, K; T) = K \cdot h\left(\frac{\ell}{K}; T\right)$$

with

$$\frac{\partial h}{\partial T} = \frac{\partial g}{\partial T}\frac{1}{K} > 0$$

where T measures the level of technology. Then equation (A-15) can be written as

$$dm = sh'\frac{\ell}{K}(n-m) + s\frac{\partial h}{\partial T}dT \qquad\qquad \text{(A-17)}$$

and $dm = 0$ if

$$\frac{\partial h}{\partial T}dT = h'\frac{\ell}{K}(m-n) \qquad\qquad \text{(A-18)}$$

5. Let

$$L = b_1 K + b_2 \ell \qquad\qquad \text{(A-19)}$$

where L is the total input of "physical-labor," K is the input of physical capital, ℓ is the input of raw labor, and b_1 and b_2 are constants which convert K and ℓ into comparable units. Furthermore, let K^* be the total stock of physical and human capital

$$K^* = K + P_H H \qquad\qquad \text{(A-20)}$$

where P_H is the (constant) amount of K forgone in producing a unit of human capital, H. Assume, as before, that

$$PdK^* = sI \qquad\qquad \text{(A-21)}$$

(a constant fraction of income is saved or invested), with

$$dK^* = dK + P_H dH \qquad\qquad \text{(A-22)}$$

If it paid to invest in both K and H, K^* would be allocated between K and H so that L and H would grow at the same rate. Then

$$m = \frac{dH}{H} = \frac{dL}{L} = \frac{b_1 dK}{L} \qquad\qquad \text{(A-23)}$$

where l is assumed to be constant over time. By the assumption that production functions are linear homogeneous in H and L,

$$\frac{dI}{I} = \frac{d(I/l)}{I/l} = g \qquad\qquad \text{(A-24)}$$

Substituting equation (A-23) into (A-22) and (A-21), we get

$$\frac{sI}{H} = P \cdot g\left(P_H + \frac{L}{b_1 H}\right)$$

or

$$g = \frac{sI}{PH}\left(P_H + \frac{L}{b_1 H}\right)^{-1} = \frac{b_1 sI}{P(P_H b_1 H + L)} \tag{A-25}$$

where the term on the right is a positive constant. (Why?) Thus by equation (A-24), the rate of growth of income per unit of raw labor (or per head) is also a positive constant.

Since $b_1 MP_1 = MP_k$, and

$$P_H \cong \frac{MP_H}{MP_K} \tag{A-26}$$

if the rates of return on H and K were equal and both kinds of capital were long-lived (Why?), then

$$g = \frac{sMP_K \cdot I}{P(MP_L L + MP_H H)} = \frac{sMP_K \cdot I}{I} = sMP_K \tag{A-27}$$

(Compare this with the formula for the "golden rule" in Problem 40.3.)

PROBLEMS

40.1. Suppose that a person knows with certainty that he will live N years. Given his utility function, income stream, prices, and so forth, he initially plans his consumption path for all N years. The following year he has only $N - 1$ years remaining and he must then plan again his consumption path for the remaining years. If his income stream and prices remain as originally expected, what conditions must be imposed on his "new" utility function in order for him to continue the consumption path originally planned?

40.2. Evaluate: One piece of evidence suggesting that human capital is more complementary to labor than to physical capital is that a rise in the amount of human capital raises earnings more than it raises the rental price on physical capital.

*40.3. Suppose there are two factors, l and K, and two industries that produce C and K. These industries use factors in the same proportion and have constant returns to scale. Let l grow at a constant rate n and let the fraction of income saved depend only on the rate of interest. The "golden rule" of steady-state growth (i.e., when capital also grows at the rate n) is to be at the labor-capital ratio that maximizes, compared to other steady-state positions, the amount of consumption per unit of labor (i.e., C/l). If capital lasts indefinitely and the "horizon" is indefinitely long,

a. What is the labor-capital ratio along the "golden rule" growth path?
b. Would a perfectly competitive economy approach this path?

General Problems

Prices and the Measuring Rod of Money

1. Economics is sometimes said to be the study of phenomena brought under the measuring rod of money. To show that economics is much broader, consider the following. Define the commodity production functions

$$Z_i = f_i(x_i, t_i) \qquad i = 1, \ldots, m$$

where the Z_i enter the preference function. To eliminate price, assume that all the x_i are freely available.

a. Find the optimal combination of the Z_i and the optimal allocation of time (the t_i).
b. Are there any "shadow" prices in the system?
c. Suppose that there is a factor-neutral shift in all the f_i by the same percentage. What is the effect of this shift on the "shadow" prices? On the allocation of time?

Spectator Enthusiasm

2. Evaluate: Holding the quality of the team fixed, the average spectator at a ball game is more exuberant, vocal, and enthusiastic in his support of the team the smaller the student body.

The Economics of Traffic Enforcement

3. Suppose that the traffic department would like to enforce parking regulations in an efficient way. Assume that each person has the choice

of parking illegally or legally; the latter costs h dollars per "day" and the former, if caught, results in a fine equal to F dollars per time per "day."

a. Assume first that the sole aim of the traffic department is to discourage illegal parking at minimal cost. Assume also that all drivers simply try to maximize expected money income. How frequently should the traffic department inspect parking in order to achieve its aim?

b. If all drivers maximized expected utility and had diminishing marginal utility of income (but there is no utility or disutility from disobeying the law), how would this affect your answer? If they had increasing marginal utility of income?

c. Suppose that the traffic department received all the fines and desired to maximize its expected income. How would your answer to 3.a be affected?

d. How does your answer to 3.a and 3.c depend on F, the size of the fine, and h, the cost of legal parking?

The Economics of Royalties

4. Authors are usually paid royalties on their books, and the royalty is usually equal to a given fraction of the gross revenue or sales of their books. Would both authors and publishers be better off if:

a. Royalties were a fixed percentage of the profits on a book?
b. Authors were paid a lump sum?

Location Theory

5. Suppose that all employed persons in a particular metropolitan area work at the center of the area and live in the surrounding territory. The real cost of commuting to the center for any particular person is assumed to be proportional to the distance from the center. Each acre of land surrounding the center is assumed to be homogeneous in all the relevant physical properties and amenities. Use these assumptions to determine:

a. The direction of the relation between the (rental or sale) price of an acre and its distance from the center.
b. Whether apartment buildings would more likely be found closer to or farther from the center.
*c. Whether higher income persons would tend to live closer to the center than lower income ones.

Location Theory and Thruways

*6. Suppose now that a thruway is introduced through one region that permits faster access to the center. Find the effect of the thruway on:

    a. The average distance lived from the center.

    b. The relation between the (rental or sale) price of an acre and its distance from the center.

    c. The relative value of land near the thruway.

    d. The incentive for higher income persons to live closer to the center.

Fluctuations in Enrollments

7. Investment in physical capital fluctuates positively and substantially with the business cycle, while investment in human capital, measured by enrollments, fluctuates inversely, rising during recessions and falling (relative to its trend) during expansions. How can you explain the very different cyclical pattern of these two kinds of investment?

The Economics of Worker Participation

8. Suppose that a firm which had been maximizing income in the usual way is converted to a workers' cooperative: it now tries to maximize the income per worker. Find the effect of this change on:

    a. The output of the firm.

    b. The amount of capital per worker.

    c. Would the direction of these effects be different if the firm were a monopolist instead of competitive?

The Sale of Votes

*9. Assume two parties, R and D, competing for office. Each party promises a platform and carries out its promises if elected. The party getting a majority of votes is elected, each person has one vote, and each knows how he will be affected by the two platforms.

    If votes are not salable, the party benefiting a majority of voters is elected. Suppose instead that votes could be bought and sold (à la a proxy fight) and that this does not affect the platforms. Assume the existence of a single market price for each person's vote.

    a. What determines this price?

    b. Could the party elected under this system differ from the one elected when votes are not salable?

    c. Which groups would gain or lose from a shift to salable votes?

The Economics of the "Brain Drain"

10. Suppose that there are three inputs in each of two countries (A and B): skilled labor, unskilled labor, and physical capital. One percent of the

skilled labor emigrates ("brain drain") during one year from A to B, the supplies of the other inputs remaining fixed. What is the effect of this on:

a. The income of persons remaining behind in A and those already in B?
b. The unit prices of the three factors in both countries?
c. The *share* of skilled labor in the total income of each country?
d. How would your answers to these questions be affected if, instead, one percent of *all* factors emigrated from A to B?
e. What is the effect of an emigration of skilled labor alone on total world incomes? Is your answer affected by whether the migration was "induced" by higher wages in B or by an "autonomous" factor like persecution in A?
f. How would the supplies of other factors in both A and B be affected by the emigration of skilled labor?

Interest-Equalization Tax

11. "United States citizens should exercise care when initiating the purchase of any foreign security. Existing law imposes an $18\frac{3}{4}$ percent tax on certain foreign stock purchased from non-U.S. sources. This tax creates an increase in the cost basis of the shares in question. Consequently, commitments entered into should be in those shares which may be purchased from a prior American owner, a fact which exempts the acquisition from the tax." (Merrill Lynch report)

a. What determines the difference in price of such a stock to an American if it were purchased from a foreign holder instead of from an American owner? Did Merrill Lynch offer good advice? What would be the difference in price to a foreigner?
b. Suppose that the tax was removed. By how much would the prices of foreign-owned and American-owned foreign stock be affected?

Bibliography—
Reading List

Review: Alchian, Armen A., and Allan, William R. — *University Economics* (Belmont, Calif.: Wadsworth Publishing Co., Inc., 1964)

Friedman, Milton — *Price Theory, A Provisional Text* (Chicago: Aldine Publishing Co., 1962)

Texts: Stigler, George J. — *Theory of Price*, 3rd ed. (New York: The Macmillan Co., 1966)

Vickrey, William S. — *Microstatics* (New York: Harcourt Brace Jovanovich, 1964)

Readings marked with an asterisk (*) are recommended, not required.

I. Introduction

Stigler — Chs. 1–2

Friedman — Pp. 6–12

Friedman, Milton — "The Methodology of Positive Economics," in Friedman, *Essays in Positive Economics* (Chicago: University of Chicago Press, Phoenix Edition, 1966), pp. 3–43

*Keynes, John M. — *The Scope and Method of Political Economy*, 4th ed. (New York: Augustus M. Kelley Publishers, 1955), pp. 1–83

*Hayek, Friedrich A. von — "The Use of Knowledge in Society," *American Economic Review*, Vol. 35 (September 1945), 519–530, reprinted in *Individualism and Economic Order* (Chicago: University of Chicago Press, 1948)

II. Demand Analysis

Friedman	Pp. 12–56
*Stigler	Chs. 2–4
*Marshall, Alfred	*Principles of Economics* (London: The Macmillan Co., 1922), Book III, Chs. 2–4, Book V, Chs. 1–2
Hicks, John R.	*Value and Capital* (Oxford: Oxford University Press, 1939), Part I
*Becker, Gary S.	"Irrational Behavior and Economic Theory," *Journal of Political Economy*, Vol. 70 (February 1962), 1–13
*Lancaster, Kelvin	"A New Approach to Consumer Theory," *Journal of Political Economy*, Vol. 74 (April 1966), 132–157
Stigler, George J.	"Economics of Information," *Journal of Political Economy*, Vol. 69 (June 1961), 213–225
*Slutsky, Eugen	"On the Theory of the Budget of the Consumer," in American Economic Association, *Readings in Price Theory* (Chicago: Richard D. Irwin, 1952), pp. 27–56
*Vickrey	Pp. 66–88
Working, Elmer J.	"What Do Statistical 'Demand Curves' Show?" *Quarterly Journal of Economics*, Vol. 41 (1927), 212–235, reprinted in American Economic Association, *Readings in Price Theory* (Chicago: Richard D. Irwin, 1952), pp. 97–115
*Wold, Herman O.	*Demand Analysis* (New York: John Wiley & Sons, 1953), Ch. 1
Stigler, George J.	"The Early History of Empirical Studies of Consumer Behavior," *Journal of Political Economy*, Vol. 62 (April 1954), 95–113
Friedman	Pp. 68–73
Alchian, Armen A.	"The Meaning of Utility Measurement," *American Economic Review*, Vol. 43 (March 1953), 26–50

III. Supply of Products

A. Cost and Supply

Friedman	Pp. 74–123
*Stigler	Chs. 6–10

Hirshleifer, Jack   "The Firm's Cost Function: A Successful Reconstruction?" *Journal of Business*, Vol. 35 (July 1962), 235–255

*Alchian and Allan   Ch. 21

*Vickrey   Chs. 4–7

*Robinson, Joan   *Economics of Imperfect Competition* (London & New York: The Macmillan Co. and St. Martin's Press, 1965), Ch. 2

*Clark, John M.   *The Economics of Overhead Costs* (Chicago: University of Chicago Press, 1923), Ch. 9

Apel, Hans   "Marginal Cost Constancy and Its Implications," *American Economic Review*, Vol. 38 (December 1948), 870–885

Stigler, George J.   "The Economies of Scale," *Journal of Law and Economics*, Vol. 1 (October 1958), 54–71

*Johnston, John   *Statistical Cost Analysis* (New York: McGraw-Hill Book Co., 1960), Chs. 2, 5, 6

Hicks, John R.   "Linear Theory," *Economic Journal*, Vol. 70 (December 1960), 671–709

*Baumol, William J.   *Economic Theory and Operations Analysis* (Englewood Cliffs, N.J.: Prentice-Hall, Inc., 1961), Chs. 5–8

Coase, Ronald   "The Problem of Social Cost," *Journal of Law and Economics*, Vol. 3 (October 1960), 1–44

Alchian, Armen A.   "Uncertainty, Evolution, and Economic Theory," *Journal of Political Economy*, Vol. 58 (June 1950), 211–221

*Alchian and Allan   Ch. 12

B. Monopoly

Stigler   Chs. 12–13

Vickrey   Chs. 7–8

Chamberlin, Edward   *The Theory of Monopolistic Competition* (Cambridge, Mass.: Harvard University Press, 1936), Chs. 3–5

Stigler, George J.   "A Theory of Oligopoly," *Journal of Political Economy*, Vol. 72 (February 1964), 44–61

*Harberger, Arnold C.   "Monopoly and Resource Allocation," *The American Economic Review, Papers and Proceedings*, Vol. 44 (May 1954), 77–87

IV. Production Functions

Friedman   Ch. 6

Vickrey   Ch. 4

*Arrow, Kenneth, et al.
"Capital-Labor Substitution and Economic Efficiency," *Review of Economics and Statistics*, Vol. 43 (August 1961), 225–250

*———
The Rate and Direction of Inventive Activity, National Bureau of Economic Research Conference (Princeton, N.J.: Princeton University Press, 1962); see especially introduction by R. R. Nelson and articles by Minasian, Marshall and Meckling, and Arrow

Griliches, Zvi
"Hybrid Corn and the Economics of Innovation," *Science*, Vol. 132 (July 29, 1960), 275–280

*Mansfield, Edwin
"The Speed of Response of Firms to New Techniques," *Quarterly Journal of Economics*, Vol. 77 (May 1963), 290–311

*Plant, Arnold
"The Economic Theory Concerning Patents for Inventions," *Economica*, Vol. 1 (February 1934), 30–51

V. Derived Demand for Factors of Production

Friedman
Chs. 7–10

Hicks, John R.
The Theory of Wages, 2nd ed. (London: The Macmillan Co., 1963), Chs. 1–6

VI. Supply of Factors

A. Supply of Labor

Friedman
Ch. 11

Becker, Gary S.
"A Theory of the Allocation of Time," *Economic Journal*, Vol. 75 (September 1965), 493–517

Becker, Gary S.
Human Capital (New York: National Bureau of Economic Research, 1964), Chs. 2–3

B. Demand and Supply of Capital

Knight, Frank H.
"Interest," in *Encyclopedia of the Social Sciences*, reprinted in *Ethics of Competition* (London: Allen & Unwin, Ltd., 1935)

Fisher, Irving
The Nature of Income and Capital (London: The Macmillan Co., 1906), Chs. 1, 2, 4, 7, 11–15, Appendix to Ch. 1

Fisher, Irving
The Theory of Interest (New York: The Macmillan Co., 1930), especially Chs. 4–11

Hirshleifer, Jack   "On the Optimal Theory of Investment,"
                         Journal of Political Economy, Vol. 66
                         (August 1958), 329–352

Stigler, George J.   *Capital and Rates of Return in Manufacturing
                         Industries* (Princeton, N.J.: Princeton Uni-
                         versity Press, 1963), pp. 3–7, 54–58, 62–66,
                         72–75

Solow, Robert M.   *Capital Theory and the Rate of Return*
                         (Amsterdam: North-Holland Publishing
                         Co., 1963), Lectures 1 and 2

Friedman   Ch. 13
*Becker, Gary S.   "Human Capital and the Personal Distribu-
                         tion of Income," Woytinsky Lecture (Ann
                         Arbor, Mich.: University of Michigan,
                         Institute of Public Administration, 1967)

Hirshleifer, Jack   "Investment Decision Under Uncertainty:
                         Choice Theoretic Approaches," *Quarterly
                         Journal of Economics*, Vol. 79 (November
                         1965), 509–536

Hicks, John R.   "Mr. Keynes and the Classics: A Suggested
                         Interpretation," *Econometrica*, Vol. 5 (April
                         1937), 147–159

Patinkin, Don   "Price Flexibility and Full Employment,"
                         American Economic Review, Vol. 38 (Sep-
                         tember 1948), 543–564

C. Economic Growth

Solow, Robert M.   "A Contribution to the Theory of Economic
                         Growth," *Quarterly Journal of Economics*,
                         Vol. 70 (February 1956), 65–94

Denison, Edward F.   *The Sources of Economic Growth in the
                         United States* (New York: Committee for
                         Economic Development, 1962), Chs. 1, 2,
                         13, 15

Hahn, Frank H.,   "A Survey of the Theory of Economic
and   Growth," *Economic Journal*, Vol. 74
Matthews, R. C. O.   (December 1964), 779–902

Index

Author Index

Subject Index

A NOTE ON THE TYPE

The text of this book was set on the Monotype in a face called
TIMES ROMAN, designed by Stanley Morison for The Times
(London), and first introduced by that newspaper in 1932.
Among typographers and designers of the twentieth century,
Stanley Morison has been a strong forming influence, as
typographical advisor to the English Monotype Corporation, as a
director of two distinguished English publishing houses, and as
a writer of sensibility, erudition, and keen practical sense.

Manufactured in the United States of America by The
Haddon Craftsmen, Inc., Scranton, Pa.

DESIGNED BY J. M. WALL